Revolution in El Salvador

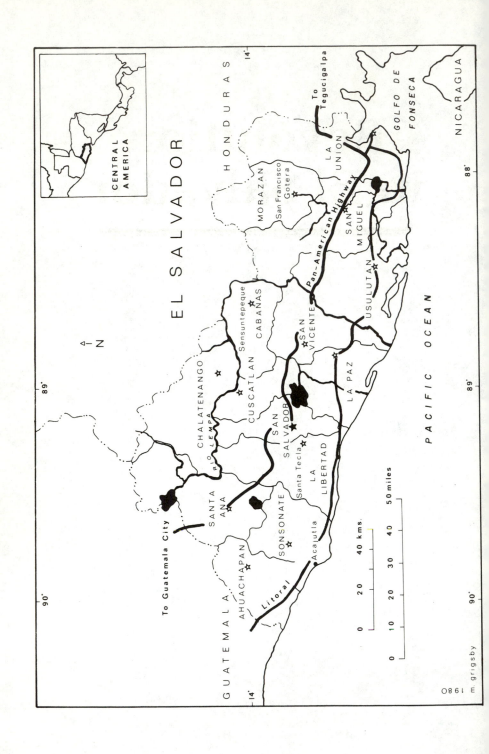

Revolution in El Salvador

Origins and Evolution

Tommie Sue Montgomery

Introduction by Román Mayorga Quiroz

Westview Press / Boulder, Colorado

The photographs, unless otherwise credited, are by the author.

Copyright © 1982 by Westview Press, Inc.

Published in 1982 in the United States of America by
Westview Press, Inc.
5500 Central Avenue
Boulder, Colorado 80301
Frederick A. Praeger, President and Publisher

Library of Congress Cataloging in Publication Data
Montgomery, Tommie Sue.
  Revolution in El Salvador.
  Bibliography: p.
  Includes index.
    1. El Salvador – History – Coup d'etat, 1979. 2. El Salvador – Politics and government. 3. El Salvador – Economic conditions. 4. Catholic Church – El Salvador.
  I. Title
F1488.3.M66 1982   972.84′052   82-8367
ISBN 0-86531-049-1   AACR2
ISBN 0-86531-386-5

Printed and bound in the United States of America

A
Oscar Arnulfo Romero y Galdámez
Presente

También a
Guillermo, Augusto, Enrique, Magdalena, Maura,
Dorothy, y Jean

Y a todos los Salvadoreños que luchan para vivir
en una sociedad de justicia y paz

Contents

Illustrations and Tables

Tables

Preface

When I arrived in El Salvador two weeks after the October 15, 1979, coup d'etat, I did not know very much about the country; I had read everything I could lay my hands on, but the most recent overall study of El Salvador had appeared in 1973 – which is indicative of general U.S. interest in Latin America's smallest country. I knew only enough to realize that the Revolutionary Junta of Government that had been installed following the coup was El Salvador's last chance for peaceful social change. If the junta failed to implement the desperately needed economic and social reforms, there would be a revolution. Everything I learned in the almost five months I spent in the country served to reinforce that initial feeling. When the government resigned on January 3, 1980, just two and a half months after its installation, it was clear that the old order had reasserted itself; that there had been a return to the status quo ante in terms of who really held the power in El Salvador. And when I left in late March, I was absolutely convinced that there would be a revolution. The question was not "if." The question was "when." That conclusion was not an expression of a personal preference; it was a political judgment based on dozens of interviews and mounds of other data.

That is my position as a political scientist. As such, however, I have never pretended to be "value free." One's values determine the subjects one chooses to investigate, the questions one asks, the way one asks them. A "political scientist" did not go to El Salvador. A human being who happens to have a Ph.D in politics went to Central America. And that human being arrived with the hope that the junta would succeed. The thought of revolution per se was not really abhorrent; I do not see the hand of the Soviet Union either creating or manipulating every revolutionary process, and there is no evidence that it is doing so in El Salvador. But I felt that a revolution in El Salvador would make Nicaragua look like a picnic, that it would be very bloody, that the human cost would be enormous. Regrettably, I was correct.

No one in his or her right mind prefers violence; so I would prefer that a path to peaceful social change in El Salvador existed. But violence was not introduced in El Salvador by the revolutionaries. Violence has been the most pervasive characteristic of Salvadorean history—from the easily identifiable repression of government forces and vigilantes in the pay of the large landowners to the more subtle violence of malnutrition, high infant mortality, illiteracy, and housing more fit for chickens than human beings.

I arrived in El Salvador objective and neutral in the sense of feeling personally detached from what was happening there. I left with my objectivity intact, but my neutrality had been buried with the bodies of those who had been gunned down, without provocation, by government security forces on January 22, 1980.

So, my objective conclusion is that the present government in El Salvador will be overthrown. This may happen, despite the Reagan administration's best efforts, soon or not for two years or five years. But it will happen and the new government will be headed by whatever leadership remains of the Salvadorean revolutionary organizations at that time. Furthermore, my preference is that the people of El Salvador determine their own future, that that future not be imposed on them either by a tiny minority of the Salvadorean population, the army, or by the government of the United States. Tens of thousands of Salvadoreans have been engaged, over the last decade, in developing their own grassroots organizations and their own leaders. They have a right to make those choices, and they have chosen, in large numbers, the constituent groups of the Democratic Revolutionary Front and the Farabundo Martí Front for National Liberation. I support their right to make that choice.

The reader also has a right to know how the research was conducted. I went to El Salvador with one basic rule: I would talk to anyone. The interviews completed for this book included people from every walk of life and covered the political spectrum from extreme left to extreme right. I talked with people from every institution of Salvadorean society: the army, the oligarchy, the church, business people, street vendors, peasants, and both the rank and file and the leadership of the revolutionary organizations. I also had many conversations with officials at the U.S. Embassy in San Salvador and in Washington, D.C., after returning. I attended press conferences at the Casa Presidencial and at the National University; read three of four newspapers each day; discovered that the dearth of information about the country in the United States is matched by the wealth of research that has been done by Salvadorean social scientists. Most of it is outstanding. Without it much of the economic analysis herein could not have been written. I also spent an additional ten months in 1980–1982 interviewing other Salvadoreans (and in some cases reinterviewing people I had met in El Salvador) in the United States, Mexico, Nicaragua, Honduras, and Costa Rica.

Because of the conditions under which the research was done, most of the interviews were privileged. All interviews have been coded; however, the symbol "†" will be used in place of a footnote to indicate such interviews.

The list of those whose help and support I would like to acknowledge is much shorter because of this need for confidentiality. I would first like to thank Ronald Hellman for referring me to Ronald Schneider as a possible author for a book on one of the Latin American nations. To both I want to say thank you for making possible the greatest (thus far) experience of my life. Robert Armstrong and Douglas Walker were extremely helpful before I went to El Salvador in providing reading material and briefings.

In El Salvador, David Mena, of the Universidad Centroamericana José Simeón Cañas (Central American University), and Edgar Jiménez Cabrera, now of the Ibero-American University in Mexico City, provided invaluable information and insights as fellow social scientists. I am grateful to them for receiving me as a colleague and later as a friend. Maryknoll Sisters Joan Petrik and Patricia Haggerty allowed me to accompany them in their work with the campesinos of La Libertad and provided information on the development of Christian Base Communities. A very wise and warm woman who has lived in El Salvador for thirty-five years introduced me to many of the subtleties of Salvadorean culture.

I want to thank all those, both in and out of El Salvador, who gave so generously of their time for interviews. I particularly want to express gratitude to those who will disagree profoundly with my analysis and conclusions (and who will probably wish they had never given me a minute). Several people read drafts of chapters or the entire manuscript, including José Alas, José Aybar, Jorge Lara-Braud, Thomas Quigley, Brian Smith, Dennis Gilbert, and Mac Chapin. I appreciate their comments and corrections although, of course, the analysis, conclusions, and remaining errors are exclusively my responsibility. Others have been helpful in miscellaneous ways: Mark Rosenberg and the Latin American and Caribbean Center of Florida International University; Gene Palumbo; Anita Colvin and Connie

Hicks, for saving me many dollars in photocopying fees; and Debbie Martin, for typing the final manuscript in very short order. I am in Mona Grigsby's debt for her maps. There are others whom I would like more than anything to name, but cannot for reasons of security. They know who they are and for now that must suffice. The Centro de Investigación y Asesoría Socio-Económica (Center of Socio-Economic Research and Advisement) in Managua welcomed me as a colleague in the summer of 1981 and has provided the requisite office space needed for additional interviewing and rewriting. Finally, this book could not have been written over the course of a year without the support of my parents, who provided love, sustenance, and maid service so that I could tie myself to the typewriter. I am eternally in their debt.

Tommie Sue Montgomery
Managua, Nicaragua
April 1982

Introduction

This new and excellent book in English about El Salvador goes a long way toward explaining not only those general background features of the country that are pertinent to revolution but also how their actual interplay led to the present situation. Going through its pages one can readily see what the author means by stating that she does not pretend to be a value-free political scientist. Although the book has been written with objectivity in the use of information and analytical tools, it also states clearly the standpoint from which it judges the facts that are described and analyzed. It combines passion with lucidity, intellectual honesty with a keen sympathy for the people of El Salvador who have suffered under oppression and exploitation.

It has been almost a decade since Thomas Anderson, David Browning, and Alastair White wrote the last and excellent books in English about El Salvador. Although the readers of those books should have been alert to the possibilities of a major social explosion in that country, it seems as if the world at large and the United States in particular were completely taken by surprise when the explosion did in fact occur.

The smallest country in the American continent has now taken on gigantic proportions in public attention, both because of the rare intensity of the human drama that is taking place there and because it has become the scene of a conflict in which different nations see important implications for their own interests. Notwithstanding the relationships that exist between the internal conflict of El Salvador and factors external to that country, the present situation has fundamentally indigenous roots. The conflict originated neither in the East-West confrontation nor through the desire of rising or middle-ranking powers in Latin America to increase their influence in the Central American region. It was basically created by causes that relate to the country's own structure and history.

The history of El Salvador is indeed a tragic one. The facts that now stun the world are part of a long chain of events that have been perceived by most Salvadoreans as a process far beyond their control.

1

Like tragedy, the process includes death, irrational destruction, intense human suffering, and the presence of forces that are superior to the individual. But unlike tragedy, where such forces are arbitrary, incomprehensible, and attributed to a mysterious destiny, the factors involved in the conflict in El Salvador are logically related to the country's social structures; and their probable behavior was not too difficult to predict.

Three factors in particular should be mentioned as major contributors to what is happening nowadays in El Salvador: first, the extreme and growing inequality of the components of the socioeconomic system; second, the sociocultural phenomenon by which the masses have perceived the structure and trends of the society; and third, the patent illegitimacy of the political system.

EXTREME AND GROWING INEQUALITY

El Salvador is a land of very sharp contrast, both geographically and socially. The vast majority of the population – certainly no less than two-thirds – live in extreme poverty. That means severely deficient nutrition, lack of medical and educational facilities, miserable housing, low wages, chronic unemployment, children without a future. It is not merely the kind of relative poverty that becomes difficult to endure when it is compared with the relative affluence of others, but a painfully objective condition in which the most basic human needs cannot be adequately met. On the other extreme of the social structure there is a heavy concentration of wealth and income in a minority that in all respects has enjoyed the goods, services, and conveniences – sometimes the eccentricities – of the most developed nations. Between the two, the very rich and the majority of the population, there has been a small but growing middle class.

If one considers the trends of growth and distribution of income, it is clear from available data that the national product has been growing over the last three decades, sufficiently to almost double average income (at constant prices) since 1950; that this increase in income has been so unequally distributed that the absolute difference between the levels of income of rich and poor has also increased; and that in the same period, rapid population growth has more than doubled the absolute number of people living under such miserable conditions.

It is, therefore, a typical situation where the rich have grown in income and the poor have grown in numbers. The roots of this situation are, of course, found in the social structures that were inherited from Spanish colonial rule and that were aggravated a hundred years ago, when practically all communal land was converted into large, privately owned plantations devoted to coffee production and, in the course of time, also to sugar and cotton. At the beginning of the century the total population of El Salvador was slightly more than one million. Arithmetically, there could be no more than one million poor; today there are probably more than four million, and the distance that separates them from the affluent is much greater than before.

This extreme and growing socioeconomic inequality is the basic structural feature that must be taken into account in explaining what is happening in contemporary El Salvador, as such a situation, when the masses became conscious of it, was bound to produce much dissatisfaction, anger, and resentment.

THE PERCEPTION OF THE MASSES

The second factor concerns the process by which people became aware of socioeconomic trends and realities. All the conditions that permit such perceptions and all the factors that influence value judgments have acted in such a way in El Salvador as to convince millions of people that they have suffered a very grave social injustice. Political agitation by local Marxist organizations contributed, of course, to such awareness, although it accounts for only a very small part of the process. The country extends over 21,000 square kilometers and is densely populated. Unlike its neighbor, Honduras, it has a rather good road and transportation system that has connected all corners of the territory. Unlike in Guatemala, there are no language or ethnic barriers. The media and the communications network have covered the entire country in the last decades and have spread demonstration effects from other countries. The school system, although still very inadequate, has also grown rapidly. There has been an increasing concentration of population in urban areas. Many peasants became rural or urban workers, proletarians, as much land along the Pacific coast was converted into commercial plantations for export agriculture and also as a result of a rapid process of industrialization, which began in the 1950s. Last but not least, a very substantial change of attitudes and social values within the Catholic Church in El Salvador took place after the Second Vatican Council and the Conference of Latin American Bishops in Medellín.

All of this not only increased awareness of the inequalities but also gave rise to the moral conviction among the people that they were the victims of deep social inequities. As people moved from consciousness to organization and from organization to political action, the third of the factors involved, namely, the rigidity of the political system, turned such action into military conflict.

THE ILLEGITIMACY OF THE POLITICAL SYSTEM

Members of the Salvadorean oligarchy ruled the country directly until 1931. As a result of a massive peasant insurrection that cost the lives of no fewer than 20,000 people, a military dictatorship established itself in the country fifty years ago. Since then the military have been directly in charge of the political system. The officers of the army, in alliance with the civilian oligarchy, adopted a rigid, inflexible attitude toward anything that would oppose their domination or that would tend to change the kind of society to which they were accustomed and from which both groups derived considerable privileges.

It is enough to point out a few of the relevant facts of the last decade to illustrate the character and consequences of the political order in El Salvador. The dominant groups committed frauds in presidential elections in 1972 and 1977 and stopped an attempt to initiate a moderate but highly publicized program of agrarian reform in 1976. Reformist political parties, including the Christian Democrats and the Social Democrats, were denied electoral victory and access to the government, not to mention the power to implement basic reforms. Their leaders were exiled, their meetings forcibly repressed, and their grassroots organizations persecuted and dismantled. Thus, the system became more and more illegitimate. The willingness of the population to cooperate with or even to passively accept the military regimes fell to a historical low. The absence of peaceful, widely accepted methods to attain and preserve political power gave birth to massive political violence, and people decided to affiliate in ever-increasing numbers with different types of revolutionary organizations. These people had already reached the conclusion that there was no way other than armed struggle to implement basic reforms in El Salvador.

Such was the political context at the end of the last decade. The events that occurred just before and after October 15, 1979, are described and analyzed in this book. Before I end this introduction, however, I wish to add a personal note on El Salvador's present and near future.

THE PRESENT SITUATION: A STALEMATE

Military stalemate characterizes the present Salvadorean situation. Neither of the two battling sides has the capacity to achieve a total military victory, although both have the ability to continue the struggle for an indefinite period, albeit at a great cost in terms of suffering, human lives, and the economic future of El Salvador.

The guerrillas grouped in the Farabundo Martí Front for National Liberation (FMLN) have shown their capacity to destabilize any scheme of government that they do not support. Despite severe repression, they destabilized the regimes of Colonel Molina and General Romero during the 1970s to the point of provoking the general's downfall. They also destabilized the successive four juntas that governed El Salvador since the coup d'etat of October 15, 1979.

The guerrillas have a heroic tenacity that leaves no doubt about their determination to fight indefinitely and to suffer extreme consequences if forced to do so by circumstances. They have also shown expertise and ingenuity, acquired in unfavorable terrain over a long period, for clandestine and semiclandestine armed struggle. They count on the active and organized political support of large segments of the Salvadorean population. In contrast to the military approaches of other revolutionary movements of Latin America, massive political fronts have developed in El Salvador that are organically linked to the military units. In addition to that, the Farabundo Martí Front for National Liberation is now allied with a variety of political parties, labor unions, and church and university groups in a broad opposition coalition, the Democratic Revolutionary Front (FDR).

All these factors not only make entirely feasible prolonged clandestine and overt resistance by the revolutionary forces; they also make it impossible to achieve a lasting stability in the country, even in the unlikely case of a direct invasion of El Salvador by U.S. troops. Such resistance would even be strengthened by the very intense nationalistic feelings of antagonism that would be unleashed by an invasion by foreign military forces.

On the other hand, it is also true that the opposing coalition lacks sufficient capacity for a military triumph over the regular army of El Salvador in the foreseeable future. This was shown, for instance, when a "general offensive" was launched in January 1981 and the opposition failed to obtain control of the country, not because they did not fight for it but because they could not win. In addition, the Reagan administration is obviously building new and powerful obstacles to a military victory of the left in El Salvador.

Thus, the present government of El Salvador finds itself in a position in which it cannot achieve sufficient control to stabilize the country, although the forces that sustain it, particularly the army, are not likely to be defeated in the near future. This situation is not a novelty and everything seems to indicate that, in the absence of a solution other than military victory, El Salvador is destined for a very long and sterile conflict.

I wish I could present a more optimistic assessment of El Salvador's future and hope that, with the passage of time, more actors within and outside the country will become convinced of the necessity of a negotiated settlement. It seems to me that a solution that fully recognizes the political and military power of the revolutionary forces is the only rational alternative to an indefinite and increasingly destructive war.

México, D.F., 1981

1

The Coup of October

Cuando no hay balazos, el golpe es malo. *

—Salvadorean saying

Everything was set to go.[1] At 6:00 A.M., October 15, 1979, the commander of each of the fourteen army barracks in El Salvador would be awakened by one of his junior officers and informed that a coup d'etat was taking place, President/General Humberto Romero was being deposed, and he himself was under arrest and confined to quarters. As each commander was arrested the officer responsible was to call Lieutenant Colonel René Guerra y Guerra at the coup's command post in San Salvador, the capital city, and confirm that the barracks were securely in the hands of the Young Military. This was a small group of officers who had been plotting for five months to overthrow a corrupt regime that had acquired one of the worst reputations for violations of human rights in the Western Hemisphere.

Except for some eager-beaver lieutenants who jeopardized the entire operation by awakening their commanders at 4:00 in the morning, then calling San Salvador (thus risking the possibility that their calls would be intercepted), the coup itself was virtually flawless. Only one person died. When the commander at San Miguel resisted arrest, a soldier was killed in the ensuing scuffle. And there was some difficulty in persuading President Romero to depart. The Young Military wanted him out of the country before the afternoon papers appeared at 3:00; he flew to Guatemala at 5:00. By 6:00 the government of El Salvador was apparently in the hands of a group of young military officers (average age thirty-two), who became known as the Fifteenth of October Movement and who were determined to change what they viewed as a rather sordid political past of corruption and gross social and economic injustice.

*When there are no bullets, the coup d'etat is worthless.

7

PRELUDES

The moving forces behind the coup were two brothers, René and Rodrigo Guerra y Guerra. Upper middle class in origin, both are engineers and both attended college and graduate school in the United States. It was unusual for someone from their social class to choose the army as a career; most officers come from the lower middle class. But René Guerra made that choice. Rodrigo Guerra, meanwhile, became a successful businessman. It was also unusual for members of the Salvadorean upper middle class to have or to exhibit publicly a social conscience and to be concerned about the extraordinary concentration of wealth and power in a very few hands while the economic prospect for 80 percent of El Salvador's population became increasingly dismal with each passing year. But the Guerra brothers shared a concern about the unequal distribution of economic resources and opportunities, about a system of corruption that helped perpetuate these inequalities, and about the need for a modern, humane private sector if the country was to develop.

With the deteriorating economic and human rights situation in El Salvador, and the concurrent growth of the Popular Organizations of the left, the Guerras began thinking out loud to each other about the possibility of once again short-circuiting an electoral system that had come to be characterized by blatant corruption, of ridding the army of its most corrupt elements, and of placing the government in the hands of competent, progressive civilians and military officers committed to implementing needed social and economic reform and to defending human rights. Similar attempts had been made in the past, most notably in 1960 (see Chapter 3), but each attempt had ended with power once again in the hands of the most conservative sector of the army.

During March and April 1979 the Guerras met with a number of civilians to try to arrange President Romero's resignation through an agreement with the director of the National Guard, Colonel José Antonio Corleto, and the president of the National Assembly, Dr. José Leandro Echeverría, a relative of the Guerras. But the colonel and the legislator did not respond to the obvious hints being dropped.

On May 2 members of the Popular Revolutionary Bloc (BPR), the largest of El Salvador's Popular Organizations, occupied the Metropolitan Cathedral in downtown San Salvador and three embassies to demand the release of five imprisoned leaders, including the BPR secretary general, Facundo Guardado. A week later the oc-

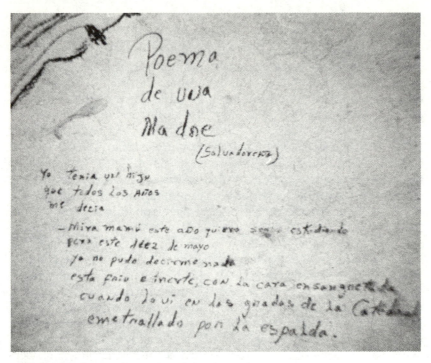

Photo 1.1 Poem of a Mother (Salvadorean).

    I had a son
    Who told me every year
    —Look, mama, this year I want to continue studying.
    But this May 10
    He couldn't tell me anything
    He was cold and stiff, his face bloody
    When I saw him on the steps of the cathedral
    Shot in the back.
    (This poem was written on the wall of a Salvadorean
    refugee center in Chinandega, Nicaragua.)

cupiers of the cathedral were joined by several hundred other demonstrators in the street outside. Suddenly eight members of the National Police opened fire on the demonstrators. When the shooting ended after twenty-five minutes, twenty-three people lay dead on the street and the steps of the cathedral. The government claimed that the BPR and its allies in the church had started the conflagration by firing machine guns from the cathedral towers, a charge refuted by many eyewitnesses, including foreign journalists.[2]

The Military Planning for the Coup

Following the massacre at the cathedral, the Guerras decided to proceed with their idea of a coup d'etat. René Guerra saw a good opportunity in a seminar on Nicaragua and Central America at the Camino Real Hotel in the capital to identify some of the more progressive officers within the army. The seminar was organized by INCAE, a graduate school of business in Nicaragua with ties to the Harvard Business School. In a masterly diversionary tactic, Guerra asked President Romero to send some of his officers. Among the officers Romero sent was Colonel Adolfo Majano, who would become one of the two military members of the junta four months later.

In July and August three critical developments occurred. First, René Guerra began consulting regularly with the archbishop of San Salvador, Monseñor Oscar Romero. Second, the Sandinista National Liberation Front (FSLN) and a popular insurrection succeeded on July 17 in driving Anastasio Somoza out of Nicaragua, thus ending a forty-seven year dynasty. With Somoza's departure the National Guard, which had been essentially the dictator's personal army, collapsed.[3]

The dissolution of the Nicaraguan National Guard, many of whose members fled through El Salvador, had a profound effect on many Salvadorean officers. They looked at the former guard officers and saw men who had lost everything: homes, money, and country. They looked at El Salvador's Popular Organizations and guerrilla forces and at their growing strength. And they saw the same fate that befell the Nicaraguans befalling them in another six to eight months. The Nicaraguan Revolution, more than any other single event, galvanized the feeling within the Young Military that there was a need for change.

In August a Military Coordinating Committee, working in tandem with a group of civilians, was formed and began feeling out officers in barracks around the country.[4] The process was extremely slow because the conspirators "were not sure who was loyal."†* Some Young Military did not trust René Guerra because they thought he was Humberto Romero's man.[5] Over the summer the committee found one young officer, either a lieutenant or a captain, in each barracks to identify and organize dissident officers, from second lieutenants through majors. The Coordinating Committee assumed the responsibility for recruiting among the upper ranks. On the morn-

---

*The symbol "†" throughout the book indicates privileged interviews (with informants who must remain anonymous).

ing of the coup, each young officer was charged with arresting his barracks commander and other senior officers identified by the *golpistas* (coup-makers) as corrupt or reactionary.[6]

Because the Coordinating Committee was concerned not merely to get rid of Humberto Romero and the reactionary elements within the armed forces but also to effect needed social and economic changes in the country, it quickly began looking for support within the civilian sector. Among the groups it approached were the Christian Democratic party, the Catholic Church, the Central American University, and the Popular Forum, a group of middle-class professionals who had been holding seminar-type sessions for months to discuss El Salvador's pressing problems and what might be done to change direction.

In August, Colonel Jaime Abdul Gutierrez, who was commander of the army's repair shop in San Salvador, learned about the plot. Guerra has said that he did not trust Gutierrez, knew he was corrupt, and had therefore not brought him into the movement. After Gutierrez got wind of the plot, two of his physicians, Drs. Alejandro Saca Meléndez and Roberto Badia, went to Monseñor Romero and tried to persuade him to pressure the Coordinating Committee to include Gutierrez. Romero, who had previously warned Guerra and the committee not to bring in Gutierrez, told them about the doctors' visit and that Gutierrez knew what was afoot; he recommended that Gutierrez be brought in so that it would be easier to watch him.[7] Later on Romero sent the committee a message that he opposed the inclusion of either Gutierrez or Colonel José Guillermo García in the new government. García was at the time commander of a small garrison in San Vicente, 64 kilometers east of San Salvador.

Civilian Coordination

While the military planning for the coup was going on, civilians were looking ahead to the problems of government and reform. Throughout the summer a group of civilians coordinated by Rodrigo Guerra worked on the Proclamation of the Armed Forces (Proclama de la Fuerza Armada), which they would issue immediately after the coup. These discussions focused on the country's problems and what steps should be taken to solve them. By October there were, in fact, three *proclamas*, the other two written by friends of Gutierrez. The first, however, prevailed as the more clear and comprehensive political document.

In June, the Guerras hinted at the possibility of a coup d'etat to the U.S. ambassador, Frank Devine. Devine indicated that this was a serious matter but that he was not disposed to oppose it. The Salvadoreans remained in sporadic contact with the embassy through the months of planning, but the United States was never involved in any way in the planning or execution of the coup. As one U.S. Embassy official said months later of this period, "We listened but we did not encourage or discourage. For once in our history we had nothing to do with it."[8] The Guerras interpreted this silence as support. They wanted to be sure that the coup would not be opposed by the United States, and that the United States would not betray them to the Romero regime. But they did not seek or desire any U.S. participation.

After the Nicaraguan Revolution the next event that concerned the Young Military was the meeting of the Organization of American States (OAS) scheduled for October 20 in Bogotá, Colombia. On the agenda for the meeting was a resolution offered by several countries condemning the Salvadorean government for its human rights violations. As October drew closer the dilemma for the Young Military in planning the coup was whether to wait until the regime was condemned and El Salvador blackened in the eyes of the world, thus providing additional justification for the coup, or to remove President Romero, make the issue moot, and go to the OAS meeting as a new government with a commitment to changing the old order.

The debate over the date for the coup continued into October. A decision was finally made to stage the coup after the OAS meeting, only to be changed at the last minute. The comedy of errors that weekend would have done justice to the Keystone Kops. On Thursday, October 11, President Romero flew to New Orleans for a physical examination. On Friday two senior officers got wind of impending disaster for Romero, whereupon they went to the military High Command. The minister of defense told them there was nothing to worry about; they called Romero and told him to return immediately.

Friday night seven officers were identified (erroneously) as being involved with the *golpistas* and arrest warrants were put out for each of them. As it happened, most of these officers were in the air force. Before the night was out, two of the seven had been arrested and the other five hid out in what are known colloquially in San Salvador as "hot sheet" motels. The word passed quickly and quietly among the conspirators that the coup could no longer be kept secret. Thus early on the thirteenth of October, the decision was made to act within forty-eight hours.

With President Romero's return the military staff of the Casa

Presidencial (the official offices of the president) went on full alert, waiting all through Saturday and Sunday for something to happen. There are stories that Romero and his closest aides spent a sleepless weekend, helped through it by "uppers." In any event, when Sunday passed quietly, the president and his fellow officers relaxed and went home to a good night's sleep. It was the last night they would spend in El Salvador.

THE COUP

As garrisons began to fall around the country the next morning, military officers assigned to the Casa Presidencial, sensing that something might happen, reported in fatigues. It was already happening. Shortly thereafter Colonel Gutierrez, in the name of the Coordinating Committee, called President Romero and the High Command. They were informed that a number of barracks were in the hands of the Young Military; that the president was no longer in office; and that the presence in the country of Romero, the minister and subsecretary of defense, the secretary to the president, and the commanders of the National Guard, National Police, and Treasury Police was no longer desired. There were guaranteed safe-conduct passes out of the country and told to leave by 3:00 P.M.

Romero did not believe it. He and Minister of Defense Federico Castillo Yanes went to the National Guard barracks in the center of San Salvador, only to learn that the National Guard, in a reversal of past behavior, was sitting it out. The subsecretary of defense, Colonel Eduardo Iraheta, went to the air force looking for support, only to discover a similar lack of enthusiasm for Romero. The president sent a helicopter over the main army barracks, San Carlos, shortly before noon. One nervous soldier shot at it with a machine gun—and missed.†

Romero's recalcitrance led the Guerras to seek assistance from the U.S. Embassy. When it became clear by late morning that the president was being stubborn, another Guerra brother, Hugo, called Ambassador Devine and asked him to call Romero. Devine declined to do so on the grounds that it was not the policy of the United States to intervene in the internal affairs of another country. After this rebuff, René Guerra called the U.S. military attaché, Colonel Gerald Walker, and asked him to stop by Rodrigo Guerra's office, which was located three blocks from the embassy. René Guerra wanted to explain the purpose of the coup to Walker and ask him to convey that information to Devine. Guerra also asked Walker to call Romero and encourage him to leave. Walker said he would call back later that afternoon; he did not call until the next morning.

There was one comical footnote. The commander and deputy commander of the San Miguel barracks, both of whom were heartily disliked by their officers and troops, were thrown into the stockade for several days. Then, someone with the authority and a perverse sense of humor to match ordered them taken out, cleaned up, and dressed in their uniforms. They were then driven into San Salvador and pushed out of the car in the middle of one of the biggest BPR demonstrations in months. The officers escaped by racing to a taxi, jumping in, and speeding off.

Formation of a Government

While military preparations were moving along in the days before the coup, political developments were proceeding apace. On October 6 Colonel Adolfo Majano was brought into the Coordinating Committee. Two days later the Young Military held a secret meeting during which they elected Majano and René Guerra the two military members of the junta. The next day, another meeting was called by Colonels Gutierrez and García. The election of Guerra was challenged on the grounds that he was too junior, being only a lieutenant colonel. Colonel Gutierrez's name was placed in nomination, and as the dissident group had managed to call all its allies, but not all Guerra's supporters, Gutierrez won the election.†[9] Guerra, on receiving the news, went to see Archbishop Romero and told him he was pulling out of the movement. Romero at first agreed that it was the right thing to do. The archbishop had second thoughts, however, and called Guerra the next day to recommend that he stay in. After Guerra met that same day with members of the Young Military in Rodrigo Guerra's office he decided to take the archbishop's advice.

Having decided to form a civilian-military junta with the civilians holding the majority of the seats, the next issue was whom to invite. The process was not as complicated as one might expect. Román Mayorga Quiroz, the rector of the Jesuit Central American University (UCA) in San Salvador, was the first choice of the Young Military. A political independent, Mayorga had written a book[10] that many of the Young Military had read. In it Mayorga had argued for a number of social and economic reforms in El Salvador with which the officers were in accord. So it was that on October 12 Mayorga met with the Young Military and laid down three conditions on which he would become a member of the junta: (1) There would have to be a clean-up of the military, with all corrupt and right-wing officers dismissed or retired; (2) there would have to be meaningful social change, including agrarian reform and nationalization of the banks and external commerce, with a consolidation of the various armed forces in support of this position; and (3) another member of the junta would have to come from the Popular Forum. The following day Mayorga met with Gutierrez and Majano in the house of Rodrigo Guerra. During this period Rodrigo Guerra showed Mayorga the three versions of the Proclama, and Mayorga liked the one ultimately selected by the Young Military, the one written by the group coordinated by Guerra.

As Mayorga had stipulated that one of the other civilians on the junta would have to come from the Forum, he called its leaders on October 16 and invited them to a meeting in San Carlos. Among those present were Guillermo Manuel Ungo, a Social Democrat, also in the UCA administration. The following day, at a meeting in the Casa Presidencial, Ungo was selected by the Forum to be its man on the Junta. The third member of the junta, Mario Andino, a moderately conservative businessman, was selected by Majano and Gutierrez after consulting the business community.

Commitment and Betrayal

Thus, on the night of October 17, 1979, El Salvador had a new government. The five members of the junta had pledged themselves to support and carry out the principles of the Proclama – yet that document already was being undermined by military officers who had other priorities but who kept them hidden until after Humberto Romero was out of the country.

The Proclama began with an acknowledgment that the previous regime had "violated human rights," had "fomented and tolerated corruption," had "created an economic and social disaster," and had "profoundly discredited" the armed forces in the eyes of the country. It then announced the formation of the Revolutionary Junta of Government and of an Emergency Program "to create a climate of tranquility and to establish the foundation on which a profound transformation of the economic, social, and political structures of the country can be sustained."

The Emergency Program called for an end to the violence and corruption through, among other things, the dissolution of ORDEN (Nationalist Democratic Organization – a right-wing paramilitary vigilante organization of armed peasants that had been formed ten years earlier to combat communism and promote "democratic" values

in the countryside); a guarantee of respect for human rights, beginning with a general amnesty for all political prisoners; implementation of a process of agrarian reform; reform of the financial sector and
external commerce; freedom for the Popular Organizations to operate;
and finally, reestablishment of relations with Honduras and improve-
ment of relations with Nicaragua.

Gutierrez gave verbal support to the Proclama. But he had his
own game plan. He was not sure just how far the Young Military intended to go in restructuring the armed forces and he was equally un-
sure how far *he* wanted the proposed economic reforms to go. He saw
himself as a minority of one on a junta that he viewed as being radical.
He wanted company. So at 1:00 A.M. on October 16, after the Proclama had been read to the nation, Gutierrez picked up the phone and
called Colonel José Guillermo García, commander of the garrison at
San Vicente. "You are the minister of defense," Gutierrez told a
pleased García. The decision to appoint García to the defense post was
made unilaterally and without consulting anyone, including Gutierrez's fellow military colleague on the junta, Adolfo Majano.[11] That the
junta, when it was fully constituted two days later, and the Young
Military accepted García's appointment as a fait accompli is indicative
of two problems that would plague the junta and the government — and ultimately bring about the government's resignation two
and a half months later. Those problems included a lack of
decisiveness on the part of certain junta members in the face of the
growing intransigence of the minister of defense and the great
political naiveté of the Young Military.

Meanwhile, Colonel García appointed his old ANTEL colleague,
Colonel Nicolás Carranza, as sub-secretary of defense. These two men
demonstrated in the days following the coup that they did not share
the priorities of the Proclama or the Young Military.

On the night of October 15, one of El Salvador's five guerrilla
forces, the Revolutionary Army of the People (ERP), occupied San
Marcos and Mejicanos, two working-class suburbs of San Salvador.
García decided to send in the army, then apprised Gutierrez and Ma-
jano of his intention. This was precisely the sort of action the Young
Military were committed *not* to take.

René Guerra was awakened on the sixteenth and told of the
ERP's action and García's plan. By his own account, Guerra im-
mediately called Gutierrez and Majano and said, "We've got to stop
García and call back the army." The two junta members agreed.
Guerra then went to the Casa Presidencial and confronted all three
men. In front of García, Guerra asked Majano "what the hell" García

was doing there. Majano said he was going to try to work with the new minister of defense. Guerra then went to see Archbishop Romero and asked him to mediate with the ERP. When Romero hesitated, Guerra reminded him of the previous week's events and that he, Guerra, was still involved in the movement because of Romero's insistence. Romero then went to talk with his advisers while Guerra phoned Gutierrez and Majano. During this time, García ordered the attack. Majano and Gutierrez did nothing.[12]

Then, at a meeting in San Carlos two days later, the Young Military began discussing the reforms proposed in the Proclama and argued that they should be implemented as peacefully as possible. According to an army officer present during the meeting, García and Carranza argued instead that the first priority should be the restructuring of the armed forces and that the reforms should be postponed until afterward. The minister and his subsecretary also argued that the focus should be on external problems, that is, "the possibility of an attack from Honduras, Guatemala, or Nicaragua."† The Young Military accepted the possibility of an attack from Guatemala but thought the other suggestions preposterous. In any event they did not want to spend time worrying about or preparing for such an attack. Throughout this discussion Gutierrez sided with García and Carranza while Majano, in the words of one young officer present, talked of nothing but "changes, changes, changes."†

By the end of the first week then, the Young Military recognized that a new division existed within the armed forces. It was not a split between corrupt, right-wing officers on one side and progressive, uncorrupted officers on the other; nor was it a division (with a few exceptions) within the officer corps. Rather it was a division between the High Command (with Gutierrez) on one side and the bulk of the officer corps (with Majano) on the other. This division became more obvious with the passage of time; it was one that would profoundly affect the future of El Salvador.

Public Reaction

Reaction to the coup ranged from shock on the part of the Salvadorean oligarchy to outrage on the part of the Popular Organizations of the left. The oligarchy, often referred to as the "Fourteen Families" but in modern times consisting of about forty (extended) families who have long controlled the economic life of the country, had been totally unaware that a coup was being planned and was stunned into silence when it occurred. The silence lasted as long as it took for its members to realize that the junta was really serious about the proposed reforms and that the army had every intention (apparently) of backing up the reforms. Then the silence turned, as it had many times before, to anguished protests and increasingly enraged attacks on the proposals for agrarian reform and nationalization of the banks and of external commerce.

The response of the revolutionary organizations was more complex. Some had been predicting a popular insurrection for January or February 1980. None believed the army was serious about the Proclama, and there was nothing in Salvadorean history to suggest that the Proclama should be taken seriously by people who had long been subjected to electoral fraud and official repression. At the same time, there were indications that the various organizations wanted to see what the new government would do.

The Popular Forces of Liberation (FPL), for example, publicly opposed the junta; but one of its clandestine members, a university professor of philosophy named Salvador Samayoa, accepted the post of minister of education. When the ERP attempted to spark an insurrection in two suburbs of San Salvador, it discovered that many people were willing to give the new government a chance. The ERP subsequently announced a unilateral cease-fire, which lasted until October 29, when twenty-one members of its mass organization, the 28th of February Popular League (LP-28), were gunned down by the National Guard in the center of San Salvador. Members of other Popular Organizations occupied the Economic and Labor ministries for two and a half weeks, thus making it impossible for the new government to get two crucial areas functioning.

The junta immediately created a special human rights commission to investigate the whereabouts of political prisoners whose release had been demanded by their families, human rights groups, and the Popular Organizations. While political prisoners still alive were freed in the general amnesty, many others whose release had been demanded had simply "disappeared";[13] the commission could find no trace of them. This provoked criticism that the new government was covering up the sins of its predecessor.[14]

Most seriously, the repression at the hands of the government's security forces did not stop. In fact, more people died in the first three weeks after the coup than had died in any equivalent period during the Romero regime.[15] The junta was not bringing the security forces under control as it had committed itself to do. This provoked harsh criticism both from the Popular Organizations and from the Catholic Church which had indicated that if the repression ceased, it was disposed to give the junta a chance to improve on the record of its predecessor.

THE ROLE OF THE UNITED STATES

The U.S. government publicly breathed a great sigh of relief that President Romero, with his appalling record on human rights, was gone. In the next breath it offered renewed economic and military assistance to the Revolutionary Junta of Government, assistance that had been largely terminated in 1977. In the following weeks U.S. policy began operating on two levels. Officially that policy was to support human rights and to encourage social, political, and economic changes that would result in a fairer distribution of the wealth and ameliorate the pressing social problems with which El Salvador has been confronted. At the same time, what in fact the United States did produced very different results from those the embassy claimed to want.

In the first place, having made a major issue of human rights from early 1977 until October 15, 1979, the United States fell silent in the face of an escalating number of massacres and assassinations at the hands of the Salvadorean security forces and civilians after the coup. Officially, according to embassy officials the human rights policy continued in force but was being pursued through quieter channels.

Second, with the growing agitation from the left in the form of demonstrations, the occupation of embassies, factories, farms, and various security forces barracks around the country, the United States began encouraging a "law and order" line within the Salvadorean military. Roughly, the argument was: "The left has to be brought under control. You cannot permit them to get away with these kinds of attacks because they will only increase in frequency and intensity and before long they will be mounting an insurrection."

It is necessary to understand the U.S. officials had a clear, liberal-democratic definition of "law and order." For them it was the maintenance of social order within a constitutional and legal framework that most of their fellow citizens enjoy most of the time within their own political system. It assumed a legal system that works and a police force that is well trained and relatively well educated and that does not serve during off-duty hours as paid assassins or vigilantes for the monied class. As none of these preconditions obtained in El Salvador, what happened was that "law and order" was instantly translated into repression, a fact that the United States either overlooked or chose to ignore. It is not clear which, as officials declined to acknowledge that this transformation was occurring. Rather, they argued that the "terrorist" activities of the left provoked harsh tactics and that when the left was brought under control these tactics would no longer be necessary. They also expressed the hope that with the resumption of military aid, which in the fall of 1979 included troop training, the Salvadorean armed forces could be made more efficient and less barbaric in their crowd-control methods. Theoretically, the difference was between using tear gas and using bullets.

Third, the U.S. Embassy, particularly its senior officials, actively supported the business community of El Salvador. A senior diplomat acknowledged that he went "to bat" for the private enterprise sector because he felt it had "been done an injustice" by the government after October 15.

What U.S. officials failed to understand was that pushing a "law and order" line on the one hand and supporting private enterprise on the other played directly into the hands of the most conservative sectors of Salvadorean society.

THE FIRST JUNTA

Informed observers have said that 90 percent of those in the government between October 15, 1979, and January 3, 1980, were the "cream of the country."† Several ministers and subsecretaries were drawn from the Central American University, including two of the civilian members of the junta and the foreign minister, Héctor Dada Hirezi. Luís Buitrago resigned as controller of the Inter-American Development Bank to return home as head of the Central Reserve Bank. Other Salvadoreans returned from exile as well to assume government posts. René Guerra accepted the innocuous post of subsecretary of the interior; his brother, Rodrigo, became director of CEL, the national power company. In short, the overwhelming majority of the people who came into the government were intelligent, well educated, competent, and honest.

But the immediate problems discussed above were compounded by Salvadorean political reality, which subverted in more fundamental ways the goals and ideals of the Young Military and their civilian allies and led directly to the resignation of the government on January 3, 1980. The key problem was that García and Gutierrez refused to take the army out of politics. Meanwhile, the Young Military, for all its commitment to ridding the army of corruption and to effecting needed social and economic changes in El Salvador, suffered from great political naiveté.

Part of that naiveté included the belief that getting rid of seventy senior army officers and installing new leadership in the Salvadorean High Command would automatically bring about control of the various security forces,[16] long notorious for the use of excessive force against the population, especially in the countryside. Unfortunately, the new members of the High Command turned out to be no more disposed to controlling the security forces than their predecessors.

The Young Military officers also shared a terror of the fate that befell the Nicaraguan National Guard—its total destruction as an institution. The fear of institutional destruction produced a situation that the oligarchy, working hand in glove with García, effectively exploited.† Through a variety of means, primarily direct contact with the High Command, members of the oligarchy set about to convince key officers, especially Minister of Defense García and his subsecretary, Carranza (who needed little convincing), that (1) the triumph of the left in a revolution would mean the dissolution of the army and security forces; (2) a revolution would mean the triumph of communism in one more country; and (3) the economic changes proposed by the junta were really communism in disguise.

Naiveté caused the army to respond legalistically rather than politically when confronted with an ultimatum by all but one of the ministers of state at the end of December. The ministers demanded a halt to the growing repression; the Young Military, however, through their self-created institution, the Permanent Council of the Armed Forces (COPEFA), rejected that demand after three days of deliberation. COPEFA's position was that it was a nonpolitical institution and therefore could not be involved in an essentially political question. COPEFA, however, had been created for a profoundly political purpose: to ensure that the Proclama was carried out.

THE GOVERNMENT RESIGNS

The crisis broke on December 26 when García appeared, uninvited and accompanied by the High Command, at a meeting of the cabinet. According to a government official present at that meeting, a "screaming match" ensued during which García told the ministers they were going too far with their proposed reforms. The ministers

Figure 1.1 As the political situation deteriorated in December 1979 a conservative middle-class organization, underwritten in part by ANEP and calling itself the Nationalist Feminine League, began placing *campos pagados* in the newspapers and staged two demonstrations demanding "Peace and Work." Caption at top reads "The valiant and dignified before the pack," referring to the Popular Organizations on the lower right. The signs read from the top: "We are with our army," "Peace and Work," "Violence, no! Order, yes!" "Changes within the law." The LP-28 member is saying (balloon), "Everyone ready! Don't forget the rocks and insults!"

responded by telling García and company that the reforms were none of their business.† In a country that had been ruled by the military for almost half a century that was an intolerable heresy.

There was a widespread feeling within the cabinet that it should resign that day. Undoubtedly García felt the same way. Instead, the ministers took their case to COPEFA which, advised by lawyers supplied by the oligarchy, declined to intervene.[17]

As the year ended, Archbishop Romero was enlisted to try and resolve the crisis through mediation. But COPEFA would not budge, and the ministers felt that to back down would leave them powerless and would betray the commitment they had made to the Salvadorean people two and a half months earlier.[18] So, on January 3, Guillermo Manuel Ungo, Román Mayorga, the entire cabinet (minus the minister of defense and his subsecretary), and all heads of state-owned companies resigned. One day later, Mario Andino also left the junta.[19]

ILLUSION AND REALITY

The coup of October appeared to alter radically the roles that each of the major actors on the Salvadorean political stage had been playing. It seemed that the oligarchy, for the first time in its hundred-year history, had been shoved into the wings. The army seemed to have cast itself in a role very different from its traditional part as handmaiden of the oligarchy. From now on, it proclaimed, it would be the servant of the people.

Until 1970 the army and the oligarchy by and large had had the stage to themselves. The Catholic Church had been a silent presence, supportive by its inaction but occasionally sallying forth to warn the faithful against the dangers of communism. But the Salvadorean church began to change in the late 1960s and began speaking out on issues of social justice and human rights. Its increasingly pointed attacks on governmental repression, coupled with its concerted efforts at evangelization through the development of Christian Base Communities (CEBs), not only made it an object of persecution by 1970 but also led (unintentionally) to its spawning the first of the Popular Organizations of 1974. These organizations from that time forced their way into the Salvadorean political arena. They were uninvited and certainly unwelcome to those who wished to maintain the status quo. But by the end of the decade, they were stealing scenes and drawing the largest crowds.

The last actor generally relegated itself to walk-on parts, which is

Photo 1.2 Lake Ilopango and San Salvador Volcano.

not to say that its occasional performances were unimportant or un-
forgettable. The U.S. government tended, like the church but for a
longer period of time, to specialize in a supporting role, although there
were occasions when it assumed directorial responsibilities. Many
Salvadoreans, regardless of political stripe, wish the United States
would go out and sit in the orchestra or, better yet, the rear balcony.

As in the past, however, the old forces reemerged in the weeks
following the coup. By mid-1980 the oligarchy, with its new allies in
the army, was doing battle with the revolutionary organizations for
center stage. The church, having lost its headliner, Archbishop Oscar
Romero, to an assassin's bullet, was deeply divided. The United
States, leaping back and forth from stage to director's chair, was trying
to convince everyone that yet another actor was present and indeed
occupied center stage: a "moderate, reformist" junta. Unfortunately,
that player was a phantom.

This book is an effort to analyze and explain these and other
lesser actors on the political stage of El Salvador. It is an attempt to
understand how a beautiful country of charming people could come to
the point of tearing itself apart through civil war or popular insurrection. And it seeks to explain why the country may have to be torn
apart before it can put itself back together again.

The next chapter provides demographic information and a history of the country between the conquest in 1525 and the 1932 peasant revolt, with attention to the rise of the oligarchy and its consolidation of economic and political power. Chapter 3 continues the story from 1932 to 1979 and focuses on the division of labor effected between the oligarchy, which continued to control the national economy, and the military, which assumed responsibility for running the state.

Chapters 4 and 5 focus on the period from 1970 to 1980, with specific attention to the two actors that have changed the course of history in El Salvador. The Catholic Church, discussed in Chapter 4, never had any intention of becoming a political actor in Salvadorean life; but in trying to be faithful to its understanding of the biblical message and of church social doctrine, particularly as it developed after 1965, it was thrust onto the stage and has never left. In Chapter 5 we look at the revolutionary organizations, their genesis, growth, programs, and errors.

Chapter 6 reviews and assesses developments in El Salvador from January 1980 to April 1982. Particular attention is paid to the United States, which has oscillated between its desire for social change and its fear of communism. The book closes with a prognosis but not conclusion. That will be written by the people of El Salvador.

2

The Roots of Revolution

Cuando la historia no se puede escribir con la pluma, hay que escribirla con el fusil. *

— Augustín Farabundo Martí

THE BOTTOM LINE

In 1981 El Salvador, the only country in the Central American isthmus without an Atlantic coast, had almost 5 million people crammed into a territory about the size of Massachusetts, thus giving it the highest population density in all of Latin America (212/sq km). Salvadoreans are privileged to live in one of the most breathtakingly beautiful countries in the Western Hemisphere: a land, except for a narrow strip along the Pacific Coast, of undulating mountain ranges punctuated by a string of mostly extinct volcanoes that begins in Mexico and runs through most of the isthmus. It is a land that has produced incredible wealth since the conquest in the mid-1520s but where 80 percent of the people still live in abject poverty.

The dimensions of that poverty can be grasped by considering the following: In 1975, 41 percent of the rural population had no land, an increase from 11.8 percent in 1950. The average annual income per landless family (of six members) was $317. If one includes families with plots of less than 1 to 5 hectares (1 hectare = 2.47 acres), income for 96.13 percent of rural families was $576 per year. The poor in the cities fared little better. The poorest 10 percent of families in San Salvador had an average annual income of $330, the poorest 40 percent, $618.[1]

At the other end of the economic scale, we find that in 1961, six families (0.0023 percent of all landowners) in El Salvador held 71,923 hectares, or 4.6 percent of all the land under cultivation.[2] In 1979, the Salvadorean Ministry of Agriculture reported that 0.7 percent of all

* When history can no longer be written with the pen, it must be written with the rifle.

27

TABLE 2.1

El Salvador: Basic Demographic Data

Land Size (Km^2)	20,935
Population (1979)	4.4 million
Projected (1985)	5.9 million
Population Density (1979 per Km^2)	212
Average Annual Rate of Growth, 1970-79	2.9%
Percent Urban (1979)	40.2
Percent Literate (1975)	60
Urban	82
Rural	47
Landless	34
Female	59
Male	65.5
Birth Rate per 1,000 inhabitants (1978)	39.7
Mortality Rate per 1,000 inhabitants (1978)	6.9
Infant Mortality per 1,000 live births (1977)	59.5
Years of Life Expectancy at Birth	62.2

SOURCE: Inter-American Development Bank; Dirección General de
Estadística y Censos, El Salvador.

property owners held 40 percent of the land. Income distribution was
equally skewed. The average annual income of the wealthiest 10 percent in the capital (and one should keep in mind that, traditionally,
virtually all large landowners have been absentee landlords living in
San Salvador or out of the country) in 1975 was greater than the combined average income of the lowest 90 percent.[3]

It is well known that data can be manipulated to support
arguments on both sides of an issue. What is striking about the presentation of data on the distribution of land and wealth in a variety of
sources is that although the exact numbers vary, the findings are consistent: The land of El Salvador is and has been for many years
concentrated in the hands of a minuscule (and shrinking) number of
proprietors, while the number of landless people has grown. Furthermore, the incomes of the poorest Salvadoreans have stagnated while
those of the wealthiest have multiplied. Tables 2.2 and 2.3 present

TABLE 2.2

Land Owners and Land Holdings, 1979

Number of Hectares	Number of Proprietors[1]	Percent	Total Hectares	Percent	Average Farm Size Hectares
Less than 1	86,798	37.20	28,126	2.55	.32
1 - 10	144,516	61.95	222,399	20.15	1.54
100 - 999	1,894	.81	636,166	57.65	335.88
1,000 or more	82	.04	216,796	19.65	2643.85
TOTAL	233,290	100.00	1,103,487	100.00	

SOURCE: Salvador Arias Peñate, "Las Perspectivas del Desarrollo Agropecuario en Relación con la Tenencia de la Tierra," Estudios Centroamericanos (ECA), No. 379, May, 1980, p. 462.

[1]The Departments of San Miguel, Morazán and La Unión are excluded from these data.

TABLE 2.3

Average Family Income in the Agricultural Sector by Size of Landholding
(1975 prices)

Size of Holdings[a]	1961	1975	Percent Increase
Families Without Land	$ 408	$ 430	5.4
Microfincas	522	583	11.7
Sub-families	734	928	26.4
Family	1,902	3,047	60.2
Multi-family Medium	9,748	16,044	64.6
Multi-family Large	39,676	89,786	126.3

SOURCE: Ministry of Agriculture. Based on figures from the Central Reserve
Bank of El Salvador and the National Census, 1961-1971. Cited in Salvador
Arias Peñate, "Las Perspectivas del Desarrollo Agropecuario en Relación con
la Tenencia de la Tierra," ECA, No. 379, May, 1980, p. 457.

[a]These categories are defined as follows: Microfincas--"farms large enough
to provide employment for one person with typical incomes, markets and levels
of technology and capital now prevailing in each region"; Sub-families--
"employment for less than two people with typical incomes . . . ."; Multi-
family, Medium--"employment for 4 to 12 people . . . ."; Multi-family, Large--
"employment for over 12 people." Source: Solon Barraclough and Arthur Domike,
"Agricultural Structure in Seven Latin American Countries," in Agricultural
Problems and Peasant Movements in Latin America, ed. Rodolfo Stavenhagen
(Garden City, N.Y.: Doubleday-Anchor, 1970), p. 48. Original source of
categories: Inter-American Committee for Agriculture Development (CIDA) Studies.

graphic evidence of this phenomenon. In Table 2.2 we find a
breakdown of landownership as of September 1979.[4] We see that
99.15 percent of the landowners held 22.7 percent of the land, while
the remaining 0.85 percent owned 77.3 percent of the land.

In Table 2.3 the financial results of this land distribution are
revealed. The most striking feature of these data is that, while the income of families in the first three categories remained essentially the
same between 1961 and 1975, income in the next two categories increased by 36.7 percent and 39.2 percent, respectively, while the income of the families with the greatest landholdings increased by 55.8
percent. Meanwhile, UN data revealed that consumer prices in-

creased between 1970 and 1977 by 181.9 percent. It is a textbook example, certainly not unique in the Third World, of the poor getting poorer while the rich become richer.

The effects in human terms of this inequality can be measured by examining the income distribution relative to the minimum amount needed to keep body and soul together in 1975. According to official sources, a family of six in that year needed an income of $704 in order to provide life's basic necessities. But almost 80 percent of Salvadorean families did not earn that much.[5] Furthermore, about 60 percent did not earn enough ($533) to provide even a minimum diet. The results are unequivocal: El Salvador has the lowest per capita calorie intake of any Latin American country; in the countryside, 73 percent of the children suffer from malnutrition; 60 of every 1,000 infants die; more than a quarter million families (39 percent of the rural population) live in one-room dwellings; and only 37 percent of families have access to potable water.[6]

These facts of Salvadorean life, although current, are not new. They are the result of developments that can be traced back to the colonial period. It is to that era that we must turn our attention before a more complete discussion of contemporary social, political, and economic realities is possible.

HISTORICAL PATTERNS

The history of El Salvador can be understood in terms of an interlocking and interacting series of phenomena that took shape during the three hundred years of Spanish colonial rule and continued after independence. These phenomena may be summarized as follows:

1. An economic cycle of "booms" and depressions that replayed itself as variations on a theme several times between the sixteenth and nineteenth centuries;
2. Dependence on a monocrop economy as the primary source of wealth, leading to dependence on outside markets;
3. Exploitation of the labor supply, first the Indians and later the peasants;
4. Concentration of the land in the hands of an ever-decreasing number of proprietors;
5. Extreme concentration of wealth in few hands, coupled with the utter deprivation of the overwhelming majority of the population;
6. A laissez-faire economic philosophy and an absolute belief in

Photo 2.1 Peasant mother and children in Santa Ana. The bloated stomachs of the children are a characteristic sign of malnutrition.

the sanctity of private property;
7. A classical liberal notion of the purpose of government – to
   maintain order;
8. Periodic rebellion by exploited segments of the population
   against perceived injustices.

These phenomena produced two persistent patterns in
Salvadorean history: (1) The distribution of resources was unequal
from the beginning, and the effects were cumulative as population
pressures exacerbated the inequities in the extreme; and (2) there was
always conflict between communal lands and private property, with
the latter regularly gaining at the expense of the former.

THE CONQUEST

First sighted by the Spanish in 1522, the land called Cuzcatlán
repelled the first wave of would-be settlers two years later. The Pipil
Indians, the dominant group among the Náhua, who had emigrated
from Mexico centuries before, sent Hernán Cortés's captain, Pedro de
Alvarado, scurrying back to Guatemala in less than a month. One year
later Pedro's brother, Gonzalo, tried again and succeeded in establishing a settlement, Villa San Salvador, only to be burned out by the
stubborn Pipiles. A third expedition in 1528 reestablished the settlement. Very soon thereafter Spanish harassment of the Pipiles caused
the Indians to revolt. The revolt produced, in turn, the first wave of
repression of the indigenous population by the colonists. Rebellions
continued for a decade but by 1539 the Spanish had sufficient control
over the territory to consider the indigenous population "subjects of
the royal service."
    The social and political system that the Spanish disrupted and
ultimately destroyed was a "military democracy organized by tribe,
with common ownership of the land."[7] Pipil society was a class society
that practiced monogamy and that included the institution of slavery.
In Cuzcatlán, however, people were enslaved as a result of war or
civil wrong and slavery was not hereditary.
    Between 1525 and 1535 most of the present cities of El Sal-
vador were founded. In 1546 San Salvador received its title as a city
from the Spanish crown. During the first seventeen years of settlement Cuzcatlán was governed directly from Guatemala and for most
of the colonial period remained part of the Audiencia of Guatemala.

THE FIRST CYCLE: CACAO

The earliest colonists in Cuzcatlán, like their countrymen in Mexico and Peru, were driven by a desire for instant wealth that could be sent back to Spain as a nest egg (after giving the crown its share) to await the master's return. Unlike other European colonizers, who came to the New World with the intention of staying, the Spaniards were interested only in what they could extract from the land that would ensure them a position of wealth and status in Iberia.

In contrast to the Mexica (Aztec) and Inca empires, there was little gold or silver in Cuzcatlán—although the *conquistadores* proceeded to extract what there was through the laborious method of panning, an endeavor that continued for approximately thirty years. Being few in number, the colonists lost no time conscripting Indian labor for this task. Meanwhile, cattle and sheep were introduced, and the cultivation of cereals for local consumption by the colonists was begun. It soon became clear that the wealth of Cuzcatlán lay in the land, and so the first search for "the key to wealth" from exports began.[8]

This search was the first step in a cycle that would play itself out in the following manner:

- discovery of a new crop
- rapid development of the crop
- period of great prosperity from the export of the crop
- dramatic decline or stagnation
- economic depression during which a frantic search for a replacement ensued
- discovery of a new crop and the beginning of another cycle

While balsam trees were discovered along the Pacific Coast of Izalcos (now Sonsonate) and became an important export crop for the Audiencia between 1560 and 1600, it was cacao that provided the first key to wealth in El Salvador. The cultivation of cacao also developed in Izalcos where the rich volcanic soil was particularly suitable to its cultivation.

The cacao plantations were owned and operated by the Indians before the conquest. They were soon forced, however, to deal only with Spanish or *mestizo* exporters. This arrangement evolved rather quickly into the *encomienda* (royal grant) system, and the export of cacao came to be dominated by three *encomenderos* by the early 1540s. With the growing popularity of cacao in Europe prices rose. The first massive fortunes for the *encomenderos*, their progeny, and between

100 and 200 creole and *mestizo* merchants who benefited from the spillover were assured.

While the plantations remained in Indian hands, the first forms of exploitation manifested themselves early on. The *encomenderos* demanded more and more cacao for export, which required more labor. The Indian farmers paid well, but the indigenous population, susceptible to imported disease, was dying in droves. Many Indians from the highlands migrated to the coast to work in the plantations but were unable to adjust to the climatic change. Meanwhile, the Spaniards were enslaving other Indians and shipping them to Panama and Peru. As the indigenous population declined the colonists began importing slaves from Africa. By 1550 there was a large Black population in El Salvador.

The primary source of exploitation in this period, however, came from the system of tribute, a carry-over from the Mexica system and a legalized form of extortion. Tribute was extracted in two ways. Formal tribute was exacted from indigenous households of married people in the Audiencia. Then there was a tribute levied on property. This was particularly directed at the cacao plantations and kept many theoretically wealthy Indian growers in virtual poverty.

The first economic cycle peaked in the 1570s and had all the earmarks of a monoculture boom. Murdo MacLeod has written that the region was "so packed with cacao trees that other crops could scarcely be grown. Food was imported and prices were high."[9]

The population decline coupled with a halt in the importation of slaves began to take its toll on the cacao plantations. The plight of the Indian growers, unable to meet production demands and therefore to pay the required tribute, had a ripple effect that became a tidal wave. Smaller *encomiendas* began reverting to the crown while the larger ones succeeded in consolidating their power. By 1600 the boom was over and the economic decline had begun. Depression hit with full force in 1610 and continued for half a century, producing the first extended economic crisis in Central America. This depression would profoundly affect the future of El Salvador by spawning two institutions that would shape the economic, political, and social life of the country. The institutions were the *hacienda* and debt peonage.

THE SECOND CYCLE: INDIGO

The decimation of the indigenous population and the migration of many of the remaining Indians either by force or because of economic exigency had three important effects. It destroyed the tradi-

tional forms of tribal organization; it spurred the development or re-
formation of indigenous villages; and it created a Spanish-speaking
peasantry for an emerging agrarian society.

The decline of cacao set off a protracted search for a replacement
crop, but as the region plunged into economic depression the creoles'
survival demanded that certain intermediate steps be taken. The
result was the establishment of self-sufficient *haciendas* in the countryside, a new emphasis on cattle breeding and the cultivation of
maize, and a consequent de-emphasis of the cities. These developments, along with the depression, weakened ties with Spain by under-
mining the existing economic links.

The quest for a substitute export crop centered for a time on
cochineal or *grana*, a scarlet dye produced by the wingless female
cochineal insect. But Central American *grana*, in spite of major efforts,
was never able to compete with that of Oaxaca, Mexico, and it waned
as an export crop in the 1620s.[10]

Another dye, however, fared much better. Indigo (*añil*), a deep
blue dye, was to become the second key to wealth in El Salvador.
Before the conquest, Indians had relied on the haphazard growth of
the hardy wild indigo plant. Demand in Europe led to its intensive
cultivation. Unlike cacao, which was a labor-intensive crop, indigo required little attention. It grew in a variety of soil and climatic conditions; the plots could be "weeded" by cattle, who ignored the indigo
plants; and the two-month period of the harvest, although requiring
increased numbers of workers, nonetheless was far better suited to a
shrunken population. Indigo had become Central America's primary
export by 1600 but it was another century before the "boom" arrived.
When it did, it lasted for almost a century and a half.

As Central America slid into economic depression, pressures
were also being exerted on the Indians and their communal lands.
From the earliest days of the colonial period Indians had been forced
from or tricked out of their lands. These methods reached epidemic
proportions in the 1590s thanks to lawyers, money, the crown's own
financial bind, and a lack of understanding on the part of the colonists
of the ecological and economic basis of Indian society. The resulting
confiscations were accompanied by efforts to persuade Indians to
leave their villages and attach themselves to an *hacienda* as *colonos* or
aparceros. *Colonos* were virtual serfs; they were given small plots
(*milpas*) on which to grow food for their families. In return they paid
the *patrono* rent or provided labor for a specified period. *Aparceros*
were essentially sharecroppers, although there were many variations
of both *colonaje* and *aparcería*.[11]

The exploitation of the *encomenderos* gave way to *repartimiento* and debt peonage. The former consisted of a rotation system of draft labor imposed on indigenous villages. Theoretically, the draft was to fall equally on all men of the village; in practice there were many exemptions and the onus generally fell on an unfortunate few. Debt peonage was a system of permanently binding the Indians to an *hacienda*, usually by tricking them into a debt they could not repay. These people became serfs, living on the *hacienda* and dependent upon the *patrono* for their very existence. Variations abounded. Sharecropping permitted a family to cultivate its own *milpa* on the *hacienda* and build its own dwelling. In return for this, husband and wife were required to work several days per week for the *patrono*.

The result of all these economic and social pressures during the seventeenth century was the establishment of patterns of land tenure that would endure into the last quarter of the twentieth century. At the same time, new pressures were being created that would lead to political unrest. The growing stability of the reestablished indigenous communities and the *hacienda* system led to a gradual population increase. The ever more extensive cultivation of indigo once again led to the need to import food. And finally, the Audiencia's laissez-faire policy permitted even greater accumulation of wealth than had occurred with cacao.

The seventeenth century depression, MacLeod has written, left its mark: "Although trade had revived and the peasant population now began to grow slowly, the Spaniards of the area had learned their lesson well. The backdrop, insurance economy of large, self-sufficient cattle estates worked by peonage, and the other system of conservative neo-indigenous villages resisting intrusion was to survive each succeeding boom and depression."[12] The economic cycle that began with the cultivation of indigo flourished for two hundred years. By the late eighteenth century between 300 and 400 families controlled the political and economic life of El Salvador.

As the rumblings of the independence movement began, there were four forms of land ownership in Central America's smallest colony. In spite of the annexations and usurpations by the Spanish, a plurality of the land continued to be held by the Indians or *mestizos* in communal lands or *ejidos*; between one-quarter and one-third of the total land area was divided among large Spanish-owned *haciendas* with an average size of 800 hectares; much of the remaining land was in the hands of small property owners; and finally, there were the squatters who had been pushed off their small plots as the *haciendas* expanded and who simply occupied whatever piece of earth they

TABLE 2.4

Ethnic Composition of El Salvador, 1780-1947

Ethnic Group	1780	1807	1947
Indian	59.0%	43.1%	5.6%
Mestizo	31.2	54.0	92.3
White	9.8	2.8	2.1

SOURCE: Roque Dalton, El Salvador (Monografía), p. 37.

could find. It is important to understand that the *ejidos* were concentrated for the most part in the central and western part of the country (see Map 2.1), which was also the area of richest soil, and that small family plots were widespread in the eastern half of the country. By independence in 1821 fully one-third of the total land area was concentrated in 400 large *haciendas*, most of which were given over to the cultivation of indigo.

As landownership became increasingly concentrated in fewer hands, the ethnic composition of the country was also rapidly changing. At the beginning of the seventeenth century the country was perhaps 85 percent indigenous, 10 percent *mestizo*, and 5 percent white. To this were added 4,000–5,000 Black slaves. That the country was well on its way to becoming a *mestizo* nation was evident by 1780 and that it had become one was clear thirty years later, as seen in Table 2.4. By the twentieth century the Blacks, who were freed in 1823, had been assimilated and officially ceased to exist as a separate racial group.[13]

THE THIRD CYCLE: COFFEE

Independence. Eduardo Colindres has written that in Central America independence was not a struggle but a "process."[14] The "First Cry of Independence" occurred on November 4, 1811, but it was another ten years before all political ties with Spain were severed. The period was characterized by repeated popular demonstrations in support of independence. In 1814 one demonstration was led by San Salvador's mayor, who organized and armed his people with what, by 1980, would be called "popular arms" – rocks, machetes, and the like.

But the era was also characterized by the efforts of newly independent Mexico to assert its hegemony over Central America. In the second decade of the century Mexico invaded El Salvador twice from Guatemala and twice was driven out.

In July 1823 the Federal Republic of Central America was created by the five former Central American colonies—Guatemala, Honduras, Nicaragua, Costa Rica, and El Salvador; it was formalized in the constitution of 1824. A year later Manuel José Arce, a Salvadorean, was elected the first president of the republic. The experiment lasted for fifteen years, then broke apart in the wake of a liberal-conservative struggle[15] exacerbated by regional economic woes—the beginning of the end of the indigo cycle.

The First Peasant Revolt. At the time of independence the orientation of the Salvadorean economy toward the production and export of indigo precluded any thought of internal development. As we have seen, the historic mentality of the *hacendados* was a single-minded desire to maximize earnings. Originally, this attitude was rooted in an understandable fear of being financially wiped out by an economic depression. Gradually, however, that attitude was transformed into a Salvadorean version of General Motors's Charles Wilson: What was good for the *hacendados* was good for the country. The best thing, in terms of profits, was the monocrop economy; until that crop required certain forms of internal development (as coffee would), development was a nonexistent issue.

The situation was complicated by growing class and ethnic antagonisms. *Repartimiento* continued, even though there was no legal ground for it. Tribute continued to be collected for several years after Spain's Cadiz Parliament abolished it in 1811. When in 1814 a parish priest told the Indians of Los Nonualcos that tribute had been abolished three years earlier and that the continuing collection was illegal, the enraged populace descended on the mayor and threatened his life if they did not get a refund. The Indians were driven off, but their rage festered. Meanwhile, incursions on communal lands became more frequent as the protection of the crown was withdrawn following independence. Insult was added to injury when the government imposed taxes on indigo harvests. All these events helped to convince the indigenous population that, for them, independence was less than meaningless.[16]

The Indians began protesting, organizing, and gathering arms. Those in the area of Los Nonualcos in the central zone of the country, led by the *cacique* Anastacio Aquino, particularly opposed the forced recruitment of men for the army and the taxes on indigo. When

Aquino's forces revolted in 1832 the government sent troops to crush the uprising; but Aquino, at the head of 3,000 peasants, helped by many *Ladinos*, repelled that and several successive attacks. Aquino's aim was to destroy the power of the white minority, who controlled the government and the economy. The rebellion continued for a year, until Aquino was captured, shot, and decapitated. His head was displayed publicly as a warning to other potential rebels.[17] It would be a hundred years before the Salvadorean peasants would again attempt to overthrow the system.

El Grano de Oro. By the middle of the nineteenth century the demand for indigo on the world market was in dramatic decline. There were three reasons for this. First, growers found that production and labor costs were far lower in Asia than in Central America. Second, the Civil War in the United States not only reduced that market but created shipping problems as a result of the Union's naval blockade. Third and most important, a synthetic dye was developed in Germany that wiped out the remunerative European market.

Well before these events occurred, however, enterprising Salvadoreans had already discovered an extremely lucrative substitute: coffee. The rich lava soils of central and western El Salvador that had given the colony its first economic boom with cacao were especially appropriate for coffee bushes, which must grow at elevations above 760 meters. Furthermore, the large *hacendados* were in a financial position to make the transition from one monocrop to another.

Unlike indigo, which is planted and harvested each year, coffee trees do not produce for three years after planting. Therefore it is necessary to have either capital on which to live during those years or the ability to get credit. The farmers in El Salvador in the best position to do either of these two things were the large *hacienda* owners who had already made a fortune from indigo.[18]

The Salvadorean government further complicated matters for the owners of communal lands by decreeing in 1856 that if two-thirds of the communal lands were not planted in coffee, the lands would revert to the state. As it happened, the largest portion of the land available for coffee cultivation was communal (see Map 2.1), and neither the government nor the financial institutions of the time were anxious to grant the credit necessary to the owners of communal land in order to make the transition. In spite of these barriers, many Indian communities made a serious effort to comply with the decree, and many tens of thousands of coffee plants were set out on these lands. But the lack of support for the communal land turned to outright opposition by the last quarter of the century.

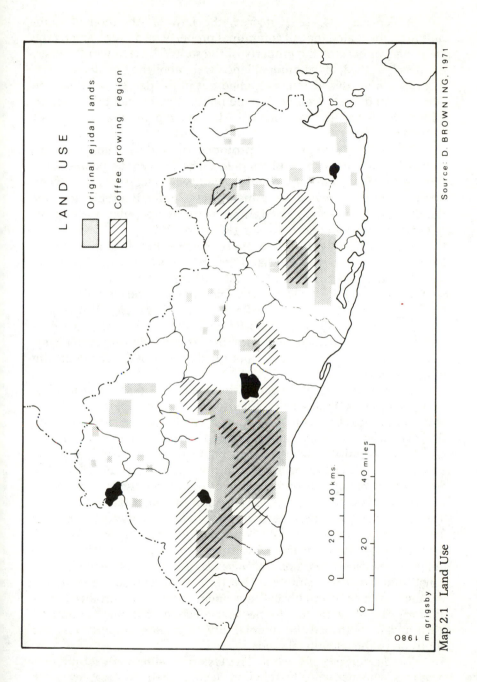

LAND USE

Original ejidal lands

Coffee growing region

Source: D. BROWNING. 1971

40 kms.

40 miles

m. grigsby

1980

Map 2.1 Land Use

A February 24, 1881, decree, the Law of Abolition of Communities, mandated that all communal property be divided among the co-owners or become the property of the state. Thirteen months later, on March 2, 1882, all communal lands were abolished by decree. The justification for this action, as spelled out in the decree, was that the common lands were "contrary to the political and social principles on which the Republic was established," i.e., the unfettered right of private property.

The 1882 decree produced profound and radical changes in patterns of landownership in El Salvador. The indigenous people were often evicted, sometimes violently, from their ancestral lands. They often resisted these evictions, sometimes violently, but it did not alter the direction of events. Indeed, there were five popular uprisings in the coffee-growing areas between 1872 and 1898.[19]

Nevertheless, within a few short years the best land in the country was concentrated in the hands of the "Fourteen Families"—who also, by then, had control of the state. In the latter part of the nineteenth century most presidents were not only generals but also major coffee growers: Francisco Dueñas, Tomás Regalado, Pedro José Escalón, Fernando Figueroa, and Francisco Meléndez. Almost a century later these remained among the names of the Salvadorean oligarchy—the families who, in 1980, continued to control the economic life of the country.

The Liberal Basis of the State. The "political and social principles" on which the republic was founded were those of liberalism. There were differences between what Alastair White has called "pragmatic liberals," who put emphasis on the economic themes of the liberal creed, and "idealists," who stressed political themes, especially free speech; but all agreed on the basic policies that would shape the Salvadorean nation: encouragement of coffee production, construction of railroads to the ports, elimination of communal lands, laws against vagrancy that permitted the state to force peasants to work for *hacendados* at low wages, and repression of rural unrest. An 1881 decree created rural justices of the peace who were empowered to oblige *campesinos* to work on the *haciendas* as they were needed.[20] The constitution of 1886 guaranteed that these policies would be pursued without obstacle; it established a secular state; it decentralized state authority by allowing for the popular election of municipal authorities; and it confirmed the inviolability of private property and the abolition of the communal lands.

The Instruments of Control. The task of dealing with recalcitrant peasants who periodically rebelled against their *patronos* was, for much of the nineteenth century, left in the hands of those selfsame *patronos*. The means employed were private armies. Elements of these would become the Rural Police and the Mounted Police, created by decrees in 1884 and 1889, respectively, in the western departments of Ahuachapán, Sonsonate and Santa Ana (the richest coffee-growing region of the country). An 1895 decree extended these two forces over the entire country.

Meanwhile, a national army began to take shape in the late 1850s when a Colombian general was invited to come in and build a professional force. In the following years French and Spanish officers also spent extended periods in the country training infantry, cavalry, and artillery units. Because El Salvador in this period lived under constant fear of invasion, the attention of the army was directed to national security, and the task of maintaining order was left to what would become known as the security forces. Not until the late twentieth century would the army be used to control the people.

The Rural Police ultimately became the National Police. To this force was added, in 1912, the National Guard. The latter was modeled after the Spanish National Guard and was formed and trained by officers from Spain. Specifically designed to function as an adjunct to the army, its duties overlapped those of the National Police: patrolling towns, villages, ports, and roads and providing police services to *haciendas*.[21] A third security force, the Treasury Police (Policía de Hacienda), was created much later, in 1936.

THE EFFECTS OF LAND TENURE PATTERNS

The positive contributions of the booming coffee market in traditional "development" terms included the construction of roads and of a railroad network between San Salvador, Santa Ana, Sonsonate, and Acajutla. The social costs of progress, however, were high. As the twentieth century began, official estimates placed the literacy rate at no more than 30 percent; most informed sources believed it to be far lower. The rate of alcoholism was extraordinary. The magnitude of the problem could be measured in the consumption of liquor, which produced *25 percent* of public revenue in 1918. Another measure was the extremely high rate of births outside marriage. By the early 1920s, 59 percent of the births in El Salvador were "natural children,"[22] as compared with 49 percent in Guatemala and 24 percent in Costa Rica. Finally, studies at the time revealed levels of malnutrition that, investigators charged, were producing unacceptably high rates of infant mortality.

Photo 2.2 Women making *pupusas,* thick tortillas stuffed with meat, cheese, or diced vegetables and fried. *Pupusas* are to El Salvador what tacos are to Mexico.

The oligarchy tended to blame these problems on the personal failings of the working class and peasants rather than on socio-economic conditions. Nonetheless, studies of the time held the economic system responsible and pointed, not only to the problem of malnutrition, but also to the fact that *maicillo,* a grain similar to millet that was used as fodder in Guatemala, was a principal food grain in El Salvador. Beef consumption in El Salvador was lower, while prices were two to four times higher, than in neighboring countries.[23]

These problems were exacerbated by the world financial crisis of 1914–1922. The difficulties of shipping, the decline in the price of coffee, and the postwar depression combined to reduce both the capital available – especially to small and medium-sized producers – and the value of the *fincas*. In this economic climate small farmers could not secure credit, and many were forced out of business. Waiting to pick up the pieces were the *hacendados*, whose wealth, access to capital, and credit were intact.

The effects of the crisis were wide-ranging. It led many farmers to experiment with diversification of their crops, which, for a time, increased the cultivation of cotton and henequen (sisal). The cultivation and export of indigo and balsam, which had never completely disappeared, were revived slightly. But the havoc wreaked by the boll weevil on the cotton crop in the years between 1926 and 1929 and a weak international market combined to virtually destroy that fledgling industry. It would not be revived again until after World War II.[24]

There was a great debate over banking reform. Until this period the government had observed a strictly laissez-faire economic policy, which had permitted the three privately held banks in the country to establish lending policies that favored the large growers and virtually excluded small farmers.[25] A lawyer on retainer to the Banco Salvadoreño described their plight:

> The Salvadorean farmer who holds title to his land is afraid to borrow the necessary capital to improve it and his fear is justified. In most cases he can obtain credit for only nine months at 10 percent interest or for a year at 10 to 18 percent. More still, the banks do not want to make small loans.
>
> The small farmers can, of course, obtain credits from the large neighboring landowners who make short-term loans at exorbitant interest rates and who really want to acquire more land. The small landowner is threatened with the loss of his parcel, which has provided his sustenance and home. He wants to improve it but he has witnessed the loss of his neighbors' land through foreclosure of their mortgages. He knows the history of the beautiful neighboring *haciendas* that inexorably come closer to absorbing his property also.[26]

Growing public demands for relief – in this case for credit – produced the radical demand for the nationalization of the banks as well as a less drastic proposal, in 1919, for a national mortgage bank that would provide the small farmer with credit sufficient to "cultivate the earth and wrest from it the rich fruit that it produces for life of man and the prosperity of the nation."[27]

But the situation did not improve. The newspaper *Patria*, which functioned as the social conscience of the time, called again in 1928 for a "People's Bank":

> We have four banks, every one of which is protected by the government and showered with prerogatives in order to serve the rich. The owner of the *finca, hacienda*, store or whatever other form of riches has a magic door. He comes and says the magic word, "Open Sesame!" and instantly receives a roll of bills that, until he needs more, satisfies his necessities and vices.
>
> We do not oppose these institutions that create fortune and security, and that convert their directors and businessmen into gods. . . .
>
> But what about the poor? Are they not part of the nation, children of the same *Patria*? Why does the government never consider that the poor also need banks? Why does it leave them enslaved to usurers, forced to borrow money at twelve *centavos* per *peso* per week in the villages and at 4 or 5 percent in the cities? Is it that the poor person does not have the right to live?[28]

These and other proposals, however, came to nought. It would be another seven years before a national mortgage bank, the Banco Hipotecario, was established (for large loans) – and fifteen years before a credit institution for small farmers and peasants, the Cajas de Credito Rural, was created.

These conditions combined to make coffee increasingly central to the economic life of the country. During the 1920s production of "the grain of gold" expanded rapidly while other crops and industries stagnated. This, coupled with growing business acumen and sophistication, brought the national economy out of the depression and into a boom. Coffee averaged between 75 and 80 percent of all exports between 1900 and 1922, then soared to a new average of 92 percent during the remainder of the 1920s. Similarly, land use increased dramatically. In 1919, 70,000 hectares were planted in coffee; by 1932 the figure had increased 34 percent, to 106,000 hectares.[29]

Meanwhile, the conditions of the average Salvadorean deteriorated. In a devastating commentary on the conditions of the time, *Patria*'s editor, Alberto Masferrer, wrote:

> The conquest of territory by the coffee industry is alarming. It has already occupied the high lands and is now descending to the valleys, displacing maize, rice, and beans. It is extended like the *conquistador*, spreading hunger and misery, reducing the former proprietors to the worst conditions – woe to those who sell! Although it is possible to prove

mathematically that these changes make the country richer, in fact they mean death. It is true that the costs of importing maize are small in relation to the benefits of the export of coffee, but do they give the imported grain to the poor? Or do they make them pay for it? Is the income of the *campesino*, who has lost his land, adequate to provide maize, rice, beans, clothes, medicine, doctors, etc.? So, what good does it do to make money from the sale of coffee when it leaves so many people in misery?[30]

But the attitude of the *hacendados* was expressed in a letter to *Patria*: "Why must one be bothered with planting maize, which produces a profit of almost 25 percent on investment, when one can plant coffee with little effort or risk? The idle lands around the volcanoes must be utilized. If the owners of these lands do not want to make use of them, they must sell them to those who would make them productive."[31] Meanwhile, many insisted that the peasants were being treated fairly – to which Masferrer with biting sarcasm replied: "Actually, there is no misery in El Salvador: The people go barefoot because they enjoy going without shoes, caressed by the fresh air; the laundry woman who earns four *colones* a week can save one-fourth of her earnings; and the child who comes to school without breakfast is convinced of the virtue of fasting."[32]

It was clear by the late 1920s that only one small sector of the nation was reaping the profits from *el grano do oro*. Everett Alan Wilson has written that "the *campesinos* were exploited by the company stores, fraudulent bookkeeping and scales, and unfulfilled promises of abundant work at distant *fincas*."[33] This situation was of concern to some, such as Masferrer, who warned that "as long as justice is not the same for everyone, none of us is safe."[34] A more pointed – and prescient – observation was tossed off by James Hill, an immigrant *hacendado* in Santa Ana: "Bolshevism? It is the tempest. The working people have meetings on Sundays and become excited. They say: 'We dig the holes for the trees, clean out the weeds, pick the trees, harvest the coffee. Who, then, earns the money? We earn it!' . . . Yes, there will be problems one of these days."[35]

PRELUDES TO REVOLT

The "problems" that Hill anticipated in 1927 exploded five years later – the result of the social and economic conditions described above, an increasingly militant labor union movement, and a flirtation with authentic electoral democracy that ended in a coup d'etat.

The Rise of Working-Class Organizations

Labor organizations in El Salvador grew rapidly after the formation of the Central American Congress of Workers, which met in San Salvador in 1911. These early organizations tended to be oriented toward mutual assistance and savings among the membership. Emphasis was placed on education, temperance, and charitable work; there were regular disavowals of political sectarianism.[36] By 1917 there were more than forty unions throughout the country, including those of masons, carpenters, teachers, shoemakers, barbers, white-collar workers, typesetters, and railway workers.[37]

The growing maturity of the labor movement was evident at a national meeting in June 1918. More than 200 union delegates gathered in Armenia for the purpose of organizing a national federation, the Great Confederation of Workers of El Salvador (COES). One measure of the significance of the gathering was the opposition it provoked. There were demands that the government post troops near the meeting hall in order to quell any disturbance that might result from the proceedings. The workers, however, conducted their business with order and decorum.[38]

In 1919, 500 union delegates met, again in Armenia, for the First National Workers' Congress. A year later COES joined the Central American Workers' Confederation (COCA) in a move to bring about greater regional unity. Soon, however, radical union organizers from Guatemala and Mexico began having some success among workers and students. These new unions did not affiliate with COES and, being consciously political, began to change the largely mutualist character of the Salvadorean union movement.[39] This influence expanded during the 1920s, and the union movement, as a consequence, became increasingly militant.

The year 1929 was eventful in several respects. It brought the onset of the Great Depression—and a resulting plunge in coffee prices. Meanwhile, the coffee growers succeeded in institutionalizing their share interests through the creation in December of the Coffee Growers' Association. This cooperative permitted the growers to more or less control production and marketing without governmental interference.[40]

The depression exacerbated social tensions, and the increasing militancy of the labor union movement, which took the form of demonstrations and strikes, inflamed the situation. What made the period all the more interesting was that El Salvador was in the midst of the first presidential administration in its history committed to allowing political organizations of all stripes to participate in the political life of the country. In this atmosphere, the Communist Party of El Salvador (PCS), the country's first revolutionary organization, was founded.

A Taste of Democracy

Thirteen years of repressive government under the minor dynasty of pragmatic liberals Carlos and Jorge Meléndez (brothers) and Alfonso Quiñonez (brother-in-law) from 1913 to 1927 ended abruptly when Quiñonez's hand-picked successor, Pío Romero Bosque, turned out to be far less pliable and far more democratic than his benefactor had anticipated. An attempted coup d'etat, engineered by Jorge Meléndez seven months after Don Pío assumed office, failed, and the latter went on to hold the most open and honest elections in Salvadorean history, first for municipal offices and then in 1930 for president.

It was in this greatly liberalized political climate that labor unions became more demanding and that the PCS was formed. It was also in this context that Romero ordered all departmental governors to let the electorate work its will and not to assume there was an official candidate. The result was the election of Arturo Araujo, a wealthy landowner who had addressed the 1919 National Workers' Congress; who had a reputation for paying his employees double the going wages; who had the endorsement of Masferrer; who, in short, had become known as a friend of the working class and peasantry.

Golpe

But Araujo's candidacy had aroused expectations among the poor and fears among the establishment, including the military whom he had implicitly courted by naming General Maximiliano Hernandez Martínez his vice-presidential running mate. No traitor to his class, Araujo was not prepared to make good on some of the more extravagant campaign promises his labor supporters had made in his name. Yet the oligarchy, which had been deeply suspicious of the free election, refused to lend its support to the new administration by accepting governmental appointments. Thus its expertise was denied the government at one of the most critical points in the country's history.

The situation deteriorated from the day Araujo was inaugurated. In July 1931 a confrontation between university students and the National Guard resulted in many injuries, arrests, and the imposition of a state of siege. The president's limited efforts to help the peasants by the purchase of land in La Libertad that was then divided into parcels and sold at low prices was little more than a Band-Aid over a gaping wound. There were 100 applicants for every parcel. The dashed expectations led to a growing number of demonstrations, especially in the western part of the country where Augustín Farabundo Martí and his organizers were having the greatest success – and where economic conditions were the worst.

August brought a new low in coffee prices. In October Araujo halted the export of gold. A November story in the newspaper *La Prensa* noted that coffee pickers were earning less than subsistence wages. The last straw seems to have been the government's inability to meet its payroll. Araujo could probably have survived – at least for a while – if the military had been paid regularly. But the president insisted on treating the military the same as the bureaucracy, which meant that no one was paid for several months.

On December 2, 1931, a coup d'etat led by a handful of young officers toppled the nine-month old regime of Arturo Araujo. The president went into exile; the military named his constitutional successor, Vice-President General Martínez, to succeed him. The United States, citing the 1923 Treaty of Washington, which had created guidelines for the recognition of new governments established under extra-constitutional circumstances, suspended diplomatic relations. Salvadoreans viewed this as another form of imperialism. Relations were not resumed until Franklin Roosevelt became president in 1933. Thus began the longest unbroken record of military rule in Latin America history.[41]

THE SECOND PEASANT REVOLT[42]

El Negro

The role that Anastacio Aquino had played in 1832 was assumed by Augustín Farabundo Martí a hundred years later. No *cacique*, Martí was the son of a *mestizo hacendado* and had attended the National University long enough to become well read in positivist, utopian socialist and Marxist-Leninist ideas. Expelled from the country in 1920 by President Meléndez for radical activities, Martí, who acquired the nickname "El Negro" because of his dark complexion, spent the early years of the decade traveling in Central America and the United States. He was a charter member of the Central American Socialist party, which was founded in Guatemala City in 1925. That same year Martí returned to El Salvador, where he worked for the

Regional Federation of Salvadorean Workers (FRTS), primarily writing political tracts and propaganda – until he was exiled by then President Quiñonez. Martí, however, slipped back into the capital and picked up where he had left off. He acquired a reputation for erudition and intellectual prowess – not to mention for implacable hostility to the existing system. When President Pío Romero Bosque had him thrown in jail, Martí went on a hunger strike. The General Association of Salvadorean University Students (AGEUS), which had been founded in 1927, supported him, and Don Pío finally had him released.

Martí then left El Salvador and a few months later joined Augusto César Sandino, who was fighting the U.S. forces in Nicaragua. In 1929 Martí accompanied Sandino into exile in Mexico, where the two men broke over ideological differences. According to Martí, Sandino "would not embrace my communist program. His banner was only that of national independence. . . . not social revolution."[43] Martí returned to El Salvador in May 1930 and immediately plunged back into political work.

Agitation and Repression

President Romero was willing to live with unions and political parties as long as they did not threaten the interests of his main support – the oligarchy. When Don Pío discovered, however, that the FRTS had quietly organized about eighty thousand *campesinos*, he issued a decree banning demonstrations, rallies, and leftist propaganda. But the decree was ignored, and the FRTS increased its organizing activities.

The government's response was to arrest, fine, or jail several hundred *campesinos* in Sonsonate for signing a petition against the decree. This led to the Campaign for the Liberation of Political Prisoners, which produced more repression and another decree – this one banning all peasant or worker demonstrations. Between mid-November 1930 and late February 1931 about twelve hundred people were jailed for various radical activities.[44]

One of those jailed was Farabundo Martí. Don Pío had decided to expel him once again, at least until after the presidential election in January 1931. So it was that Martí was put aboard a steamer in La Libertad and spent most of the next two months at sea. Finally, El Negro jumped ship in Corinto, Nicaragua, and made his way back to El Salvador, arriving in the capital on February 20 – after Araujo's election.

Insurrection and Massacre

The following months were filled with organizing and propagandizing among the peasants in the central and western part of the country and among university students. There were also demonstrations and strikes that were put down with increasing brutality. Legislation in March giving the security forces greater authority to deal with the unrest led to raids on leftist headquarters and mail searches for subversive material. Martí was again jailed on April 9 after receiving a large quantity of Marxist literature that had been sent from New York. After a month, Martí began a hunger strike that lasted twenty-six days and finally led to his release. He was carried from the hospital, where he had been taken from jail, on the shoulders of his supporters – an authentic hero among the Salvadorean masses.

For the next several months Martí kept a relatively low profile as the political situation deteriorated and the demonstration-repression cycle escalated. Interestingly, the left greeted the coup on December 2 with cautious optimism, but leftist hopes were dashed as the legislative and municipal elections in early January were once again characterized by fraud. In the western part of the country, where the Marxists were strong, the elections were suspended. In Santa Tecla, Sonsonate, and other towns, the PCS claimed victory, but the government refused to certify the elections.

Martí, the other radical leaders, and the PCS concluded that the Martínez regime had no intention of letting them participate or hold office through legal means; they then set the date for the insurrection. The plan called for simultaneous uprisings in several towns and army barracks on January 22, 1932. Unfortunately for the revolutionaries, everything went wrong. The authorities learned of the plan several days in advance.[45] Farabundo Martí was captured on January 18, along with two student supporters. Then communications broke down when other rebel leaders attempted to call off the revolt.

The result was an unorganized, uncoordinated uprising that met with a swift and brutal response. Five of the smaller towns in the western region fell to the insurgents, but security forces in Sonsonate, Ahuachapán, and Santa Tecla easily repelled the attacks of *campesinos* armed with little more than machetes. Within three days the captured towns were retaken. Then the massacre began. Anyone in Indian dress, any one running from the security forces was fair game. When the carnage was over 30,000 people were dead. Less than 10 percent of those had participated in the uprising. Martí and the two students were tried by military tribunal and shot.

The insurrection occurred in the central and western part of the country; the eastern half was virtually untouched by the events of late January and early February. The military consolidated its hold on the government, and there was no more pretense of popular political participation. *Campesino* unions were outlawed and all other political organizations were prohibited. The oligarchy achieved the social peace it wanted and considered necessary to rebuild a shattered economy.

The significance of these events in the history of El Salvador has been captured by Jorge Arias Gomez:

> December 2, 1931, marks an era in the political life of the nation which has continued for almost 40 years. On that date, the oligarchy ceased to govern directly. If before the coup d'etat the political idea that only civilians must serve as president had triumphed and been consolidated, afterwards the opposite idea was pursued. If before, forces of the oligarchy were thrown into the struggle for power, organizing more or less successful parties and electoral movements; exciting the masses; afterward the entire oligarchy withdrew from the political game in order to leave it to military tyranny. . . . In a few words, political power passed, on December 2, 1931, into the hands of the army. That was transformed, in practice, into the great elector and into a type of political party permanently in arms.[46]

In the next chapter, we will examine more closely the roles of the oligarchy and the armed forces in the life of El Salvador since 1932.

3

The State:
A Division of Labor
1932-1979

We have traditionally bought the military's guns and have paid them to pull the trigger.

— A Salvadorean oligarch, 1980

Just as a cyclical pattern of economic development had evolved in the colonial period, so a cyclical pattern emerged in El Salvador's political life after 1932. Where the first pattern had served to consolidate economic power in a few hands (those of the oligarchy), the second pattern served to perpetuate political power in other hands: those of the army. Meanwhile, the economic situation continued unchanged and what reforms did occur in no way affected the sources and distribution of wealth or the control of the national economy.

THE POLITICAL CYCLE

The political cycle, although its time span varied considerably, operated as follows:

1. Consolidation of power by the new regime
2. Growing intolerance of dissent and increasing repression
3. Reaction from two quarters: the public and, more important, a progressive faction within the army officer corps, culminating ultimately in a
4. Coup d'etat, led by progressive officers
5. Promulgation of various reforms
6. Reemergence, within the army, of the most conservative faction
7. Consolidation of that power once more.

Constants

Throughout these cycles, there were certain constants that emerged in the regime of Hernandez Martínez. The first was the establishment of the official party.

Created by Martínez and named, in its first incarnation, "Pro-Patria" (for the homeland), the official party was not a traditional political party. Salvadorean political scientist Rubén Zamora has noted that although the party occasionally fulfilled some of the traditional functions of a political party, in fact its real purpose was to be an instrument of social control. In an interview Zamora argued that, before 1932, the oligarchy controlled the people through two mechanisms: the security forces that operated as personal instruments of repression; and, more subtly, through *compadrazgo*, a social institution that created family-like ties between *patrono* and *campesino*.[1] After 1932, Zamora continued, "the mechanisms of *compadrazgo* gradually passed to the state." Indeed, Pro-Patria did not have a life of its own but functioned as the personal instrument of Martínez, who kept the peasants in line during the 1930s through a highly personalistic style of rule.[2]

The second constant in Salvadorean life was the use of repression to maintain order when persuasion failed. The security forces continued to serve at the beck and call of the oligarchy and were particularly effective in the countryside. Both security forces and army units were used in the cities whenever demonstrations by university students or labor unions threatened domestic tranquillity. As the years passed, the techniques of repression became more sophisticated, as many leftist leaders would learn firsthand in the 1960s and 1970s.[3]

In each political cycle, a time came when the government, feeling itself under siege, would with increasing frequency and vigor label all dissent "subversive" and the work of "communists." These were also the favorite labels of the oligarchy for anyone in El Salvador who advocated any social or economic change that would, in any measure, affect its economic interests adversely. Over the years, the labels have been applied to army officers, members of centrist political factions, church leaders, labor unions, and to openly leftist mass organizations.

Each cycle brought some measure of social and economic reform, although it was never enough to either deal adequately with El Salvador's growing numbers of poor people or to tamper with the economic status quo.

One of the most effective means the oligarchy devised after 1932 to ensure that its interests would be protected by the state was an elaborate and pervasive system of corruption. Key army officers were systematically bought off with money, land, and business investments. Indeed, corruption was a key element in the political cycle, for it guaranteed the reemergence of the most conservative officers, who could be counted on to stop any reforms that the oligarchy perceived as going too far.

Ultimate Goals

Throughout the decades following the assumption of power by the military, two goals remained paramount. One was the protection of the interests of the oligarchy. The second was the preservation of the institution of the army. Indeed, the latter would determine whether it was progressive or conservative factions deciding at a given moment to take matters into their own hands.

Between December 1932 and November 1979 El Salvador was convulsed six times by the cycle of consolidation of power by conservatives, growing dissent and repression, a coup d'etat by a progressive faction within the army, the reemergence of the conservatives, and their reassumption of control of the government. We saw in the previous chapter that the coup that installed General Maximiliano Hernandez Martínez in power was a response not only to deteriorating economic conditions that directly affected army personnel, but also to growing agitation from the masses for major economic reforms and the willingness of the Araujo government to tolerate these activities.

THE FIRST CYCLE: 1932–1944

Martínez moved quickly and decisively to consolidate his power. After order was restored following the insurrection of January 1931, the government developed four means of keeping the population in line. First, it effected an administrative reorganization throughout the country that centralized decisionmaking and all public works and services. Second, Martínez further consolidated this control by replacing civilians with military officers at the local and national levels.[4] Third, labor unions, which had flourished during the Romero Bosque and Araujo presidencies, were officially discouraged on the grounds that they were subversive. Last, all peasant organizations were banned, as was the Communist party. Indian cofradías (fraternal societies) were similarly accused and suffered a corresponding decline.[5]

Virtually all political opposition disappeared for several years.

Although Alastair White reported stories of *campesinos* being killed for failure to kowtow to the demands of landowners for long hours and low pay,[6] by and large there were few ripples to disturb the imposed political calm.

Economic Concerns

Dependence on a single crop continued as before. Government policy after the 1932 uprising was directed to protecting the interests of the coffee growers. Laws designed to discourage mechanization were drafted, and investment was encouraged only in industries that did not threaten artisan production, such as shoemaking. There was fear that industrialization would destroy such crafts and revive the alliance between peasants and workers that had led to the 1932 insurrection.[7] Not until after World War II was there any significant diversification of export crops.

In the financial area, a general moratorium on debts was decreed, and it was stipulated that debtors should not be prosecuted. In 1934 the Central Reserve Bank was created, and private banks were barred from issuing currency. Theoretically the Central Bank was to help nationalize the country's economy. In fact the bank, like those already in existence, was controlled by the oligarchy. The Coffee Growers' Association provided 36.5 percent of its capitalization; the two existing banks, owned by members of the oligarchy, held 27 percent; and the balance was retained by private stockholders. The creation of the Central Bank, then, merely ensured that the coffee growers' interests would be protected by guaranteeing that their land would not be foreclosed and that sufficient capital would be available for the further development of coffee production.[8]

A year after the Central Bank was founded, the government created the Banco Hipotecario, or national mortgage bank. Ostensibly, its purpose was to make mortgages more easily obtainable for small farmers and business people. In fact, it quickly became yet another financial instrument by which the oligarchy extended its economic tentacles.

The economic policies of the Martínez government included nationalization of all the public utility companies and assertion of the right of eminent domain over municipal power companies. Following compensation to the previous owners, the new National Electricity Commission assumed responsibility for their operation.[9]

Ultimately these policies, which in no way helped small entrepreneurs either recover from the depression or establish new businesses, bred discontent among the Salvadorean bourgeoisie. At the same time, conditions in the countryside were turning El Salvador into an urban nation; by 1935 more than one-third of the population lived in cities.[10] This migration created growing pressures for jobs and services that the government was ill-prepared – or ill-disposed – to alleviate. It was also unable to control political dissension in the cities, as the National Guard so effectively did in the countryside.

Foreign Policy

Official Tilt Toward the Axis Powers. Martínez and other senior officers were attracted by the fascist governments of Germany and Italy. This attraction grew out of the failure of the liberal governments of Romero and Araujo, the communist involvement in the 1932 insurrection, and the resulting belief that what the country needed was a more elitist government. By 1936 army officers had begun training in Germany and Italy. Officers openly sympathetic to the Axis powers could be found in major government and military positions until late 1941.[11] During 1938 Italy sent El Salvador planes with spare parts, tanks, and tractors capable of being converted into armored cars – all in exchange for $200,000 worth of coffee. In the same year a German colonel became director of the Military Academy.

Two years later, after Germany had marched into Poland, Austria, and Czechoslovakia, Martínez decreed it a crime to express support for the Allies.[12] This sympathy for the Axis powers was not universally shared in El Salvador. When Italy declared war in June 1940, 300 Black Shirts marched in downtown San Salvador. But they were greeted with denunciations – a response that was rapidly repressed by the police.

There was also less than total support within the army. Three times betwen 1935 and 1939 plots to overthrow the Martínez regime were uncovered. In 1936 the would-be *golpistas* were shot. Three years later twenty-five plotters were merely imprisoned and the two ringleaders, a colonel and a general, were exiled.[13]

Ultimately, Martínez was forced to abandon his flirtation with Germany and Italy, not on ideological grounds but out of necessity. Trade with the Axis for both military and domestic goods became increasingly unreliable. The decline in exports produced a 20 percent unemployment rate by late 1940. Opposition to Martínez's policy built within the military, and in October of that year Martínez abruptly reversed his foreign policy. In a public statement he condemned totalitarianism on the continent and praised the Allies.[14]

Meanwhile, the United States had already indicated its willingness to become El Salvador's primary source of arms. In June 1940, when the minister of defense asked the U.S. military attaché, Col. J. B. Pate, for 35,000 rifles, Pate assured him that the means would be found "to help our exceptionally loyal friends in this matter."[15]

The Causes of Dissension. It cannot be assumed that the tilt toward the Axis powers was the main reason for dissension within the army. Rather, the primary cause of disaffection was the perception that power, privilege, and opportunity were concentrated in an ever-smaller clique. The best positions were held by Martínez's cronies, and there was no policy of advancement that permitted other officers to aspire to better conditions. Thus, the younger officers in particular gradually came to view the dictatorship as an obstacle to their personal ambitions.†

The End of a Regime

Reaction Brews. In January 1944 a Constitutional Assembly was convened, ostensibly to amend the constitution so that German property could be expropriated. The hidden agenda, however, was to change the succession laws in order to permit Hernandez Martínez a fourth term as president. This was the last straw for disenchanted army officers and increasingly restive members of the bourgeoisie. On April 2 an attempted coup was staged by army and air force officers. Martínez, with the support of the National Guard and National Police, survived the revolt at a cost of at least 200 lives. Martínez then turned his vengeance on the conspirators. Ten officers were executed the morning of April 10 on a street in downtown San Salvador. Thirty-three more executions followed. Martial law was imposed throughout the country.

The retribution exacted by the regime was too much for the people. Students at the University of El Salvador struck in protest. They were quickly joined by high school students, clerks, and professionals. By the end of April the general strike had brought San Salvador to a standstill.[16] In a last-ditch effort to preserve his regime, Martínez attempted to mobilize workers and peasants. With the help of loyal *hacendados,* 800 *campesinos* armed with machetes were trucked into the capital in early May. Government broadcasts coupled with the appearance on the streets of armed *campesinos* were enough to rekindle unhappy memories of 1932 and inspired sufficient fear to send some workers back to their jobs.[17]

Martínez Resigns. It was, however, too little, too late. On May 8, 1944, Maximiliano Hernandez Martínez addressed the nation by radio and announced his resignation.[18] The next day, with the general strike still in progress, the nation learned that its new provisional president was General Andrés Ignacio Menéndez. Menéndez quickly named a cabinet that included representatives from the several political factions that had emerged since 1941. Freedom of the press was reinstated; a general amnesty was declared for all political prisoners and exiles; and Martínez's hated secret police was abolished. Menéndez appeared bent on opening up the political process.

The Liberals Win . . . Briefly. In the following weeks civilians became ever more vocal in their demands for free elections, for the removal of Martínez appointees, and for guarantees of fundamental civil liberties. Political parties were created or emerged from clandestine activity, precipitating a period of political ferment such as had not been experienced since the 1931 presidential election.

Most notable in this regard was the emergence from clandestinity of the Salvadorean Democratic Association (ADS). The ADS had been formed in September 1941 as a forum for discussion of international issues. It was driven underground almost immediately by government charges that it intended to engage in activities designed to subvert the existing order.[19] ADS reemerged with the fall of Martínez. In an effort to ensure the victory of a civilian candidate in the presidential election scheduled for January 1945, ADS spearheaded the formation of a coalition that nominated Arturo Romero, a young doctor who had been a civilian leader of the April revolt. Romero and his supporters were frankly committed to the restoration of civilian government and to sweeping economic and social reforms. With this commitment they were riding the crest of the antimilitarist wave that swept the country between May and October 1944.[20]

THE SECOND CYCLE: 1944–1948

The power of the progressive forces was not, however, consolidated. The continuing antimilitarism, public demonstrations, and lively campaigning finally convinced the conservatives that El Salvador was not yet ready for civilian rule. So, on October 21, 1944, a coup d'etat was led by the *martinista* director of the National Police, Colonel Osmín Aguirre y Salinas. He met no resistance from the army. Indeed, there are indications that Menéndez may have invited the coup as he was not in a position to lead it. Arturo Romero went into exile in Costa Rica. What remained of the presidential campaign was a minor right-wing candidate and the official candidate, General Salvador Castaneda Castro, who had replaced Menéndez as provisional president immediately after the coup. The outcome was predictable.[21]

Four Years of Stagnation

If the Castaneda government was not as repressive as that of Hernandez Martínez, neither was it inclined to carry forward the modest economic and social reforms Martínez had implemented. Castaneda was willing to permit some of the political organizations created in the ferment of 1944 to continue. Upon formally assuming the office of president in March 1945, he issued a general political amnesty, opened the borders, and undertook a reorganization of the government and army.

Within four months this shake-up provoked former police director Aguirre, who had been moved by Castaneda to the innocuous position of director of social security, to twice attempt a coup—and twice fail. Castaneda's politics of stagnation was challenged in September when another general strike closed businesses, transportation, and newspapers in San Salvador. The masses and progressives within the middle class had seen an opportunity in the internecine military fights to force economic and social changes. But the president responded primarily with diversions.

Reforms as Reaction. On the one hand, he instituted a variety of toothless reforms as a sop to the liberals; on the other, he began limiting the freedom of liberal spokespersons and organizations in order to pacify the conservatives among his colleagues. After June 1945 the country operated almost continually under a state of siege.

Castaneda's diversions included a new constitution in November 1945 that was virtually identical to that of 1886; a program of public works, which included paving streets and building a bridge over the Lempa River; and various social programs in the area of health, hygiene, and orphanages. With all of these, the emphasis was on construction of facilities that would produce the greatest political return.[22]

Castaneda dramatically reduced the number of junior-grade officers and shipped a large number of young officers out of the country for training or service as diplomatic attachés between 1945 and 1948. Castaneda thus created short-term relief but a long-term disaster for himself. The young officers who were sent abroad were among the remaining progressives in the Salvadorean army. Indeed, that was a prime reason for their official "exile." These men returned as the 1948 presidential campaign began. But the time they had spent out of the country served only to exacerbate a growing split within the officer corps.

The Noncampaign. The Castaneda administration had bred

nothing if not malaise among Salvadoreans. As the presidential campaign opened, there were no civilian candidates and little discussion of issues. As the weeks passed, it was commonly believed that Castaneda would somehow contrive a second term, in spite of his public assertions to the contrary. What finally rattled the army and the people was the selection of an official candidate by the National Union Party (PUN), successor to Martínez's Pro-Patria. General Mauro Espinola Castro was a close ally of Castaneda but was also understood to be a coward; he had reportedly deserted his position during the 1931 coup and had hidden during the April 1944 revolt. At sixty-five he was allegedly living with a woman of twenty and was known to be drinking heavily.

The political opposition finally had something to inspire it. News sheets appeared charging that the Ministry of Defense had become a political campaign headquarters, that military and government vehicles were being used for campaigning, and that the opposition was being denied access to radio while the PUN had all the broadcast time it desired.[23] Unfortunately, the opposition had not done much better with its candidates, who included Colonel Aguirre y Salinas. As Espinola began losing support within the army and other sectors, flyers and posters appeared demanding Castaneda's continuation in office. When Espinola showed no sign of taking the hint, Castaneda moved to rescind the ban on reelection.

The 1948 "Revolution". As the National Assembly met on December 13 to call for the formation of a new constitutional assembly that would permit Castaneda to succeed himself, a coup that had been in the works for months took final shape. The next day fighting broke out in San Salvador between National Police loyal to the president and rebels in El Zapote barracks next to the Casa Presidencial. By the time Castaneda sought refuge in the National Police headquarters, it was all but over. Soon after his arrival, leaders of the insurrection took control of the building and devoted the remainder of the day to convincing a stubborn president that his career was at an end.[24]

THE THIRD CYCLE: 1948–1960

The nation was stunned. The identity of the *golpistas* was a mystery. Government ministers and the National Assembly president adjourned to the U.S. Embassy to try and learn the identity of the rebel leaders. The embassy shared their ignorance. The director of the Military Academy, a U.S. Army colonel, was annoyed with his sub-

director, Lieutenant Colonel Manuel de Jesus Córdova, that morning;
Córdova was obviously distracted.

When the Revolutionary Council announced itself later that day
Córdova, who had been one of the key *golpistas,* was a member. He
was joined by two majors and two civilians. From its initial
statements, the council asserted its break with the past. It ended the
state of siege, declared an amnesty, and announced the restoration of
political rights. The council proclaimed its determination to initiate
needed economic and social reforms. It also affirmed its determination to remove the army from politics and to make that institution a
defender of the constitution.[25] In spite of ex-President Castaneda's un-
popularity, these announcements were greeted with less than overwhelming enthusiasm by the Salvadorean people. They had heard it
all before.

Undeterred by popular apathy, the Revolutionary Council acted
quickly to institutionalize its break with the past. The council
abrogated the constitution and reserved all legislative and executive
powers to itself. It called for a freely elected constitutional assembly.
The council then moved against former government officials and
seventeen civilians whom it accused of malfeasance and corruption.
Within two months of the coup the council issued the "Law of Honesty," an ex post facto anticorruption law. A tribunal was created to try
the accused, who had their bank accounts sealed and were barred
from leaving the country or seeking refuge in foreign embassies.

The Revolutionary Council maintained itself in power for fourteen months. The new ministers, all of whom save the minister of
defense were civilians, were, like the council members, relatively
young, well educated, well traveled, and middle class. The council
created a momentum in its first weeks that demonstrated its commitment to both institutional and social change. Yet while this momentum was building the old games once again began within the army.
Less than a month after the coup Córdova resigned from the council
and took himself into exile in Honduras. Major Oscar Osorio, another
council member, quickly emerged as the new strong man. In
February the council granted itself a substantial pay raise. Young officers who had supported the coup from the beginning were promoted. The Ministry of Defense budget enjoyed a significant increase.

The motivations of the officer corps were complex. As in 1944,
there were two groups among the rebels. One recognized that some
moderate reforms had to come in order to preserve peace, stability,
and the institution of the army. The second group was committed to
reform for its own sake. Both groups undoubtedly felt pressured by

developments in Guatemala, where a 1944 revolt had succeeded and a progressive government, headed by the army, was making significant social and economic reforms.

Those among the middle class who supported both the 1944 and 1948 movements did so out of essentially personal motives; they wanted to modernize and diversify the national economy, agriculture, and the system of national credit. They also wanted the government to facilitate the development of some industry.†

The Presidential Campaign

Nine months after the coup a new election law was decreed. All political parties based on religion, sex, class, foreign financial support, or communist affiliation were banned.[26] In January 1950 the council called for a national election in March to select a constitutional assembly and a president. It also established an autonomous Central Election Council (CCE), which was charged with collecting and counting the votes. Other decrees granted women's suffrage and instituted the secret ballot.

As preparations got under way for the campaign in the fall of 1949, Oscar Osorio resigned from the Revolutionary Council to form the newest official party, the Revolutionary Party of Democratic Unification (PRUD). Osorio then became its candidate for the presidency. With only nominal opposition from an old colleague who ran under the banner of the progressive Renovating Action Party (PAR), Osorio easily won with 60 percent of the vote. The PRUD captured a decisive majority in the Constitutional Assembly.

Osorio was inaugurated in September 1950. That same month the Assembly issued a new constitution, thus fulfilling one of the Revolutionary Council's original promises. Under the constitution the army acquired a new name, the Armed Forces, and had its strength set at 3,000 men. Neither the number nor the name, however, included the security forces, which retained their separate identities.

Reform and Economic Change

Once inaugurated, Osorio wasted no time before embarking on a series of public works and programs intended to encourage industry and trade, increase production, and diversify agriculture. Housing construction, health care, and sanitation projects were initiated. Labor unions were legalized in 1951, although demands for agricultural unions were ignored. A year later collective bargaining was instituted under government regulation.

When the oligarchy began complaining about the reforms, the

government reminded it of the "communist threat" in Guatemala, where a populist socialist military regime was moving even faster, to the growing consternation of its neighbors and the United States. The grumbling died away.[27]

Developmentalism and Reform. The model embraced by the Osorio regime and economic elite may be termed "developmentalist"; that is, policies were adopted to encourage the growth and modernization of the industrial sector. The laws passed in the 1930s that had severely limited industrialization were scrapped. Other measures followed: strong incentives in the form of tax breaks, repeal of laws restricting the process of capital accumulation, income taxes on a larger proportion of personal income (a measure that affected the small but growing middle class more severely than any other sector), an increase in the tax on the exportation of coffee, creation of a social security system, and the granting of permission for (state-controlled) industrial organizations. The state did not stop there. It embarked on a road-building program and constructed the November 5 Dam on the Lempa River, which boosted energy output dramatically while cutting the cost of electricity by 25 percent. It also built the Puente de Oro (Bridge of Gold, so named because of its high cost), an 800-meter span across the Lempa on the Litoral Highway in south central El Salvador.

By 1955 José María Lemus, who would succeed Osorio in the presidency, was praising the accomplishments of the 1948 "revolution":

> The dispossessed classes have progressed in cultural and spiritual respects that concern the value of work and the enjoyment of human treatment regulated by law. And there has not been present, in the course of this great experience, the explosions of angry capitalists or the dangerous condition of mass discontent. The Revolution has constructed modern school buildings, raised educational standards in the most remote regions, sought a solution to the problem of urban housing by providing facilities for the proletariat and middle class, and has organized Rural Communities through which the problems of housing, work, and production in some zones have been resolved.[28]

This glowing assessment ignored what Alastair White recognized in his 1973 study of El Salvador – that the administrations of Osorio and Lemus,

> in attempting or appearing to effect a general expansion and improvement through industrial development . . . tended to achieve only an ex-

pansion of job opportunities for a new salaried middle class, and in attempting or appearing to introduce modern government provision for social development . . . tended to create a relatively privileged sector within the working class, those with access to such innovations as social security, collective wage bargaining through the legal unions, and the government urban housing and rural land settlement schemes. These benefited a very small percentage of the poor, but could be represented demagogically as a social revolution being carried out by the government.[29]

As for economic changes, nothing was done to upset the fundamental control by the oligarchy over the economy. The process of industrialization, which had been officially discouraged in the 1930s, found new life in the late 1940s and early 1950s. This was due not only to a regime change but also to increased coffee production and skyrocketing prices.[30] The oligarchy had to do something with its profits. Thus the traditional alliance between military and oligarchy acquired a new dimension, and others, including the existing (if minuscule) industrial sector and technocrats, were brought into the process.

Import Substitution. The precise character of the development model invoked was that of "import substitution" – establishing industries that produced goods that had previously been imported and were, by and large, capital- rather than labor-intensive. This created further external dependency, for now foreign capital, primarily from the United States, joined that of the oligarchy to finance the new industrial growth.

It also created an internal contradiction. The import-substitution model implicitly assumed an expanding domestic consumer market to absorb the goods that were being produced. But the linchpin of the oligarchy-state alliance was an understanding that El Salvador's first key to wealth, the land, was untouchable. Thus the possibility of developing through agrarian reform a class of small farmers who would become sufficiently affluent to acquire purchasing power was negated. Furthermore, El Salvador continued to be a significant net food importer. As prices rose the problems of the poor, which Masferrer had condemned in the 1920s, were exacerbated rather than reduced.

Agricultural Diversification. The coastal zone of southeastern El Salvador could not be exploited until drugs and insecticides were developed to combat rampant problems with malaria and insects. The availability of these commodities, along with the need to develop a domestic textile industry during World War II, combined to en-

68

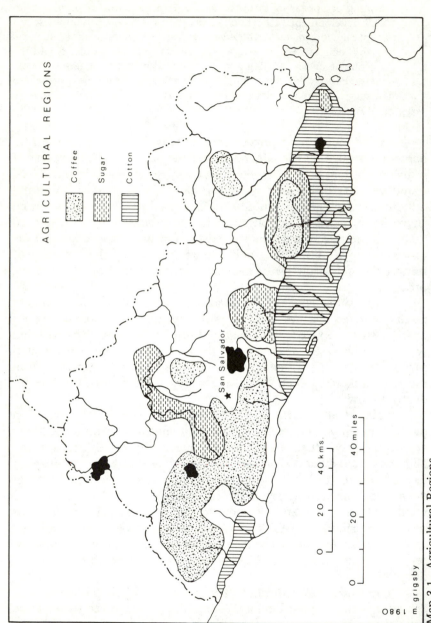

AGRICULTURAL REGIONS

Coffee

Sugar

Cotton

San Salvador

0   20   40 kms.

0   20   40 miles

1980   m grigsby

Map 3.1   Agricultural Regions

courage the cultivation of cotton. In 1940 the Salvadorean Cotton Growers' Cooperative, an organization to which all cotton growers were required by law to belong, was created. Officially, it was given wide powers to regulate all aspects of cotton production and processing and was the sole purchaser, processor, and marketer of the crop. In reality the cooperative concerned itself almost exclusively with the commercial aspects of production and with protecting the interests of the growers.[31] The amount of land under cultivation grew from 9,800 hectares in 1942 to 19,030 hectares in 1951; by 1960 it had increased to more than 43,000 hectares and five years later had tripled to 122,300 hectares. This expansion took place at the expense of forests, cattle ranching, and subsistence farming and of both tenants and squatters. From the perspective of the growers, however, the return was well worth the price: By 1964 cotton accounted for 24 percent of El Salvador's total exports. This, however, was the apogee of Salvadorean cotton production. By 1969, overuse of fertilizer and insecticides and rising costs forced out speculators and dramatically reduced the area planted to half that in 1965.[32]

The costs of intensive cotton cultivation were described by David Browning in 1971:

> The cotton farmers, in introducing an agricultural system, the techniques of which they are not familiar with, into a natural environment whose balanced structure they do not understand or appreciate, have failed to adapt their methods of farming to local environmental conditions and thereby have abused and destroyed the area's natural ecological balance. . . . Whereas coffee farmers realized that sound techniques of cultivation based on applied research were a necessity for the long-term future of the crop, the cotton farmers cleared and cultivated the coastal plain in an attempt to gain maximum and immediate profits with little thought of the long-term effects of their activities.[33]

Sugar cane developed even later than cotton. Grown for internal consumption since the sixteenth century, cane was cultivated on the low hills in the central part of the country that were too low for coffee and too high for cotton. It did not become a significant export crop until the 1960s.

An additional cost accompanied agricultural diversification. The cultivation of cotton and sugar cane for export took place at the expense of tenant farmers and squatters, thousands of whom were pushed off the land that had previously provided them with subsistence crops.[34] William Durham, echoing Masferrer, argued in his

Photo 3.1 Usulután. During the six weeks of the cotton harvest, workers migrate into the southeastern region of the country. They bring their own hammocks, which they hang under sheds like these.

study of the ecological origins of the 1969 war between El Salvador and Honduras that "from a balance of payments point of view the country as a whole is better off with land in export crops. But the problem is . . . that most Salvadoreans do not derive much benefit from export production."[35]

National Politics During the Osorio Regime

Under Oscar Osorio the promise of the Revolutionary Council to remove the army from politics was soon proved empty. The president and his colleagues were loath to allow any significant opposition. The PRUD emerged as a political actor in its own right when, in 1952, the CCE lost its autonomy and came under PRUD control for the National Assembly elections.

In that year and in 1954 the regime so restricted the activities of opposition parties in the Assembly election campaign that they withdrew their candidates. Osorio's justification for this renewed interference was that an open campaign would permit communism to flourish in El Salvador.[36] The increasing radicalization of the Guatemalan government was a source of major concern to military and oligarchy alike, and there was agreement between them that radical elements in El Salvador should be given no opportunity to gain a toehold in the country's political life.

By mid-decade army officers once again held a large number of government posts, including a majority of the departmental governorships and key offices in new institutes that had been established to develop and carry out various reforms. So when Osorio announced that the man he had chosen to succeed him was a civilian, a large delegation of officers immediately informed the president that, although civilian participation in the government was acceptable, a civilian president was not.[37] Osorio then turned to Lieutenant Colonel José María Lemus.

The 1955 Election. Opposition came from five candidates, two of them civilian. It was, however, a lackluster campaign; issues were all but ignored and party platforms were monotonously alike. Nonetheless, the government and the PRUD did not take any chances. The campaign was filled with irregularities. The National Guard repeatedly disrupted rallies and meetings of the opposition. Two months before the March election the opposition formed two coalitions in an effort to create a meaningful contest, but the CCE disqualified three of the five opposition candidates. On election day the army was very much in evidence, and army officers thought to be loyal to anyone other than Lemus were detained. To no one's surprise, Lemus won.[38]

The Lemus Regime

The heavy-handed tactics and fraud perpetrated by the government and the PRUD in the 1954 and 1955 elections created tensions both within the armed forces and between civilian and military sectors. Meanwhile, economic pressures were growing in the form of rising production costs and falling yields and prices. When Lemus spoke on the eleventh anniversary of the "revolution" in December 1959, he could do no better than rail against the communist threat. The crowd booed and jeered.[39]

Resurgence of Popular Unrest. The 1950s, despite increasing repression,[40] provided sufficient political latitude to permit the development of several center-to-left-leaning organizations. As these groups became more vocal in their demands for reform the regime grew more defensive. Repression increased, producing opposition.[41] In an act of desperation Lemus attempted to rally popular support by announcing in July 1960 a sweeping program of social and economic reforms. Three weeks later 20,000 peasants were trucked into the capital by the government for an anticommunist rally. Archbishop Luís Chávez y González concluded the rally with a mass.[42] The following day students held a rally of their own in the Plaza Libertad in downtown San Salvador. They praised the Cuban Revolution, attacked government repression, and strongly criticized the church for getting involved in politics. Security forces rounded up and incarcerated demonstrators. Lemus closed the National University, provoking even greater demonstrations. In September one student was killed and several (including the rector of the University of El Salvador [UES]) were arrested in a confrontation with police. Newspapers that had long supported the government broke with it over the growing repression.[43]

Coup d'Etat

In that same month *Osorista* officers and civilians began conspiring to overthrow Lemus. Osorio himself acted as a go-between for the conspirators, although he was ultimately excluded from the execution of the coup and the new government. The revolt itself, which occurred on October 25, 1960, was quick and bloodless. The new six-man junta included three civilians.

THE FOURTH CYCLE: 1960-1972

The junta dissolved the National Assembly and the Supreme Court. Like its predecessors, it lifted the state of siege, opened the borders to political exiles, and released Lemus's political prisoners into the arms of a waiting and jubilant crowd. According to junta member Fabio Castillo, "the Governmental Junta attempted to create a democratic climate and elaborated political and social guidelines which stressed development of a [completely open] electoral process and an educational program with the objectives of suppressing illiteracy and raising the educational level of the population."[44]

Visits by the members of the junta to the various army barracks to introduce themselves revealed the concerns of the officers. Would transfers occur without approval of the officers affected? Would the army continue its preeminent role in the national life? How would the regime deal with increasingly vocal communist and leftist groups?[45]

The presence of Castillo on the junta did nothing to assuage their concerns. A professor of pharmacology at the National University, Castillo was an unabashed supporter of the Cuban Revolution. The appointment of a largely civilian cabinet caused further worry as the growing public clamor for change intensified. When the junta announced its intent to hold truly free elections and to permit the participation of all political groups, consternation moved the officers to action.

Counter-Coup

Three months to the night after the ouster of Lemus, officers in the San Carlos barracks commandeered the country's communications system and announced a revolt. Two members of the junta fled to Guatemala; the others, including Castillo, were arrested. It was all over within twelve hours, whereupon the successful rebels gathered at San Carlos and selected Colonel Julio Adalberto Rivera to head a new junta. Rivera asserted that the character of the revolt was anticommunist and anti-Cuba.[46]

The Role of the United States. The October coup had occurred just days before the U.S. presidential election in which John F. Kennedy defeated Richard Nixon. Thus it was a lame duck Eisenhower administration that decided to withhold diplomatic recognition of the civilian-military junta.

Fabio Castillo, in testimony before the U.S. Congress in 1976, recounted his own experiences with the U.S. chargé d'affaires who, Castillo charged, intervened openly. On one occasion the chargé, accompanied by oligarch Ricardo Quiñonez, visited Castillo and told him that "the U.S. Embassy did not agree with the holding of a free election and added that the Embassy would agree to a 'free election' held with two candidates previously approved by them." Castillo rejected the proposal, whereupon "Quiñonez, unable to control his anger, turned to the chargé and said: 'You see, they are Communists, we have to go ahead.'"

Two weeks later the chargé approached Castillo, who was also minister of education, at a diplomatic reception and tried again. "I guess, you don't really want to go ahead with those plans to teach the people how to read and to educate them as you have previously announced." Castillo responded that "that was the explicit wish of the people of El Salvador who had been left in great ignorance and poverty." The chargé, who by this time was, according to Castillo, quite angry, replied, "Don't you know that educated people will ask for bread?" Castillo answered, "What's wrong with hungry people wanting bread and work?"

Castillo charged that from that time on "members of the U.S. Military Mission openly intensified their invitation to conspiracy and rebellion." He further asserted that "members of the U.S. Military Mission were at the San Carlos Headquarters on the day of coup." Castillo affirmed that he "was able to see them there at 1:30 p.m." when he talked with Colonel Rivera.[47]

The new Kennedy administration immediately recognized the Rivera government.

The Rivera Era

On January 25, 1961, El Salvador had yet another government. The Civilian-Military Directorate, composed of Rivera, another colonel, and three civilians, was created. Two of the civilians resigned in April, partly in opposition to proposed reforms, partly because they were figureheads. In September Rivera resigned from the junta and joined with dissident Christian Democrats who had recently formed the latest incarnation of the official party, the National Conciliation Party (PCN).[48]

The two remaining members of the Directorate set the election of a constitutional assembly for December 17. Only the PCN and five minor conservative parties were allowed to participate. To no one's surprise, the PCN garnered an overwhelming victory. A month later the Constitutional Assembly revised the 1950 constitution, gave itself the status of a national assembly, and scheduled a presidential election for April. The PCN nominated Rivera. AGEUS, the university student organization, provided Rivera's only competition: a donkey.[49]

If Rivera's regime was not to go the way of Lemus's, he would have to do something different. Under pressure from the United States through its ambassador, Murat Williams, and to the dismay of the oligarchy, President Rivera opened the electoral process to opposition parties. He established proportional representation in the National Assembly, thus guaranteeing the opposition representation commensurate with its electoral strength.

The Christian Democratic Party. After the Cuban Revolution the United States cast about for an alternative to right-wing military dictatorship and left-wing revolution in Latin America and discovered Christian Democracy, which promised a "third way" to "revolution in liberty" through social and economic reforms via the developmental model.[50] Thus the United States was only too happy to encourage the fledgling Christian Democratic party in El Salvador during the 1960s. Some U.S. officials envisioned a process of democratization that would culminate in a peaceful transition from military to civilian rule. U.S. hopes and Rivera's strategy coincided from 1962 to 1964, leading to gains by the opposition in the National Assembly and in mayoral and local elections as the decade progressed.

The Salvadorean PDC incorporated three distinct ideological positions from its founding. All came from Catholic thought, but one

TABLE 3.1

Christian Democratic Party Electoral Results in Municipal and Assembly Elections 1964 - 1970, based on official government figures.

	1964	1966	1968	1970	1972	1974	1976[a]
Seats in National Assembly (of 52)	14[b]	15	19[c]	16[d]	8	15	0
Mayors	37[e]	83[e]	78[f]	8[e]	17[e]	17[e]	0
Percent Popular Vote	26	31	42[g]	27	57	NA[h]	--

SOURCES: Stephen Webre, José Napoleón Duarte and the Christian Democratic Party in Salvadoran Politics 1960-1972, pp. 81, 98, 102, 136, 147, 187. Rubén Zamora, "Seguro de vida o despojo? Análisis político de la transformación agraria." ECA XXXI, No. 335-336, Sept. - Oct. 1976, pp. 514, 517.

a. In 1976 the experiment in democracy was over. The opposition abstained for the first time since 1962 in protest against the manipulation of the electoral process by the PCN and government.
b. The PAR won six seats in addition.
c. Other opposition parties gained six seats in addition.
d. Other opposition parties won two seats in addition.
e. Including San Salvador.
f. Including San Salvador, Santa Ana, and San Miguel, the three largest cities.
g. Sixty percent in San Salvador.
h. The government never published the election returns. According to Webre, "An independent student of Salvadoran politics calculated that the UNO would have come out of a fair race with a majority in the Legislative Assembly" (p. 187).

was reactionary and the other two were progressive. The reactionary faction split off and formed the PCN. Of the remaining two, one was inspired by the most progressive social doctrine of the Catholic Church and programmatically shared much in common with the international social democratic movement. The other, although it supported social and economic change, was conditioned in its thinking by a strong dose of anticommunism. The roots of future dissension and division were firmly planted when, early in the party's existence, the man who emerged as its principal theoretician, Roberto Lara Velado, came out of the first group, while the man who would become its dominant public figure, José Napoleón Duarte, belonged to the latter.[51]

From a small electoral showing in the 1964 municipal and Assembly elections the PDC eclipsed other opposition parties and by 1968 was challenging the PCN for control of the National Assembly (see Table 3.1).

Economic Reforms Under Rivera

Measured by some indicators, President Rivera succeeded, not only in reversing the economic decline El Salvador endured during the late 1950s, but in setting the country on an economic course that created "boom" conditions. For example, the annual rate of growth of value added in the industrial sector between 1962 and 1967 was as much as 11.7 percent. In fact, the conditions that produced the "boom" and "bust" under Osorio and Lemus remained unchanged.

The substitute for agrarian reform was the economic integration of Central America. The reasoning, at least in El Salvador and Guatemala, the two most developed countries in the area, was that the unrestricted flow of capital, people, and goods throughout the isthmus would create additional markets for industrial products, new opportunities for investment, and a means of relieving the growing population pressure. Supported by the United Nations Economic Commission for Latin America (ECLA), the idea was at first opposed by the United States because ECLA had suggested a limited and strongly regulated role for foreign investment as well as an emphasis on planned and balanced development and the elimination of competition and duplication of industries. These plans had to be dropped before the United States came around in the late 1950s.[52]

The result was the creation in 1961 of the Central American Common Market. CACM's impact was soon apparent. Intraregional trade increased 32 percent each year between 1962 and 1968, and the increase averaged 26 percent between 1960 and 1972. The nature of the goods being traded changed from unprocessed agricultural products to nondurable consumer goods.[53]

In El Salvador, furthermore, the nature of industry had shifted by this time from import substitution to industry for export—that is, the assembly or packing of imported components.[54] For companies like Texas Instruments and Maidenform this technique significantly increased their profit margin because Item 807 of the U.S. Tariff Code required that duty be paid only on the "value added" to the product, that is, the cost of labor. At salaries averaging $4.00 per day, these companies' imports from El Salvador began growing: By 1975 their value was $12 million; four years later it had more than doubled, to $25.9 million.[55]

The Effects of Industrialization. The economic reforms of the early 1960s began attracting both domestic and foreign investment. The Alliance for Progress helped create the "boom time" aura through the allocation of funds for housing, school construction, health facilities,

Figure 3.1 This cartoon is from a book prepared for army recruits in 1980. The caption reads, "For a just and secure peace." The sign says, "We work together for the peace of our territory."

and water and sewage projects. The army began providing manpower for various public construction projects—which, while they demonstrated that the army was "working for the people," also denied hundreds of civilian jobs in a country where the unemployment rate ranged between 30 and 57 percent.[56]

Industrial expansion occurred without commensurate growth in the level of employment because factories brought in the most modern machinery, which required few workers. Furthermore, the government provided no incentives for labor-intensive industry. On the contrary, the stated objective of the 1965–69 Development Plan to promote "the use of modern equipment and methods" was officially encouraged by at least two means: the tariff-free importation of capital equipment and the provision by the Salvadorean Institute for Industrial Development, of loans at low rates for the purchase of machinery.[57]

In industry as in agriculture, the oligarchy's primary interest was the profit margin. According to two independent Salvadorean economic analysts, Salvadorean investors were in the habit of earning a 25 to 40 percent rate of return on investment, as compared with an expectation in the United States and Europe of 10 to 12 percent. As they had investment alternatives both within and outside the country this was a realistic goal.†

The foreign-born part-owner and general manager of a large hotel in the capital, who immigrated to El Salvador in 1975, said he came in with the attitude that on a $1 million investment he would lose 5 percent the first year and 2 percent the second and make 3 percent the third and 12 percent thereafter. But Salvadoreans, he said, "thought I was crazy. They wanted a 100 percent return the first year." He added that by 1980 most Salvadorean businessmen were willing to accept a return of three or four points over the going interest rate†—but by then investment had plummeted, a casualty of the growing political unrest.

Changes in Agriculture. A minimum wage law for agricultural workers in May 1965 theoretically was to bring a new, higher standard of living for Salvadorean peasants. Its effect, however, was to create many thousands more landless and underemployed or unemployed people. As we saw in Chapter 2, *colonos* and *aparceros* had formed, from colonial times, an integral part of the *hacienda* system. In 1965, however, the government decided it was time to abolish that vestige of feudalism. As David Browning noted, provision of food and a *milpa* for each worker was "officially discouraged and the *colono* or *aparcero* [was] expected to become a laborer whose sole

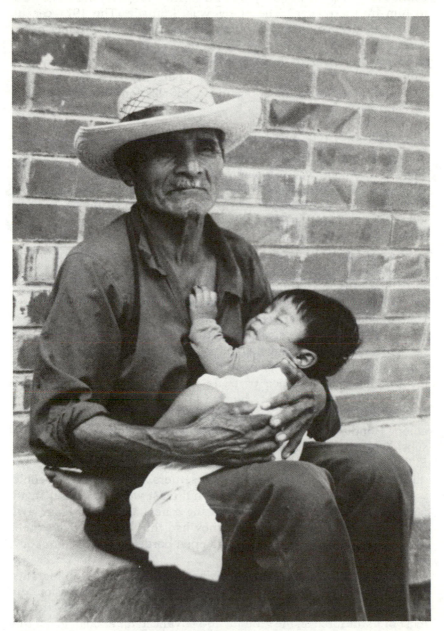

Photo 3.2 A *campesino* and his grandson.

connection with the property that he worked on [was] the wage paid to him by the owner." The effect was dramatic. The 1971 census recorded a decline during the preceding decade in the number of *colonos* from 55,769 to 17,019. At the same time the number of landless *campesinos* increased from 30,451 (11.8 percent of all rural Salvadoreans) in 1961 to 112,108 (29.1 percent) ten years later. By 1975 the figure had climbed again, to 166,922 landless people (40.9 percent).[58]

Origins of the "Soccer War"

A second reason for the dramatic increase in landless peasants was the 100-hour war between El Salvador and Honduras in 1969, which left several thousand dead and at least 100,000 Salvadoreans homeless. Dubbed the "Soccer War" by foreign journalists because it followed a series of bitterly contested games between the two countries during the qualifying rounds for the 1969 World Cup, the mini-war was, in fact, the result of at least three other, far more profound issues.[59]

First, the two countries were at odds over their border—a dispute that extended all the way back to independence. Second, they were at odds over the effect of CACM on their respective economies. While El Salvador saw its balance of trade within the isthmus increase markedly as it began producing industrial goods for export, Honduras was watching its balance of trade decline. Meanwhile, Honduras enjoyed a favorable balance of trade outside the region—thanks to bananas, lumber, and meat—but suffered a great imbalance within Central America. This state of affairs caused increasing resentment among Honduran leaders as they realized their country was, in effect, subsidizing the industrial development of its neighbors, in particular El Salvador.[60] Third, and most important, was the presence in Honduras of at least 300,000 Salvadorean settlers. Many of these people were second-generation immigrants, and most were successful small farmers. In April 1969 Honduras, using a new agrarian reform law, notified Salvadorean farmers that they had thirty days to leave their land. In June Honduras reversed its open-border immigration policy and closed its border.

El Salvador responded by closing *its* border to the immigrants and filing a complaint with the Inter-American Commission on Human Rights. On July 14, El Salvador invaded Honduras, destroyed most of its air force on the ground, and advanced far enough to cut the roads to Nicaragua and Guatemala. Five days later the war ended, thanks in part to a cease-fire arranged by the Organization of

American States, but due largely to U.S. pressure on the Salvadorean government in the form of threatened economic sanctions. Within El Salvador the war was enormously popular and served to take people's minds off the country's growing economic problems.

Those problems emerged in the last years of the Rivera administration. World market prices for coffee dropped; disease and drought severely affected the cotton crop; sugar cane surpluses increased as world demand plummeted. Private investment declined as budget and international payment deficits mounted. The government was forced to curtail many public works projects and social welfare programs. Unemployment grew. These conditions bred popular unrest as the unemployed took to the streets for the first time since 1959 to demand relief.

The 1967 Presidential Election

It was in this context that President Rivera dictated to the PCN national convention his choice of General Fidel Sanchez Hernandez as successor. Although the PDC offered a candidate, the only opponent who received any attention from Sanchez was the PAR candidate, Fabio Castillo. Castillo had become rector of the National University in 1963. During his four-year tenure, he significantly upgraded the quality of education, expanded enrollment, and began providing scholarships for needy students. Sanchez Hernandez set the tone of the campaign by declaring that the people had a choice between communism and liberty.[61]

The Catholic Church jumped into the fray with a condemnation of the PAR by the bishop of San Vicente, Monseñor Pedro Aparicio.[62] Aparicio also threatened to excommunicate parishioners who had the temerity to ally themselves with the PAR. Finally, the Episcopal Conference issued a declaration two weeks before the election reminding the flock of the church's blanket condemnation of communism.[63]

The outcome of the election was at once predictable and surprising—predictable, because Sanchez Hernandez won; surprising because the PAR garnered 14.4 percent of the national vote, while the Christian Democrats ran second with 21.6 percent, and the PCN led with 54.4 percent. In the Department of San Salvador, however, the PAR led the PDC 29 percent to 25 percent, with the PCN gaining only a plurality, 41 percent.[64]

The Man on Donkey-Back

The economic woes that Sanchez Hernandez inherited grew worse. Labor unions joined the protests and many teachers and workers went on strike. The president responded by naming a colonel as minister of labor and charging that the unrest was communist-inspired.[65] Meanwhile the army began demanding a larger budget and new equipment and began receiving "counterinsurgency" training that had been offered by the United States in the mid-1960s. The growing political unrest in El Salvador and the restiveness in the army, coupled with the intraregional economic issues, provided Sanchez with all the excuses he needed to invade Honduras on July 14, 1969.

The Benefits and Costs of War. In the short term, Sanchez succeeded in distracting his countrypeople from their economic woes. The most famous picture to come out of the four-day battle was that of the president astride a donkey at the Salvadorean-Honduran border. In the long run, however, Sanchez Hernandez's little war only exacerbated the deteriorating economic conditions within the country. The war itself was expensive: About $20 million—or one-fifth of El Salvador's annual budget—was expended in those four days.[66]

The Honduran market, which in 1968 had taken $23 million in Salvadorean goods, vanished. El Salvador's route via the Pan American Highway to Nicaragua and Costa Rica, its other CACM trading partners, was closed for a time. The Common Market itself was a shambles. El Salvador suddenly found itself with tens of thousands of new landless and jobless citizens inside its boundaries.

Agrarian Reform. Sanchez Hernandez, who prided himself on being a "moderate," decided to capitalize on his popularity by initiating a series of mild reforms, the most significant of which was to be a "democratic program of agrarian reform."[67] The president argued that this reform had long been needed and was made even more necessary by the recent influx from Honduras. Enrique Alvarez Córdova, one of the more progressive members of the oligarchy, was minister of agriculture.[68] Alvarez was among those who most strongly influenced the proposed reform.

The National Assembly, operating with a coalition of opposition and progressive PCN members, and with both government and PDC agrarian reform bills on its agenda, called a National Agrarian Reform Congress. Composed of delegates from all sectors of Salvadorean society, the congress met in San Salvador in January 1970. During the first session the entire private sector walked out after losing a roll call vote on the question of whether the congress should pass resolutions and make recommendations. The private sector opposed this, arguing that agrarian reform was a technical, not a political, issue and that there was therefore no sense surveying national opinion on the question—the very point of the congress.

The delegates then went far beyond anyone's expectations by identifying the concentration of land in few hands as the major barrier to full employment and development of national resources and by concluding that, under these circumstances, it was "not only a right of the state but a duty" to institute "massive expropriation in favor of the common good."[69] The delegates also tackled another taboo—the long-proscribed *campesino* unions—and argued that the only way agrarian reform would work was to ensure the participation of the projected beneficiaries, the peasants. The delegates argued that the only way to achieve this was for the government to restrain the *hacendados* and their minions within the armed forces while defending the right of the *campesinos* to organize.[70]

The 1970 National Elections

Two months after the Agrarian Reform Congress, national elections reduced the opposition's seats in the National Assembly from almost half to barely a third. As shown in Table 3.1, the Christian Democrats and other progressive opposition parties had come within two seats of a majority in the Assembly in the 1968 elections. The PDC also controlled mayoralties in El Salvador's three largest cities. Following the war however, the PDC and other opposition parties lost seven seats, while the PCN swept seventy of the seventy-eight mayoralties that the PDC had held during the previous four years. No more was heard about agrarian reform until the mid-1970s.

The decline in the electoral fortunes of the opposition was, in a sense, temporary. The economic problems described earlier persisted in spite of a short-lived surge in coffee prices, thanks to a blight in Brazil in 1969–1970. Meanwhile, the opposition parties decided to form a coalition for the 1972 presidential elections.

The Critical Election of 1972

Stephen Webre, in his study of the Christian Democratic Party in Salvadorean politics, observed that "the real question facing El Salvador in 1968 was not whether the opposition would continue to make gains, but what the PCN would do when the electoral solution became absolutely incompatible with its survival as the dominant party."[71] The answer to that question came with the 1972 presidential election.

The Opposition Comes Together. In the late 1960s two other opposition parties were formed. One was the Revolutionary National Movement (MNR), which affiliated with the Socialist International. Its secretary general was a lawyer, Guillermo Manuel Ungo, whose father had been one of the founders of the PDC a decade before. The other party was the Nationalist Democratic Union (UDN), which described itself as the "noncommunist" left but was, in fact, the legal front for the proscribed Salvadorean Communist Party.[72]

In September 1971 the PDC, MNR, and UDN announced their intention of forming a permanent coalition, the National Opposition Union (UNO), not just for the coming election but to work together on a continuing basis. "We have a common goal," they stated in their joint manifesto, "capable of transcending the problem of differences of ideology and strategy; we desire a positive change in the existing structures of political and economic power which have demonstrated their injustice and have had a clearly retrogressive effect on our development."[73] The PDC had long opposed coalitions, but by 1971 it recognized that the greatest problem facing the opposition was its disunity. In addition the PDC, as the largest of the three parties, negotiated with the other two from a position of strength.

The Campaign. To no one's surprise, José Napoleón Duarte, who had served for several years as mayor of San Salvador and was far and away the most popular opposition figure in the country, was chosen to lead the UNO ticket. Duarte asked for and got Ungo as his vice-presidential running mate. UNO's platform was modest. "We do not promise to create a paradise overnight. We merely intend to start the country down a different road from that which it has followed for so long and which has brought it to such grave and overwhelming difficulties."[74]

As in the past, President Sanchez Hernandez dictated his choice of successor to the PCN and the army: his own secretary, Colonel Arturo Armando Molina. Two other candidates, both to the political right of Molina, graced the ballot. One, José Antonio Rodriguez Porth, was the candidate of that sector of the oligarchy which had diversified its holdings into industry and commerce. The other, General José Alberto Medrano, was the choice of the landed oligarchy. Medrano was a hero of the Soccer War, a former director of the National Guard, and the founder and guiding light of ORDEN.[75] The year before, Medrano had been arrested for killing a policeman on the general's own doorstep. The policeman had been sent to arrest him for complicity in an attempted coup. Medrano pleaded self-defense and a jury acquitted him.

Attention focused on Molina and Duarte, both of whom mounted vigorous national campaigns. As the campaign heated up, Duarte and Ungo became the objects of ad hominem attacks intended to call their honesty and competence into question and to portray them as communists or at least fellow travelers. Despite the polemics, there was only one direct physical attack. Duarte's campaign caravan was fired on by unidentified assailants in eastern El Salvador in late December 1971, and the driver of the lead car was killed. President Sanchez condemned the killing and ordered an investigation, but nothing came of it.

Mayoral and Assembly elections were scheduled for March, after the presidential election. The PCN did not fear losing the presidency, but it did fear losing its majority in the National Assembly. To avoid such an outcome, the CCE disqualified on technicalities UNO Assembly slates in the six largest departments in the country – including San Salvador, where UNO strength was greatest. Thus, before the balloting for president, the PCN had ensured that there was no way UNO could win a majority in the Assembly.

February 20, 1972. The cancellation of the UNO slates, the bitter campaign rhetoric, and the murder of the UNO driver merely set the stage for election day. Turnout was heavy, and as the returns began coming in from the rural departments, Molina took a commanding lead. Then the tide turned. Duarte carried San Salvador, with 30 percent of the nation's voters, two to one. The government immediately prohibited further announcement of returns. Finally, almost twenty-four hours after the polls closed, the CCE announced that Molina had won by a margin of 22,000 votes. UNO had a different count. Its figures, taken directly from election boards around the country, showed Duarte 9,500 votes ahead.[76] Molina agreed to a recount. Duarte and Ungo announced they would ask the CCE to nullify the votes and schedule a new election. As Rodriguez Porth and Medrano had garnered 100,000 votes between them, neither Molina nor Duarte had an absolute majority. The constitutional procedure in such an event was to throw the election into the National Assembly, which hastily convened on February 25 and elected Molina president.

March 12, 1972. Duarte and the UNO then called on voters in the Department of San Salvador to deface their ballots in the Assembly elections. Under Salvadorean law, marred ballots were counted as null votes, and if they exceeded the number of valid votes the election, theoretically, was nullified. Almost 75,000 voters heeded the UNO's call, a clear majority of the 144,101 votes cast. The UNO asked the departmental electoral board to nullify the election and on March 23 it did. The CCE promptly overturned that decision.

Coup d'Etat

Shortly after midnight on March 25 the San Carlos and El Zapote barracks in the capital revolted. Led by Colonel Benjamin Mejia, the rebels quickly gained control of San Salvador and captured President Sanchez Hernandez and his daughter. With San Salvador secure, Mejia went on national radio and announced "the triumph of the military youth." His announcement was premature. Although he had the solid support of the army in San Salvador, the air force and all the security forces remained loyal to the government. Even as Mejia was speaking the Air Force began bombing the city. The National Guard converged on the capital from all points, and the initially bloodless coup became a bloody fight for San Salvador. Duarte, at Mejia's request, issued an appeal by radio for listeners to support the rebels.[77]

As rebel positions crumbled, Duarte sought refuge in the home of the Venezuelan Embassy's First Secretary. After Sanchez Hernandez regained his office, soldiers found Duarte and carted him off. The Christian Democratic government of Venezuela threatened to break diplomatic relations if Duarte was not freed. The Salvadorean government's announcement of plans to try and to shoot all *golpistas* brought concerted protest from the diplomatic corps. Sanchez Hernandez agreed to ship the plotters off into exile. Duarte took up residence in Venezuela, and Molina was duly inaugurated.[78]

As Stephen Webre observed in a masterpiece of understatement, the logical flaw of the electoral solution of the 1960s was that it "encouraged an active opposition but, by definition, forbade that opposition to come to power."[79] The army had been willing to lose some of its support from the most reactionary elements of the oligarchy, as symbolized in the candidacies of Rodriguez Porth and Medrano. It was not, however, willing to give up one iota of real political power.

Corruption as an Instrument of the Status Quo

It is impossible to understand the relationship between the oligarchy and the military after 1932 without understanding the institutional system of corruption that guaranteed that key army officers would become and remain loyal, not to the interests of the whole country, but to their benefactors.

A part-owner and general manager of one of San Salvador's largest hotels asserted during an interview that the private sector was "more corrupt" than the army. He explained that as long as officers were in the barracks there was no opportunity for them to become corrupt.[80] When they assumed positions in state-owned companies

TABLE 3.2

Monthly Salaries for Members of the Salvadorean Armed Forces, January 1980

Officers		Noncommissioned officers and troops	
Colonel	$1120	Sergeants	$200*
Lieutenant Colonel	980	Sub-sergeants	140*
Major	840	Corporals	100*
Captain	800	Soldiers	80*
Lieutenant	700	National Guard	320*
Second Lieutenant	600	*Plus uniforms, meals, and bed	

such as ANTEL, however, opportunities for corruption abounded. The businessman described how the system might work for him: An officer would be invited to dinner at the hotel, to return and bring his family, to use hotel facilities (gratis, of course) for a birthday party or similar event—followed by an invitation to spend the weekend at the manager's beach house. Later the officer would be offered the opportunity to buy 10 percent of a business with guarantees that if he needed a loan one would be available at attractive interest rates, courtesy of a bank owned by members of the oligarchy. This, the businessman concluded, was only one example of how a "very elastic system" of corruption worked.†

Members of the army provided further confirmation of the system. A lieutenant colonel suggested that low salaries "led directly to corruption," then added that the military "were poorly paid intentionally—in order to make them ripe for corruption." Those salaries, in January 1980, were as shown in Table 3.2.

An officer who had been a senior official of ANTEL for a time in the late 1970s related how, at a funeral, he had been approached by a member of the cabinet and offered $80,000 to help a certain supplying company win a bid from ANTEL. The officer declined the offer, but later a company official offered him $40,000 more, telling him that the country was close to collapse and the money could be a *"colchon"* (literally, a mattress, a cushion) for him. Again, the officer said, he refused. He concluded by saying that "corruption has been a tool of the oligarchy [which has] yielded economic profits to the oligarchy—ultra right—and political profits to the far left."†

THE FIFTH CYCLE: 1972–1979

Alastair White observed in his 1973 study of El Salvador that the years after 1932 were characterized by an erratic oscillation between "concession and repression," with little effort to maintain a balance between the two. White noted that Araujo in 1931 and Menéndez in 1944 fell after making too many concessions to popular demands; on the other hand, Martínez in 1944, Castaneda in 1948, Lemus in 1960, and Sanchez Hernandez in 1972 all went too far in the opposite direction.[81]

After the aborted coup and the inauguration of Molina it appeared for a brief time that the balance had been restored. But 1972 proved to be a watershed. The army-dominated government had increasingly infuriated most of the oligarchy by its modest reform efforts; and it had alienated many workers, peasants, and youth by the inadequacy of those reforms and by the blatant fraud that paraded as an election.

Molina, his legitimacy weakened by the attempted coup, searched desperately for a means to reinforce his authority. He found it, as so many of his predecessors had, in "anticommunism" and "law and order." The scapegoat for his campaign became the University of El Salvador (UES), a target of increasingly frequent right-wing attacks. Charging that UES "had fallen into the hands of the Communists," Molina induced the National Assembly in July to issue a decree ending the university's autonomy[82] and ordered its campuses in San Salvador, Santa Ana, and San Miguel occupied by security forces. Many professors, students, and administrators were arrested; foreigners among them were expelled, and a good number of Salvadoreans were exiled. The university was reopened in September 1973 under government control and with a government-appointed rector.[83]

Molina scored points among Salvadorean conservatives, who viewed the university (not without reason) as a hotbed of revolution. But the repressive character of this action undoubtedly contributed to the increasing radicalization of thousands of young Salvadoreans and provided one more reason for them to believe that meaningful social, political, and economic change was impossible under the existing regime.

And Now . . . Miss Universe

In the midst of these developments, El Salvador won the privilege of hosting the 1975 Miss Universe pageant. Apart from the perceived prestige associated with the event, Salvadorean government and business leaders saw in it an opportunity for worldwide publicity that would promote a nascent tourist industry. Thousands of other Salvadoreans saw it differently. They saw a set of warped priorities that led the government to spend about $30 million on the pageant in the face of massive social needs.[84] So it was that UES students in Santa Ana demonstrated in protest; the demonstration was forcibly disbanded by the National Guard. At that, more than 2,000 UES students in San Salvador marched in solidarity from the university to the Plaza Libertad downtown. They suddenly found themselves surrounded by units of the National Guard, with all avenues of escape cut off. The troops — without provocation, according to eyewitnesses — opened fire on the demonstrators, leaving at least thirty-seven dead and several dozen more "disappeared."[85]

This massacre occurred at a time of increasing violence at both ends of the political spectrum. On one side, guerrilla organizations created at the beginning of the decade were kidnapping members of the oligarchy with increasing regularity and holding them for enormous ransoms. On the other, security forces were engaging in official repression, such as the massacre in the hamlet of La Cayetana in November 1974. Peasants there had been engaged for some time in a land dispute with a neighboring *hacendado*. The National Guard and National Police, accompanied by members of ORDEN, surrounded the town and opened fire. Six farmers were killed; thirteen "disappeared"; and twenty-five were arrested.[86]

In August 1975 an extremist organization, the FALANGE, made its appearance with a public commitment to exterminate all communists and their sympathizers in El Salvador. The FALANGE would be joined by several other groups[87] in the following years, all of which have three things in common: They have all been connected with certain army officers; their membership has consisted primarily of off-duty National Guardsmen and National Police, supplemented by some ORDEN members and occasional mercenaries; and they all have received money from various members of the oligarchy.[88]

Electoral Fraud Redux

The mayoral and Assembly elections in 1974 were marked by even more blatant manipulation than had been evident two years earlier. The CCE never published official returns, but the government announced that the UNO had won fifteen seats in the Assembly, while the PCN controlled thirty-six.

In 1976 UNO nominated no candidates, refusing to dignify what it was certain would be another electoral farce. Thus, for the first time in fourteen years, the opposition deliberately abstained.

Agrarian Reform . . . Again

On the heels of the 1976 election Molina and the National Assembly decreed a modest agrarian transformation ("reform" was a word they avoided) and nationalized almost 61,000 hectares in the Departments of Usulután and San Miguel. Most of this transformation zone was either cow pastures or planted in cotton, and the aim was to divide it among 12,000 *campesino* families. The decree followed a 1974 law that permitted, under certain conditions, the forced rental or even expropriation of fallow or insufficiently exploited land and a 1975 law that created the Salvadorean Institute of Agrarian Transformation (ISTA).

The first two laws had raised howls of protest from the oligarchy, which failed in an attempt to have them struck down in court. With the creation of the transformation zone the oligarchy, through its various interest groups like the National Association of Private Enterprise (ANEP), launched a massive opposition campaign. As in the past, ANEP insisted it was "not against agrarian transformation" but charged that this particular project (like all others before it) was precipitous; that it had been rushed through without sufficient forethought or consultation; and that the planners were "divorced from national realities."[89]

But the oligarchy did not stop with *campos pagados* (paid political advertisements). Minister of Defense Carlos Humberto Romero had already been chosen by Molina as his successor, with the understanding that Romero would support the agrarian reform. But Romero had other loyalties: He went to Molina and threatened him with a coup d'etat if the agrarian reform went forward.† Molina, seeing the proverbial handwriting, met with members of the oligarchy and arranged a "compromise" that effectively emasculated the program.[90]

Industrial Growth During the 1970s

While the oligarchy was winning its political battles, it was also continuing to expand its economic interests. We saw earlier that industrialization resulted from an alliance between the oligarchy and the military and incorporated other elements in Salvadorean economic life. The primacy of the coffee-growing families in the industrial sector and their alliance with foreign investment is important because it confirms the concentration of wealth and economic control in the country.

Table 3.3 reveals the extent to which coffee-growing families

TABLE 3.3

Economic Groups by Economic Sector, 1974

ECONOMIC SECTORS	Coffee Growing Oligarchy		Non-Coffee Growing Oligarchy		Other Businessmen		Total
	Number of Businesses	%	Number of Businesses	%	Number of Businesses	%	Number of Businesses
Agriculture	65	86.5	10	2.6	27	10.9	102
Mining	--	---	2	1.2	4	98.2	6
Construction	49	55.1	36	32.1	39	12.8	124
Industry	156	72.7	98	15.9	161	11.4	415
Commerce	185	53.3	92	28.5	199	18.2	476
Transportation	9	8.7	10	28.6	40	62.7	59
Services	82	72.9	32	10.2	130	16.9	244
Total	546	66.0	280	18.7	600	15.3	1426

SOURCE: David Mena, Universidad Centroamericana José Simeón Cañas, 1980.

controlled the industrial life of El Salvador. They had invested a total of $278 million by 1974, more than 50 percent of it in industry. Meanwhile, noncoffee-growing members of the oligarchy had $79 million invested and nonmembers of the oligarchy $64.27 million. Table 3.4 demonstrates the extent of the alliance between foreign investment and the coffee-growing members of the oligarchy. Only one group of foreign investors—other Central Americans—invested their money in any significant amount outside this group.

In El Salvador the U.S. economic presence was strong. Although in the context of Latin America, U.S. investment was minuscule (less than one percent of total U.S. investment in the hemisphere), within El Salvador the impact was powerfully felt. That investment climbed from $19.4 million in 1950, of which about 25 percent was invested in industry, principally textiles, pharmaceuticals, chemicals, petroleum, paper products, and food. Gross U.S. investment for 1974 was $9.2 million, of which 56 percent was invested in industry. One must also keep in mind that most "Panamanian" investors were subsidiaries of U.S. concerns; hence total U.S. investment was considerably larger than the $9.2 million figure. (Fully 63 percent of all foreign investment in 1974 was in industry, with services in second place at 27.6 percent.) In 1975, however, U.S. investment climbed to $42.8 million.[91]

Effects of Investment Patterns. The industrial investments in El Salvador were concentrated in the urban zones, which did nothing to alleviate the growing underemployment in the countryside and exacerbated the population problem in the cities (especially the capital) as people moved in looking for work. Further, as industrialization was capital- rather than labor-intensive and no effort was made to strike a balance between the two, the number of persons employed by the industrial sector remained tiny (see Table 3.5) relative to the pool of available labor. In 1961 the industrial sector absorbed 12.8 percent of the total available work force; in 1970, the figure was 20.9 percent. By 1975, however, that percentage had dropped precipitously to 9.9 percent.[92] Meanwhile, urban unemployment in San Salvador in 1974 was 14 percent, a figure that did not decline in succeeding years.

Another phenomenon was at work as well. As Table 3.5 reveals, while the number of industrial employees was inching upward, the number of businesses that employed them was shrinking. In other words, there was a growing centralization of production.[93] The old saying that "money follows money" was never truer than in El Salvador, as these data reveal. These investment patterns not only contributed to an ever-greater concentration of wealth, but confirm

TABLE 3.4

Distribution of Foreign Capital by Country and Economic Group, 1974 (millions of dollars)

Countries	Coffee Oligarchy $	%	Non-Coffee Oligarchy $	%	Others $	%	Total $	%
United States	$ 9.2	80.8	$ 1.0	8.7	$ 1.2	10.5	$ 11.4	100.0
Panama	8.3	76.0	.7	6.4	1.9	17.6	11.0	100.0
Canada	15.3	88.5	---	---	2.0	11.5	17.3	100.0
Japan	10.8	93.5	.15	1.3	.6	5.2	11.5	100.0
Europe	8.0	66.2	2.3	19.1	1.8	14.7	12.1	100.0
Latin America	1.7	92.4	.04	2.2	.099	5.4	1.8	100.0
Central America	.8	34.7	.02	.9	1.5	64.4	2.3	100.0
Others	---	---	.014	100.0	---	---	.014	100.0
TOTAL/AVERAGE	$ 54.1	80.3	$ 4.2	6.3	$ 9.1	13.4	$ 67.5	100.0

SOURCE: David Mena, Universidad Centroamericana José Simeón Cañas, 1980.

TABLE 3.5

Industries and Employment, by Year

	1967	1970	1975 (Apr-June)
Total Number of Industries	515	541	478
Number of Industries Producing more than 50% of total production	153	150	136
Total Number of Employees	17,420	24,492	34,934
Number of Employees in Businesses with majority of total production	11,199	13,715	20,783

SOURCE: Carmen Sermeño Zelidon. "Las Nuevas Formas de Dominación política en El Salvador," Thesis for the Licenciatura in sociology, University of Costa Rica, 1979, p. 69.

that the traditional developmentalist assumption that wealth generated through industrialization or modernization will "trickle down" in developing nations is groundless.

The 1977 Election—and After

The UNO decided to enter the political fray once again in 1977. With Duarte still in exile, the coalition turned to a retired colonel, Ernesto Claramount, to head its ticket and chose the former PDC mayor of San Salvador, José Antonio Morales Erlich, as his running mate. Romero won handily in an election marked once again by fraud. Ballot boxes were already stuffed when the polls opened on February 20. UNO poll watchers were arrested or physically removed from numerous polling places. Still, in many locations where UNO observers remained, Claramount led by a significant margin.[94]

As the UNO denounced the stolen election, Claramount, Morales Erlich, and at least 15,000 supporters gathered in the Plaza Libertad, where the colonel announced his readiness to "remain in the plaza as long as the people want me to." Three days later the crowd had grown to 50,000, and talk of a general strike was in the air. On the night of February 27-28, the National Police moved in in armored cars and opened fire. At least four dozen people were killed as Claramount and 1,500 supporters raced into El Rosario Church, which fronts the plaza. Claramount was persuaded by friends to go into exile. As he left El Rosario in a Red Cross ambulance on his way to Ilopango airport and Costa Rica, he issued a warning. "This is not the end," he said. "It is only the beginning."[95]

The Romero Regime

Between July 1, 1977, and October 15, 1979, El Salvador was buffeted by a rising spiral of mass demonstrations and protests, government repression, left-wing kidnappings, labor strikes, and death-squad murders.

The new Carter administration, placing emphasis on human rights as a criterion for determining whether or not a government would receive military assistance, so angered the regime that it cut off all U.S. military aid packages before the Carter administration could act.

Finally, the sixth cycle began on October 15, 1979, with a coup d'etat. Throughout the 1970s the economic conditions under which the majority of Salvadoreans lived and the increasing repression fostered growing opposition from two not entirely unrelated quarters: the Roman Catholic Church and the revolutionary organizations. The next two chapters focus on these institutions, for they have changed the course of Salvadorean history.

4

The Church

Si me matan, resucitaré en la lucha del pueblo salvadoreño. *

—Oscar Arnulfo Romero

When the National Assembly convened the Agrarian Reform Congress in January 1970, governmental, nongovernmental, labor, and business groups were invited to participate. Among the nongovernmental groups that accepted was the Roman Catholic Church. Archbishop Luís Chávez y González handpicked a progressive group of priests and laity to represent the church, and Father José Inocencio Alas, a young diocesan priest, was chosen to present the church's position on the issue. It was a position so strongly in support of agrarian reform that it created a very "strong commotion", according to Monseñor Arturo Rivera Damas, the then auxiliary bishop of San Salvador. Hours after Alas made his presentation, he was abducted by men in civilian clothes in front of the National Palace. Eyewitnesses immediately called the Arzobispado (archdiocesan offices), and Rivera Damas, on receiving the news, got in his car and went to see the president of the National Congress. Rivera announced that he was going to the Ministry of Defense and would stay there until Alas was produced.

When Rivera told Minister of Defense Fidel Torres that he was going to sit in his office until Alas appeared, Torres "blanched," then picked up the phone. After each of several calls Torres reported the same response: "We don't have him." Rivera reminded Torres that in the history of El Salvador there were frequently situations like this and the response was always the same: *"No lo tenemos."* Rivera was soon joined by Monseñor Ricardo Urioste, who declared he would stay with Rivera. Torres attempted to strike a bargain: He would notify them of Alas's whereabouts at 9:00 P.M. (it was then 5:30 P.M.)

*If they kill me, I will be resurrected in the struggle of the Salvadorean people.

but the priests would have to leave. Torres promised that Alas would not be killed. Rivera and Urioste, unimpressed, did not move. Two hours later Torres provided sufficient information about Alas to assure Rivera and Urioste that he was alive and would be released unharmed. Satisfied, the two prelates departed.

Meanwhile, the radio station of the archdiocese, YSAX, had begun broadcasting the news of Alas's abduction. It stayed on the air all night relaying the news and calling on priests and parishes to pray for Alas. Years later, Rivera Damas said that "in those days we only asked people to pray; we did not know how to denounce."

Alas was beaten, drugged, and left naked on the edge of a cliff in the mountains south of San Salvador. His abductors apparently hoped he would roll off the cliff, but he rolled the other way. When Monseñor Urioste subsequently asked Alas if he had been thinking about being rescued, Alas replied, "No, I was thinking about the resurrection."[1]

This incident represented several "firsts" for the Salvadorean church. It was the first time the church had participated in a political event of this type and the first time it had taken a policy position on the question of agrarian reform. Alas's abduction was the first direct attack by government agents on the church, and it signaled (though one could not know it at the time) the beginning of a history of persecution that would be characterized by both random and systematic violence directed at both clergy and laity. Finally, Minister of Defense Torres's experience of having a cleric sit in and make demands was very likely the first such confrontation in Salvadorean history. In short, the Agrarian Reform Congress marked a turning point, not only in church-state relations, but even more significantly, in the church's role as a political actor in El Salvador.

VATICAN II AND MEDELLÍN

The events of January 1970 marked a turning point, not a beginning. The beginning can be dated from the Second Vatican Council (Vatican II), which convened in 1962 under Pope John XXIII and closed three years later under Pope Paul VI. Prior to Vatican II, national churches in Latin America presented a uniformly traditional religious image, accompanied by sharply conservative social and political attitudes. Virtually everywhere, including El Salvador, the church was allied with the regime.

Vatican II changed this state of affairs almost overnight. The council, strongly influenced by Pope John XXIII's social encyclicals, especially *Pacem in Terris,* asserted in its closing document *Gaudium et Spes* two new principles that would have particular impact in Latin America. They asserted that the church is in and of the world, with concerns well beyond the purely spiritual. They also emphasized that the church is a community of equals by baptism. The prelates refused to condemn communism per se, joining criticism of certain of its practices with an equally strong critique of capitalism's abuses.[2]

Three years after the end of Vatican II bishops from all over Latin America gathered in Medellín, Colombia, for the Second Episcopal Conference (CELAM II). Penny Lernoux correctly noted that Medellín was "one of the major political events of the century: it shattered the centuries old alliance of Church, military, and the rich elites."[3] At Medellín the bishops called upon the church "to defend the rights of the oppressed"; to promote grassroots organizations; "to denounce the unjust action of world powers that works against self-determination of weaker nations"; in short, to make a "preferential option for the poor."[4]

The primary means of accomplishing these ends was the development of Christian Base Communities (CEBs). It can be argued that these communities are the most revolutionary development in the Latin American church because, for the first time in history, the masses of the people began participating in and taking responsibility for important aspects of their own lives and for each other; they were no longer merely observers at a ritual conducted for their benefit by a resident or visiting priest. This form of participation, however, has had social consequences. With a growing frequency that disturbs traditional members of the church, CEB members have moved beyond purely religious concerns to political issues. Nowhere in Latin America has this been more true or had more profound consequences than in El Salvador.

Thus when one speaks of the "Salvadorean church" one must specify whether one is referring to the hierarchy (the bishops) or to what came by 1980 to be known as the *iglesia popular* (popular church)—that is, the tens of thousands of people, most of them poor, who came to believe that "liberation" is not only something one achieves at death, but also something which, with God's blessing, one can struggle for and possibly achieve during one's lifetime.

POLITICAL DIVISIONS WITHIN THE SALVADOREAN CHURCH

The reaction in the Latin American church to the conciliar and Medellín documents is usually described as falling into one of two categories. One hears references to the "historical" church and the "institutional" church, or the "Church of the Gospel" and the "Church of Rome." The former refers to the church at the base, the local church when it existed as small communities of believers without any institutional or bureaucratic superstructure. The latter refers to the bureaucratic church, with its own institutional interests that often have little to do with the fundamental values of Christianity, especially as those values are interpreted by liberation theology. Whatever the labels, Medellín initiated a dynamic process of reflection that encouraged Catholics (as well as Protestants) throughout the continent to rethink their faith. Most important, the emphasis on identifying the church with the poor led to assumption of a more prophetic attitude toward politics and society.[5] That prophetic attitude has been expressed in a theology of liberation that has interpreted the gospel as demanding that Christians be a force actively working to liberate the great majority of the people from poverty and oppression. By the mid-1970s the theology of liberation had become the "common coin of discourse"[6] among progressive Christians.

Division Within the Hierarchy

In El Salvador, as elsewhere in Latin America, two strains of liberation theology developed. While four of the six members of the Salvadorean hierarchy adhered to an institutional, sacramentalist view of the church's role in society,[7] the remaining two prelates, both in the archdiocese of San Salvador (and Archbishop Oscar Romero before his death), accepted and promoted the positions of Vatican II and Medellín from the beginning. (The archdiocese encompasses four departments, 40 percent of the population, and 57 percent of the priests and religious [brothers and nuns] in the country.)

Before his assassination, Archbishop Romero suggested that the key to this division within the church was stated at the Third Conference of Latin American Bishops in (CELAM III) in Puebla, Mexico, during January 1979: "In Latin America not all members of the Church have converted to the poor." Romero then continued:

> I believe that there is where the path to unity is, a "preferential option for the poor." If bishops, priests and laity would take this option—we found Jesus Christ among the poor and there was no problem—but the thing is that we do not believe much in that.
>   . . . The Pope in Puebla called attention to the divisions within the Church: an institutional church and a charismatic one that arises from the people. I always preach respect for the institution, to the hierarchy, but I say, "don't say the 'real church' if we only save the institution."[8]

Two Interpretations of Liberation Theology

While Romero reflected one strain of liberation theology, about 30 percent of the younger priests, in the words of one, "use the analysis of Marxism because it is objective and scientific. But we are not Marxists. We are not able to understand Marx as a religion because we are Christians."†

Within the archdiocese a clear pastoral line was laid down by Archbishops Chávez and Romero: Priests were to be guided by church doctrine issuing from Rome and CELAM; clergy could (indeed, were obliged to) *accompany* their people, but they could not take a political stance. During the early 1970s this pastoral line held little difficulty for even the most committed priests; as the political situation deteriorated toward the end of the decade, however, disagreement developed between Romero and the younger priests. The position of the latter, in the words of one during a monthly priests' meeting with Romero in December 1979 was, "You cannot have a pastoral line without having a political option. You [Romero] have got a political option, and we do too."† In the view of these priests, their archbishop's option was to support the junta, a charge that was unfair if understandable. To them, a logical extension of the defense of the people's right to organize was support of the organizations they had created. And since, as we shall see in the next chapter, many members and leaders of these organizations came out of the parishes' Christian Base Communities, there was yet another reason to support the organizations and the option for change that they represented.

This division within the archdiocese, although heated at times, never produced an open split like that in the hierarchy. Within the archdiocese, both sides of the liberation theology debate have taken great care not to create a situation in which reconciliation would be difficult or impossible.

In the discussion that follows, the "church" refers to that group of bishops, clergy, religious, and laity who follow Medellín and Puebla in committing themselves to a "preferential option for the poor."[9] It is this part of the church that became a major political actor in El Salvador during the 1970s.[10]

THE BEGINNINGS OF CHURCH ACTIVISM

With Vatican II and Medellín as doctrinal guides and support, Archbishop Chávez began immediately to encourage adherence to and development of new pastoral approaches. Such episcopal encouragement was confined largely to the archdiocese. In other dioceses the bishops continued to behave as though Vatican II and Medellín had never occurred. This unwillingness to move with the times would have profound consequences. For the moment, however, it is sufficient to note that the archdiocese became the locus of ferment within the Salvadorean church and that its impact and influence reached into every corner of the country.[11]

Archbishop Chávez, according to Arturo Rivera Damas, was very "anxious to put into practice the social doctrines that came out of the Council and to have them diffused and practiced." So it was that on August 6, 1966, the archbishop issued a pastoral letter, "The Responsibility of the Laity in the Ordering of Temporal Life," which put some distance between the church and the military government, "which saw in it support for the Christian Democrats . . . and criticism of capitalism."[12] It also occasioned something close to a rupture with the oligarchy, which not only disliked the perceived attack on capitalism but also recognized the social and political danger if all the laity should become involved in civic affairs. To a group of people used to having things their own way, the specter of politicized masses was disturbing, to say the least.

The ferment that began with this pastoral letter received an official impetus with the decision to hold a "pastoral week" in July 1970. Convoked by agreement of the Salvadorean Episcopal Conference (CEDES), only the three bishops of the archdiocese participated. The remainder of the hierarchy subsequently denounced, then diluted, the final document. The flap was the first open rift within CEDES; it would not be the last. The dissident bishops found the conclusions too extreme, motivated "by youthful fervor." One of the points that bothered the prelates most was "the denunciation of their connivance with the Salvadorean oligarchic minority, which oppressed the great majority of *campesinos* and workers." These bishops were also disturbed by the "necessity to promote lay pastoral agents as an indispensable means to bring the Gospel to the *campesino* masses." CEDES took the final document and diluted the first part, which contained an analysis of the structural injustice and institutionalized violence in El Salvador. In the second part, a theological reflection on these data, the bishops "emphasized the vertical (person-God) dimension while reducing to almost nothing the horizontal (person-person) dimension." But all CEDES changed were words. "In practice, the final conclusions were not touched."[13]

Christian Base Communities

In practice there was an explosion of pastoral activity throughout the archdiocese,† leading within a few years to the establishment of hundreds of Christian Base Communities. The work was spearheaded by a nun, a priest, and two prelates in the Arzobispado who provided the necessary coordination and support for priests and religious working in parishes from the Pacific Ocean to the Honduran border. CEBs were intended as a mechanism by which church doctrine developed during Vatican II could be implemented: to bring the laity into the life of the church, to teach that the Christian community is a community of equals before God in which all have obligations to each other and responsibilities to share. CEBs are small groups, usually no more than twenty or thirty, within a parish who meet regularly for Bible study. An initial course will be led by the priest or religious working with the CEB, but the group is encouraged to develop its own leadership–a necessary step in a country like El Salvador where the ratio of priests to parishioners was 1 : 10,000 during the 1970s.[14]

The people soon elect their catechists (lay teachers) and "delegates of the Word" (lay preachers). The catechists assume responsibility for one specific area, such as baptism, catechism, or marriage preparation classes. They receive additional training, but their responsibility is to lead the community in weekly worship services. Catechists and delegates are selected not only for their leadership qualities but also for their moral rectitude and their Christian commitment. There is a strong tradition against electing someone who is inclined to be overbearing or authoritarian. Willingness to be of service to the community is crucial.

The Training of Lay Leaders

Between 1970 and 1976 seven centers were established in El Salvador for the training of catechists and delegates. Over the course of the decade approximately 15,000 leaders were trained. According to Walter Guerra, a Salvadorean priest who spearheaded the development of these centers, the content of the courses emphasized "an integral formation" and spanned topics from Bible study and liturgy to agriculture, cooperativism, leadership, and health. This broad training, Guerra said, was necessary because "the catechist, among us, is a man who works not only as a religious person, but assumes leadership that is also social, including, at times, political in our rural communities."[15]

Guerra noted that a 1978 survey of the catechists and their work in the diocese of Santa Ana found that they "really made a great contribution" to their communities. After as little as three or four months, Guerra found in his visits that "the people were changing; communities were engaging in dialogue to resolve their problems (something that had never happened before); and there was religious renewal as well."

The process of study and selection of leaders is closely bound up with the content of the courses in which the people are involved. The message is a radical break with the past: that it is not God's will that the people be poor; that they are equal before God to the large *hacienda* owner down the road; that they have a basic human right to organize in order to begin taking control of their own lives; and that throughout human history God has been a God of justice who has always acted on behalf of the poor and oppressed.

Once peasants recover from the shock of hearing these words, amazing things begin to happen that those in power inevitably call "subversive." Said Maryknoll Sister Joan Petrik, who worked with *campesinos* in the mountains above La Libertad, El Salvador, for seven years: "When I first arrived in Tamanique, every time a child died the family would say, 'It's the will of God.' But after the people became involved in the Christian communities, that attitude began to change. And after a year or so I no longer heard people in the communities saying that. After a while they began to say, 'The system caused this.'" Sister Joan also observed that, after a time, one could walk into a village where CEBs had been established and identify the people who are members of the communities simply by the way they carry themselves. "They walk upright, their heads held high, with self-confidence," she noted. The other peasants shuffle along, with their heads bowed.[16]

Aguilares and Rutilio Grande

Nowhere did the development of CEBs have a faster or more profound impact than in the small town of Aguilares, 35 kilometers north of San Salvador. There, in September 1972, Father Rutilio Grande and three fellow Jesuits arrived to take up pastoral duties. What happened in Aguilares in the succeeding four and a half years was replayed in many locales throughout El Salvador, sometimes with equally dramatic results.

Grande and his fellow priests divided Aguilares into ten mission zones and the surrounding countryside into fifteen other zones. They talked with residents of each zone about the best place to locate the mission center, then visited the families in each zone to learn about individual and community problems. In short, they conducted a socioeconomic survey of the parish, with many religious and cultural questions included.

Later, in each mission center, they conducted evangelizing sessions with children, then adults, the purpose of which was to give the people a basic outline by which they could continue celebrating the word of God on their own. In this way the priests were able to begin a process of "self-evangelization," of building a community, and of selection by the community of catechists and delegates of the Word. The delegates subsequently received additional weekly training and instruction from the priests.

Between September 1973 and June 1974 the priests and their collaborators[17] established ten urban and twenty-seven rural CEBs, training 326 catechists and delegates for various responsibilities, including prebaptismal instruction (37); catechists (38); youth work (18); musical groups (72); founding and encouraging new CEBS (58, of whom 17 moved on to continue the work in other communities); and assisting in various courses (29).[18]

It cannot be emphasized too strongly that the work of Grande and his associates was consciously, deliberately, and exclusively pastoral, never political. At the same time the content of their evangelizing message, although always drawn from the Bible and the social doctrine of the church, was profoundly radicalizing in a political as well as a religious sense.

Beginning with the assertion that God was "not in the clouds, lying in a hammock," detached from and uncaring about his creation, the priests sought to convey to their parishioners the notion of a God of justice and love who acts on the side of the poor and oppressed. Beginning with the Exodus story (Exod.: 3) and running through the Old Testament, God is consistently portrayed as one who cares passionately about his people, especially the poor, and wreaks his vengeance on the rich and powerful who became and remain that way through the exploitation of others.

This message continued in the New Testament, with the proclamation of the "good news" in Luke 4: "The Spirit of the Lord is upon me, because he has chosen me to bring good news to the poor. . . . To proclaim liberty to the captives and recovery of sight to the blind, to set free the oppressed."[19]

Jesus' "preferential option for the poor," the message ran, did not mean that he hated the rich. On the contrary, he had many wealthy friends. In this sense, Grande continued, Jesus was the "liberator" of all people, poor and rich alike. This liberation results in a totally integrated human being, a person transfigured (converted) so that all aspects of one's life — family, business, pleasure — are a unified whole. Such liberation, Grande preached, would free the oppressed from their oppression, and their oppressors from oppressing.

It does not require much imagination to understand the impact of such a message on poorly educated *campesinos* for whom the biblical message until this time had been "accept your lot here on earth because your real reward will come in the hereafter." The *campesinos* lost little time relating the gospel message to their own "situation of misery and injustice. They began to emerge from their *conciencia mágica* realizing that the will of God was not to maintain things as they were. They took confidence in themselves, losing their complexes of bashfulness and incapacity, they discovered that they had words [*tenian una palabra*] and that they could think [*opinar*]."[20]

The results were electric. Eight months after the arrival of the priests in Aguilares, on May 24, 1973, 1,600 workers in the La Cabaña sugar mill struck on payday for six hours because they did not receive an orally promised salary increase. The strike was peaceful and ended when management granted a raise, albeit less than that which was originally promised.

The strike was not organized by the parish, but many of the workers were members of the CEBs and some of the leaders were delegates of the Word. This produced in Grande a tension with which he would live for the rest of his life. "He saw clearly that his mission was to evangelize and not political organization, but at the same time he understood that conscientization in a situation of injustice and oppression would necessarily lead to organization." The tension was exacerbated by the Christian Federation of Salvadorean Campesinos (FECCAS), an organization founded in 1964 in the wake of the Christian Democratic Party. Its purpose was to defend the rights of the *campesinos,* and it had established a base in Aguilares prior to the arrival of Grande. FECCAS quite naturally found a receptive audience among the people in the CEBs, and it had participated in the strike at La Cabaña. In 1973 and 1974 FECCAS expanded rapidly throughout the country, quite independently of what was happening in the parish of Aguilares. Nevertheless, Rutilio Grande was considered by the government and the oligarchy to be responsible for everything from the strike at La Cabaña and subsequent similar actions elsewhere to the growth of FECCAS.[21]

By mid-1975 the priests of Aguilares were being called "subversives" by a *"grupo fantasma,"*[22] the Conservative Religious Front. By Christmas President Molina was making public statements against what he termed "liberationist clerics." In the meantime, Father Rafael Barahona, a diocesan priest from San Vicente, was taken into custody and transported to National Guard headquarters in San Salvador. There he was severely beaten as his assailants "used profanity to insult me as a priest. One of them struck me and said mockingly: I am excommunicated, I am excommunicated.'"[23] Barahona's bishop,

Monseñor Aparicio, obliged not only the soldier, but all the other government officials responsible for Barahona's incarceration. "The torturer who clamored for excommunication now has it," a furious bishop wrote the national government. In one of his rare defenses of the pastoral work of his priests, Aparicio inquired if "the Constitution of El Salvador has two interpretations, one for the authorities and the other for the people? We would like a response, if it would not annoy you, Honorable Authorities, so as not to teach our students a mistaken lesson."†

THE CENTRAL AMERICAN UNIVERSITY
JOSÉ SIMEÓN CAÑAS

While the church at the parish level was beginning to resocialize the people from a religious perspective, a new national university was founded in 1966 with the intention of teaching the children of the ruling class about the social and economic reality in which a majority of their fellow citizens lived, creating a sense of responsibility for changing this reality, and giving them the education necessary to do so. That, at least, was the intent of the Jesuits who formed the intellectual and administrative backbone of the Central American University (UCA). Their benefactors, the self-same oligarchy, had different objectives. They did not want their children to attend and be corrupted by the University of El Salvador, which was perceived as a hotbed of Marxism and revolution. The oligarchs wanted for their children a good, conservative, Catholic education that would prepare them to continue in their fathers' footsteps.†[24]

The Salvadorean oligarchy contributed heavily to the construction of the new campus on the southwest side of the capital and thus felt a strong sense of proprietorship. But in 1970, at the time of the Agrarian Reform Congress, the Superior Council of UCA issued the first in a series of manifestos concerning various issues confronting the country. In this document the Jesuits in effect told the oligarchy that UCA was not its university and proceeded to take a strong position in favor of agrarian reform.†

Luís de Sebastián, an economist and vice-rector of UCA, has said that when the university began to speak out through its manifestos, some sources of funding dried up. He has also said that although UCA's "political line" was not clear in 1970, by 1975, when security forces fired point-blank at a student demonstration, killing at least thirty-seven, the university's political position of opposition to the government and its policies had become unambiguous.

Figure 4.1 The wall hanging reads: "The Jesuit is Beelzebub, who departed from Hell." Dario is Ruben Dario, Nicaragua's greatest poet. Ironically, Dario wrote these words at a time when the Catholic Church, including the Jesuits, was allied with the regime.

POLITICAL EFFECTS OF CHURCH ACTIVISM

President Molina's decree of a limited agrarian reform in March 1976 received strong support from the church and UCA.[25] When the vituperative opposition of affected economic interests forced Molina to hastily withdraw his proposal, UCA published an editorial, "*A sus ordenes, mi capital,*"[26] in its journal, *Estudios Centroamericanos* (ECA). The university's reward for its efforts was a bomb at the administration building – the first of six that year – for which right-wing groups took responsibility.

In this period the right began looking for scapegoats on which to blame Molina's lapse and found one in the church, which, they decided, was "inciting the people to revolt." To appease the oligarchy, Molina and Minister of Defense Humberto Romero arrested five priests and expelled eighteen others, including two Jesuits from UCA. The climate was such that by May 1977 fliers urging Salvadoreans to "Be a Patriot! Kill a Priest!" were circulating in the capital. By then two priests had been assassinated, one of them Rutilio Grande as he drove with two parishioners from Aguilares to El Paisnal to celebrate mass on the afternoon of March 12, 1977. The three Jesuits who had been working with Grande were expelled.[27]

The murders of Grande and of Father Alfonso Navarro a month later came in the midst of a wave of persecution the like of which the Latin American church has rarely experienced. Between February 21 and May 14, 1977, ten priests were exiled; eight were expelled, with five of them tortured beforehand; two were arrested; one was beaten; and another, Rafael Barahona, was again picked up and tortured.

Barahona's incarceration occurred the day before Oscar Romero was installed as archbishop of San Salvador, succeeding the aged Chávez. The day after his installation, Romero went to the Casa Presidencial and requested the release of his priest. President Molina's response was: "I will release Barahona but you cannot ask us to treat them any differently until they go back to their basic business which is religion. These priests of yours," Molina continued, "have become politicians and I hold you responsible for their behavior." Romero looked Molina straight in the eye. "With all due respect, Mr. President," the archbishop said, "we take our orders from someone higher."†

OSCAR ARNULFO ROMERO BECOMES ARCHBISHOP

The selection of Monseñor Oscar Romero, bishop of Santiago de María, as archbishop of San Salvador was greeted with widespread dismay throughout the archdiocese. The old archbishop, priests, religious, and laity had hoped that Arturo Rivera Damas, the auxiliary bishop since 1960, would be chosen. But Rivera had too many enemies going back to the mid-1960s, when the oligarchy had accused him (erroneously) of ghosting Archbishop Chávez's pastoral letters. Then he had incensed the government when he confronted Minister of Defense Torres over the abduction of Father Alas in 1970. In the meantime he had strongly supported the pastoral line of the archdiocese and had spoken out forcefully against official repression. So when the papal nuncio, being of a mind similar to that of the oligarchy and the government, asked the minister of justice which candidate he preferred, the choice of the powerful was Romero.† Romero, who was born in San Miguel, three hours to the east of the capital, had spent most of his priestly life in the eastern section of the country. He was considered to be quiet and noncontroversial. His detractors considered him an ally of the oligarchy and were extremely worried that he would halt or even try to reverse the process of evangelization that had been developed during the previous eight years.†

A month before Romero's installation, Rivera Damas was in Rome, where he was informed why he had been passed over. "We don't want anyone who is going to oppose the government," a cardinal with some responsibility in the selection process told him.†

Romero's "Transformation"

As we have seen, Romero stunned everyone by wasting no time declaring where he stood. But it was the assassination of Grande only three weeks after his installation that turned Romero into an unflinching prophet of the church. In an interview three months before his death, Romero described his process of "transformation":

> I have always tried to be faithful to my vocation, my priesthood. My fidelity to the Church's orientations (and to those encyclicals and council documents that asked for a larger service to the people) has always been the rule of my priesthood. The poor people didn't take me by surprise; I have always felt a preference for the poor, the humble, and believe that in the trajectory of my priestly life it has been like one facet. I wasn't aggressive against the powerful classes when the government was, perhaps, a little diplomatic, and I still have some friends among the very powerful, but a lot have been lost.
>
> There were times when the old archbishop, Mons. Chávez, was suffering the expulsion of priests and couldn't make himself understood with the government; they wouldn't pay attention to him. I felt we

should defend this position; the following month after my arrival Fr. Rutilio Grande was killed, which also reinforced my decision because Fr. Rutilio, before his death, was with me by my side in a priests' meeting, the first one I had.

I asked them to help me carry on with the responsibility; there was a lot of enthusiasm from the clergy to help me and I felt that I would not be alone taking care of the situation but that I could count on all of them and that union with the clergy vanquished all our fears. They had the idea that I was conservative, that I would maintain relations with the government, with the rich, and that I would ignore the people's problems, the repression, the poverty; I found here many committed clergy and communities that thought a lot about the situation in the country. Some of them feared I would stop everything and asked what I was thinking of doing. My response was that they should continue and that we should try to understand each other well, and to work in a promotion of the Church's work as Vatican II and Medellín had asked us to do.

Fr. Grande's death and the death of other priests after his impelled me to take an energetic attitude before the government. I remember that because of Fr. Grande's death I made a statement that I would not attend any official acts until this situation [who had killed Grande] was clarified. I was very strongly criticized, especially by diplomats. A rupture was produced, not by me with the government but the government itself because of its attitude.

I support all of the priests in the communities. We have managed to combine well the pastoral mission of the Church, preference for the poor, to be clearly on the side of the repressed, and from there to clamor for the liberation of the people.[28]

Romero understood well why this commitment would cause him and other priests to be labeled subversives; the moment the issue of defense of the poor is raised in El Salvador, he remarked shortly before the inauguration of President Romero, "You call the whole thing into question. That is why they have no other recourse than to call us subversives—that is what we are." Archbishop Romero declined to attend the inauguration of President Romero on July 1, 1977, reasoning that it was preferable to risk exacerbating hostilities than to appear and thereby bless a system characterized by fraud, corruption, and repression.†

During Oscar Romero's three years and one month as archbishop, the role of the church in the political life of the country expanded with each succeeding crisis. At the same time, under ever-increasing difficulties brought about by waves of persecution against priests, religious, and CEB members, the church itself was growing and was having a greater and greater impact on the life of the average Salvadorean – which is to say, the poor. While Christian Base Communities multiplied, the focus increasingly was on the diminutive archbishop of San Salvador, both within and outside the country.

"The Voice of Those Who Have No Voice"

Romero's message reached into almost every corner of the country (as well as Guatemala, Honduras, and Nicaragua) via the radio station of the archdiocese, YSAX. Within a short time, the 8:00 mass on Sunday morning became the single most listened-to program in the nation. In second place were YSAX's commentaries, written by as many as twenty different people whose identities were a carefully guarded secret. In third place was Romero's weekly interview. All these programs were broadcast three times in order to reach the largest possible audience.†

Romero's Sunday morning mass provided many lessons; but for the social scientist perhaps the most striking was that the mass had become a means of socialization. Although the mass rarely lasted less than two hours, hundreds came and sat on hard wooden pews for the duration – or were glued to their radios. Philip Land, a U.S. priest, related that having been given the extraordinary advice not to attend the mass because the people were too restive and one could never tell what might happen, he wandered into San Salvador's Central Market, where he found that almost every stall had a radio – and every radio was tuned to YSAX.[29] It was a common practice in villages, when no priest was present, to gather in the church and turn on the radio. In some villages the mass was broadcast over the ubiquitous loudspeaker system in the plaza.

All of these people were waiting for "Monseñor's" homily, which generally ran an hour and a half. Each sermon had an invariable pattern: He began with a theological exposition – always with three points – on the scriptural readings of the day. Then he would relate the scripture to the reality of life in El Salvador. This was followed by church announcements, then a recitation of the events of the week just ended, including a reading of every documented case of persons who had been killed, assaulted, or tortured (by *any* group on the left or the right) or who had disappeared. The Salvadorean reality, however, ensured that the list of attacks at the hands of the government's security forces and the right-wing terrorist groups was many times longer than those by left-wing guerrillas.[30] When an event, such as the coup of October 15 or the promulgation of the agrarian reform, warranted it, Romero would conclude with a "pastoral position" on the question.

Photo 4.1 Building that housed the transmitter for the archdiocesan radio station YSAX after the second bomb of 1980.

Photo 4.2 Archbishop Romero is speaking into the telephone during the mass on March 9, 1980, two weeks before his assassination. After the archdiocesan radio station had been destroyed by a bomb and all other radio stations in El Salvador refused to broadcast the Sunday morning mass, a station in Costa Rica transmitted Romero's homily live by telephone.

These homilies, then, were not only religious instruction for the people, but they were oral newspapers as well. As such they were a potent force in El Salvador from 1977 onward. Just how potent can be measured by the fact that the YSAX transmitter or antenna was bombed ten times in three years—twice in January and February 1980. It should be added that the archdiocesan newspaper, *Orientación,* was also the recipient of several bombs after Romero became archbishop. In spite of or perhaps because of the attacks, circulation almost tripled in the first half of 1977 and had surpassed 12,000 copies per week by early 1980.[31]

THE COST OF COMMITMENT

We have seen that the church in El Salvador, against opposition in its own ranks and from the larger society, became a powerful advocate of political and economic change in Salvadorean society. Its emergence as a political actor during the 1970s was the result of a political and economic reality that contradicted in every respect the traditional social doctrine of the Catholic Church as laid down in encyclicals and conciliar documents and by the Latin American church itself. Its increasingly vocal opposition to and condemnation of official repression and the refusal of the government to implement desperately needed reforms; its unequivocal support of the right of the people to organize themselves to demand better wages and working and living conditions; and its criticism of the oligarchy for condoning and cooperating in the repression while opposing the right of organization—all brought down on the church the wrath of the government and oligarchy alike. The fact that Archbishop Romero also condemned the terrorist activities of the left was ignored by the right.

The price the church has paid for its effort to be faithful to its understanding of the Bible and of church doctrine is high indeed. Rutilio Grande is usually counted as the first assassinated priest; but Father Nicolás Rodriguez was abducted by the National Guard on January 2, 1972. His dismembered body was found several days later. Arturo Rivera Damas has said that at the time the church accepted the government's explanation that Rodriguez's death was the work of unknown assailants because "we couldn't believe that they could kill a priest."† Between March 1977 and June 1981 ten more priests and a seminarian within a month of ordination were assassinated. At least sixty priests were expelled or forced into exile. Some of these, along with many others who did not leave, were picked up and beaten or tortured. The Jesuits' house in San Salvador was sprayed with bullets and bombed on three occasions.

Nuns have not escaped. In January 1980 two Mexican nuns working in the parish of Arcatao, Chalatenango, were recalled by their superior after they were taken and held in the local National Guard barracks for several hours. Only when Archbishop Romero demanded their release were they brought into San Salvador and given into his custody. In June a Salvadorean nun was attacked with a machete and sustained severe cuts on her face and neck.[32] On December 2 three U.S. nuns and a lay missioner were murdered by the National Guard.

The assassination of Archbishop Romero during a Mass on March 24, 1980, by a professional "hit-man" hired by the extreme right,[33] was only the most heinous of the attacks on the church. His death silenced the most forceful voice for justice in El Salvador. But if those responsible for his murder thought they would silence the church by silencing "the voice of those who have no voice," they were mistaken. They did not understand what Oscar Romero knew very well: "I am not the Church," he would say, "The hierarchy is not the Church; the Church is the people."

The church's advocacy of social justice operated at three levels: (some of) the hierarchy, the Catholic university, and the parish. The first two levels often have received the most attention both in and outside El Salvador, but it has been at the parish level that the transformation of the church has been the most extensive and most pervasive and has had the greatest impact on political developments within the country.

THE CHURCH AND THE POPULAR ORGANIZATIONS

We have seen in the example of Aguilares that many people, once they shed their *"conciencia mágica,"* moved quickly to political action by joining or supporting an existing *campesino* organization. It is less well known that the church, at the parish level, spawned the mass popular organizations that in less than six years brought El Salvador to the brink of revolution. To understand the connection between the church and these organizations, it is necessary to review the experience of the parish of Suchitoto and its priests, José Inocencio (Chencho) Alas and his brother, Higinio.[34]

Chencho Alas arrived in Suchitoto, a town 48 kilometers northeast of San Salvador, in December 1968. Within two months several

Christian Base Communities were functioning; the number would grow to thirty-two in a short time. In February 1969 the priest began a two-month course in which the CEBs discussed biblical themes and the form of the CEBs. The objective of the course, according to Alas, was "to prepare the people, following Medellín, to succeed in constructing their own destiny." At the end of the course the CEBs elected nineteen *campesinos* as delegates of the Word. The delegates then received additional training and a course in public speaking.

While these courses were going on the ubiquitous problem of land tenancy was coming to a head in Suchitoto. Roberto Hill and Miguel Salaverría, two of the country's wealthiest oligarchs, had in 1969 created the Parcialaciones Rurales de Desarrollo (Rural Subdivisions for Development), a private company, ostensibly to provide financing for individuals to purchase plots of land. In reality, it provided loans to already wealthy landowners to purchase large farms at a low price, then subdivide them and sell the small parcels at exorbitant prices.

In Suchitoto Robert Hill purchased the Hacienda La Asunción for $97 per *manzana* (1 *manzana* = 0.7 hectares), subdivided it, and put it back on the market for $280 to $680 per *manzana*. This so outraged the *campesinos* that they mobilized the entire town, and 3,000 people demonstrated in front of the *hacienda* to demand lower prices for the land. Receiving no response, 400 campesinos then demonstrated in San Salvador—the first such demonstration (not staged by the government) since 1932.

As it happened, a monthly clerics' meeting was being held in the Arzobispado at the time of this demonstration, and Alas took advantage of the opportunity to ask his fellow priests and Archbishop Chávez to support the *campesinos*' cause. Alas recalled that Chávez, not having been confronted with such a request previously, "did not know exactly what to do. Yet he did not oppose the idea." The result, according to Alas, was a "very violent meeting because, for that era, it was very difficult for the clergy to accept such a task. It was believed that the work one must do in the countryside was evangelization, defined as administering the sacraments." In the end, Chávez and two other priests, Alfonso Navarro and Rutilio Sanchez, who was working in Suchitoto with Alas at the time, supported Alas and the *campesinos*' demand for a price of $200 per *manzana*.

The demonstration moved the National Assembly, where the opposition parties were just two votes shy of a majority, to pass a law obliging Hill to sell the land for $200 per *manzana*. Hill and the oligarchy were livid, but among the *campesinos* a "very positive atmosphere was created."

In April 1969 Alas began a weekly course for the delegates of the Word on justice and peace, a major theme of Medellín. These sessions, Alas said, always began with "the Celebration of the Word and communion." Out of this and succeeding courses grew a recognition of "the necessity to form an organization of the people to deal with the state." During the next five years Alas, who was joined by his brother Higinio in 1972, continued to hold courses for the CEBs, primarily on biblical themes. But by 1973 they began to study systematically socialist and capitalist ideology. Alas has said that before 1973, explicitly political themes were occasionally addressed, as during the 1972 presidential election when they discussed agrarian reform, but there was never a systematic study of these issues.

In October 1972 the government announced its intention of building a second dam, the Cerron Grande, on the River Lempa below Suchitoto, a project that would flood thousands of hectares. That, plus the blatantly fraudulent municipal and national elections in March 1974, served to convince the *campesinos* of Suchitoto that they needed a more formal organization to press their demands on the national government. Following those elections, *campesinos* and FUERSA, ANDES-21, and FECCAS held two meetings in Suchitoto to create a national organization. That organization, the United Popular Action Front (FAPU), was formally established in April 1974 during a meeting of José Alas, a group of *campesinos,* and representatives of the Unitary Union Federation of El Salvador (FUSS), the Salvador Allende University Front of Revolutionary Students (FUERSA), the National Association of Salvadorean Educators (ANDES), the PCS, and others in the Basilica of the Sacred Heart in San Salvador.[35]

Thus for the first time in Latin American history a popular mass organization came directly out of the evangelizing efforts of the Roman Catholic Church. As we shall see in the next chapter, although the umbilical cord tying the church and FAPU together was quickly cut, the influence of the church would continue to be strongly felt.

5

The Revolutionaries

The Left wants power, not reforms.

— Frank Devine,
former U.S. ambassador to El Salvador

There is an image of the Latin American revolutionary that is particularly prevalent in the United States: that of the bearded fanatic who takes to the mountains where, motivated by blind hatred, he carries out "terrorist" attacks against the existing regime. This caricature, no doubt created or at least promoted by the life and legend of "Che" Guevara, bears little resemblance, however, to the character of the current revolutionary struggles in Central America or to the thousands of people who have chosen to commit their lives, their fortunes, and their sacred honor to the struggle for a different society and political order.

Observers often date the struggle to overthrow the civilian-military government in El Salvador from 1970, when the first of five Political-Military Organizations (OP-Ms) was founded. As we have seen in earlier chapters, however, El Salvador has a long history of struggle against economic oppression and political repression that, for four hundred years, was unshaped by any political ideology. The resistance of the Pipil Indians in the 1520s, the Indian/*Ladino* uprising in 1832, and the revolts against land usurpation by the oligarchy in the late nineteenth century were all reactions to real and perceived wrongs committed by the powerful. Not until 1932 did the struggle acquire overtones of a political ideology — the Marxism-Leninism of the Communist Party of El Salvador (PCS). Even then, as the historical record makes clear, the PCS, whose leadership was exclusively Salvadorean, provided a means of organizing and a vision of a new society; it did not create the conditions that led to revolt.

Thus one can say that, historically, the necessary conditions for revolution in El Salvador have been economic oppression and political repression. The sufficient conditions, however, have varied. In 1832 the sufficient conditions were forced conscription and onerous taxes on indigo. In 1932, the sufficient condition became a stolen election. By the late 1960s and early 1970s there was once again electoral fraud at the end of a decade of increasing political competition. There was also one other, new element: the church.

THE POLITICAL-MILITARY ORGANIZATIONS

After 1932 the PCS was outlawed and its members were subjected in the ensuing decades to severe repression. Yet, as the party noted in a declaration on the fiftieth anniversary of the 1932 uprising, "In spite of everything, [it] was the only revolutionary organization capable of resistance during decades of repressive assaults by various governments that linked the cruel chain of reactionary dictatorship."[1]

Its leaders were often jailed and tortured. One, Salvador Cayetano Carpio, wrote of his experiences in the jails of the "reformist" government of Oscar Osorio.[2] In the 1960s, Cayetano Carpio became secretary general of the PCS, and when a debate arose over whether the moment had once again come for armed struggle, Cayetano led the faction within the party that believed the time was ripe. He explained in a February 1980 interview what happened:

> After a long process of ideological struggle within the traditional organizations [political parties] it became evident that they stubbornly refused to lead the working class and the people in general in the new stages of struggle that needed to be undertaken. . . . Concretely, the traditional organizations denied the possibility and necessity of the Salvadorean people undertaking the process of revolutionary armed struggle. They also denied the mounting element of revolutionary violence in the struggles of the broad popular masses. . . .
>
> By the end of 1969 it was very clear that El Salvador, its people, needed an overall strategy in which all methods of struggle could be used and combined in dialectical fashion.[3]

But the PCS was not prepared to lead the fight. As the party itself acknowledged in the January 1982 declaration, "tendencies appeared that, evaluating the [1932] insurrection only on the basis of its results, renounced the armed struggle thereby giving birth to and perpetuating reformist positions."[4] Noted Carpio, "If there had not arisen a stubborn majority that at all costs blocked the advance towards the political-military strategy that the people needed for moving towards new stages of struggle, no need would have arisen to create a revolutionary organization such as the Popular Forces of Liberation."[5] Carpio resigned from the PCS, went underground with a small group of comrades, and began building the first of the Political-Military Organizations, the Popular Forces of Liberation (FPL).

It is no accident that "Political-Military Organization" is the self-description of El Salvador's revolutionary organizations, for they were, from their inception, more than armed bands. Each had a clear political line to which it held tenaciously. By the late 1970s that tenacity was impeding the process of unity that they all recognized would be necessary if they were to ever achieve victory.

Meanwhile, in 1972 a second Political-Military Organization was created. The Revolutionary Army of People (ERP) also came out of the PCS, but its composition was broader: Juventud Comunista (Young Communists), youth from the Christian Democratic party, and elements from the radicalized sector of the Salvadorean bourgeoisie. In contrast to the youth of most ERP members, Carpio was fifty at the time of his resignation from the party.

Both the FPL and the ERP had a strongly militaristic conception of the revolutionary struggle. As Carpio put it in his interview, "the armed struggle would be the main thread running through the people's revolutionary fervor and would become in the process the basic element for the destruction of the counterrevolutionary forces." Although the FPL did recognize the need for a "political-military strategy," the political aspect would, for several years, be treated as less important than the military. For the ERP the armed struggle was all that mattered, and the party clung to that belief for nearly a decade.[6]

The leadership of these and subsequent organizations came, to some extent, out of the church. Carpio studied for a time in El Salvador's Conciliar Seminary. Many among the ERP leadership were Christian radicals of the 1960s. A large number within the National Resistance (RN), an ERP faction, were Protestants, and at least two were Baptist ministers.

Within the ERP two tendencies were present from the beginning. One, as suggested above, thought the revolution could be won principally through military means. The other tendency, the National Resistance, believed that political as well as military action was necessary. The members of the RN quietly worked with the campesinos of Suchitoto in 1973–1974, particularly as the Cerron Grande Dam project got under way. Without the knowledge of Father José Alas, they quietly encouraged the formation of FAPU in 1974.[7] So, although it is accurate, as stated earlier, to say that the first of the

Popular Organizations came out of the church, it is also true that some members of the young Political-Military Organizations were working toward the same end: the organization of the people.

The differences in political lines within the OP-Ms led directly to a split within the ERP. The RN faction that had helped spawn FAPU included Roque Dalton, El Salvador's leading contemporary poet. Dalton's insistence on the need for a political as well as a military line led the hard-line faction to charge him with treason, try him in absentia, find him guilty, and condemn him to death.

Dalton's assassination in May 1975 by a handful of extremist leaders (who were subsequently expelled from the ERP)† split that organization wide open. The RN immediately created a revolutionary or vanguard party and named its armed branch the Armed Forces of National Resistance (FARN). FAPU, established the year before, automatically became the mass organization. Thus the RN had, from its inception, a more formal structure than the other OP-Ms. Not until early 1978 did the ERP finally decide that an affiliated mass organization was necessary and spawn the 28th of February Popular Leagues (LP-28). Then, two years later the ERP/LP-28 created a revolutionary party, the Party of Salvadorean Revolution (PRS).

The fourth OP-M was the PCS. As we have seen, the PCS during the 1960s chose to follow a "reformist" course in Salvadorean political life by participating in the electoral process through its legal front, the UDN. Following the February 28, 1977, massacre in the Plaza Libertad, however, the PCS changed its policy; it concluded, as the other OP-Ms had done years before, that the time had once again come for armed struggle.

After the massacre it began to create militias, which toward the end of 1979 became the Armed Forces of Liberation (FAL). While the UDN participated in the government of the first junta following the October coup, the PCS was moving toward unity with other OP-Ms. During the last week in December 1979 the PCS formed a coordinating body with the RN and the FPL. A week after the government's resignation, the UDN joined with other mass organizations to form the Revolutionary Coordination of the Masses (CRM).

The fifth OP-M developed from a different conception of struggle. The Revolutionary Party of Central American Workers (PRTC) was created at the end of a founding congress on January 26, 1976. Many of its members were involved in the initial nuclei that, in 1972, became the ERP. Some members also came out of unions that were under PCS influence. Its conception of the struggle was regional, rooted in the history of Central America that recalled, among other events, the Central American Federation of the early nineteenth century; the regional struggle against William Walker in the mid-nineteenth century; the Central American Workers' Confederation which enjoyed a brief life in the 1920s; and the struggle of Augusto César Sandino in Nicaragua, which was joined by other Central Americans, including Farabundo Martí. Until late 1980 the PRTC remained a regional party; on October 29 of that year, however, the national units of the party separated, although they maintained ties with each other.

THE POPULAR ORGANIZATIONS

The need to build a base of support among the people led, as we have seen, to the formation of FAPU in 1974. Yet, it would be misleading to suggest that there were no mass organizations in El Salvador before the founding of FAPU. In fact FECCAS, whose strength was in Aguilares, Chalatenango, and San Vicente, had been created in the early 1960s during the period that saw the emergence of the Christian Democratic Party. In response, the government, worried about the increasing "agitation" in the countryside caused by peasants demanding their rights, created ORDEN.[8]

The government also created, in 1966, with the assistance of the American Institute for Free Labor Development (AIFLD), the Salvadorean Communal Union (UCS), whose membership by 1980 was estimated at 120,000. The UCS was seen by the government and the U.S. Embassy as a vehicle for co-opting a significant number of peasants into the system through the creation of a privileged class among the *campesinos*. The object was to head off any "radical" or "communist" agitation in the countryside. The UCS functioned as intended for more than a decade. In mid-1980, however, after several UCS leaders had been killed by security forces and one UCS cooperative had been invaded by the National Guard, which then proceeded to line up and assassinate eleven of the twelve *campesino* directors of the coop (the president survived by fleeing), the UCS began distancing itself from the government. By August it had split into two factions. One was cooperating with the government's agrarian reform that had been promulgated the previous March. The second, with strength in the three western departments of Sonsonate, Santa Ana, and Ahuachapán, as well as in Cabañas, allied itself, after 1978, with FAPU.[9]

There were two important differences between the government-sponsored UCS and the Popular Organizations (OPs) during the 1970s.

TABLE 5.1

The Farabundo Martí Front for National Liberation (FMLN)

Political-Military Organization	Mass Organization	Armed Forces
Popular Forces of Liberation (Fuerzas Populares de Liberación) (FPL - 1970*)	Popular Revolutionary Bloc (Bloque Popular Revolucionario) (BPR - 1975)	Popular Forces of Liberation (Fuerzas Populares de Liberación) (FPL - 1970)
National Resistance (Resistencia Nacional) (RN - 1975)	United Popular Action Front (Frente de Acción Popular Unificada) (FAPU - 1974)	Armed Forces of National Resistance (Fuerzas Armadas de Resistencia Nacional) (FARN - 1975)
Party of the Salvadorean Revolution (Partido de la Revolución Salvadoreña) (PRS - 1977)	28th of February Popular Leagues (Ligas Populares 28 de Febrero) (LP-28 - 1978)	Revolutionary Army of the People (Ejército Revolucionario del Pueblo) (ERP - 1972)
Communist Party of El Salvador (Partido Comunista de El Salvador) (PCS - 1930)	Nationalist Democratic Union (Unión Democrática Nacionalista) (UDN - 1967)	Armed Forces of Liberation (Fuerzas Armadas de Liberación) (FAL - 1979)
Revolutionary Party of Central American Workers (Partido Revolucionario de los Trabajadores Centroamericanos) (PRTC - 1976)	Popular Liberation Movement (Movimiento de Liberación Popular) (MLP - 1979)	Revolutionary Party of Central American Workers (Partido Revolucionario de los Trabajadores Centroamericanos) (PRTC - 1976)

*Years cited are dates of founding.

The first was ideological. The UCS was viewed by those who created it as a means of controlling the peasantry by giving its members a piece of the pie—or at least giving them some reason to believe it would be possible to obtain a piece. In other words, the UCS represented a deliberate effort to maintain the economic and political status quo. The Popular Organizations, on the other hand, were dedicated from the beginning, not to getting a piece of the pie, but to making a different pie.

The second difference was structural. The UCS was organized from the top down. Local leaders were generally hand-picked, not by their fellow *campesinos,* but by national officers or U.S. AIFLD advisers. In sharp contrast, the Popular Organizations were completely indigenous and were developed from the grassroots. As with the Christian Base Communities, the people were encouraged to select their own leaders.

Sectarian Differences and Divisions

We have seen that FAPU was founded by a priest and *campesinos* with the participation of other groups. Traditional parties like the PDC and the MNR also joined as observers but withdrew when they discovered they could not control FAPU. The organization grew quickly but its unity was short-lived. FAPU, like the ERP, contained two factions. One was oriented toward the RN, the other toward the FPL. While the organization grew rapidly the differences between the two tendencies increased, producing by July 1975 a split and a new OP, the Revolutionary Popular Bloc (BPR).

The Causes of Division. The differences within FAPU were political, strategic, and tactical. First, there was disagreement over the definition of the fundamental struggle. FAPU's perspective was that the struggle to effect political change should be viewed in the short, medium, and long term, with actions appropriate to the historic moment. Those in the BPR thought in terms of *la lucha prolongada,* a prolonged struggle in which all actions were directed toward the ultimate goal—the overthrow of the existing regime.

Second, especially during the 1970s, the debate focused on how best to build the popular organizations. Both the FPL and the RN considered an alliance between workers and *campesinos* to be the fundamental and necessary force in the struggle. But the BPR and FAPU divided over which to emphasize. Both originated in the countryside, FAPU among the peasants of Suchitoto and the BPR among the *campesinos* of Aguilares, where FECCAS was strong. But the RN tendency believed that its organizing emphasis should be among the most strategic unions, such as the electric workers, Port Authority workers, and coffee, cotton, and sugarcane laborers. Meanwhile the FPL tendency considered that the emphasis should be on the *campesinos.*

Third, the two tendencies parted company over the role of the progressive sectors of the middle class and the military. The FPL discarded any possibility of alliance with the military and placed less emphasis on work with the middle class, while the RN considered both important and directed part of its effort to developing alliances with them.

In tactical terms, for example, FAPU's conception of working with unions was to build support from the base—the membership—through its political schools (a tactic the RN shared with the PCS). The FPL approach was to try and seize control of a union from the top. These different approaches may be explained by the fact that all three organizations were competing with each other for hegemony in the unions; the BPR's tactics were related to its lack of the resources for working at all levels because of its emphasis on the countryside.

The result of these different strategies was that by 1980 the BPR had become the largest of the mass organizations, with a total membership of more than 60,000 and nine affiliated organizations. FAPU's membership was estimated at half that size, and much of its leadership was older, more middle class, and in the unions.

FAPU acquired a reputation for incisive analysis of the Salvadorean reality and for its theoretical publications. Through this work it exerted a profound impact on the development of a unified political program in 1980. Ultimately, FAPU's insistence on revolution *and* democracy, as well as on forming alliances with progressive sectors of the church and political parties, the UCA, progressive labor unions, and elements of the private sector, became the official policy of the FMLN/FDR.

The *28th of February Popular Leagues.* The third of the Popular Organizations, the 28th of February Popular Leagues, was founded by ERP sympathizers within the National University in February 1978. This date was the first anniversary of the massacre that occurred when the National Police cleared the Plaza Libertad of Colonel Ernesto Claramount and his supporters. LP-28's founding was the result of a belated recognition by the ERP that if it did not create its own mass organization it was going to be left in the dust by the FPL and the RN. LP-28 was also third in size, with about ten thousand members. During the late 1970s the organization was considered by others on the left to have the least well-developed political program.†
This was not surprising, given the ERP's overly militaristic view of the struggle.

As a result of the failure to think through the relationship between political thought and action, and the need to make its presence felt powerfully and quickly, LP-28 historically resorted to such actions as the occupation of embassies, ministries, farms, and the like without much thought for the consequences. The most memorable of these acts may have been the occupation of the Spanish Embassy in San Salvador in February 1980 without consulting the other members of the recently formed CRM. This occurred after Guatemalan government forces had attacked Spain's embassy in Guatemala City, which had been occupied by a large group of Indians who were protesting government repression and the detention of fellow Indians in their home province of Quiché. Thirty-seven died in the assault. LP-28 announced that it was protesting this attack and issued a series of demands, including the release of several political prisoners. LP-28 clearly never stopped to analyze the effects of its action; it alienated a country whose support on the international level the left needed. It also handed the Salvadorean government a public relations victory, for that regime kept its troops out of sight and was thus able to project an image of responsible behavior compared not only with the actions of the Guatemalan government, but also with the behavior of LP-28 – and by extension, the entire left.

Popular Liberation Movement. The smallest, and youngest in membership, of the Popular Organizations was spawned by the PRTC in late 1979. The Popular Liberation Movement (MLP) was initially kept out of the CRM by FAPU's opposition. FAPU maintained, in the face of BRP support for MLP membership, that the new organization had to demonstrate its capacity to organize and mobilize the people. By May 1980 the MLP had satisfied FAPU's criteria and joined the CRM.

National Democratic Union. As we saw in Chapter 3, the legal front of the PCS, the UDN, was created in the 1960s so that the proscribed party could participate in electoral politics. At the same time, the PCS also exerted hegemony over teacher and student organizations, as well as labor unions. Thus the UDN was also, in a very real sense, a popular organization, even though its political line appeared to be more "reformist" than "revolutionary" for much of the 1970s.

Unity Announced. One may conclude from the above discussion that the most prominent characteristic of the Salvadorean left was its sectarianism. By the end of 1979, however, a direct correlation between proximity to power and a reduction in sectarianism – a phenomenon that had occurred in Nicaragua in 1978–1979 – was becoming stronger and more apparent. On January 11, 1980, the Popular Organizations of El Salvador papered over their remaining differences, called a press conference, and announced the creation of the Revolutionary Coordination of the Masses.

In a document issued that day, *Nuestras Organizaciones Populares Marcha Hacia la Unidad* [Our Popular Organizations march toward unity], the CRM described, in language remarkably free of ideological rhetoric, the "profound economic and political crisis" of the country, then argued that the "revolutionary alternative is the only solution to the crisis." "The People have created riches and live in poverty," it stated, a situation that is the result of a "political and economic structure" that cannot be corrected by a government that is a part of that structure and does not have the support of the people.

The press conference itself revealed something of the character

Photo 5.1 January 11, 1980. Opening of the press conference called to announce the formation of the CRM, the unity of the Popular Organizations.
This press conference, like most held by various revolutionary organizations
prior to the closing and occupation of the National University in the summer
of 1980, took place in the auditorium of the law school.

of the left. One incident in particular is worth noting because it suggested the profound nationalism of people who have been accused of
being tools of an "international communist conspiracy" and the pup-
pets of Cuba. Before the conference began a young man brought the
Salvadorean flag on to the stage. (The flag was rarely present at a
gathering of the left.) At first no one noticed, but by the time he was
halfway across the stage the audience began whistling, then cheering.
At that point a young woman took the microphone and said she
wanted to give a word of explanation. She asserted that "the flag is not
the property of the oligarchy" and that "it is the only symbol of unity
for us." Her words were greeted with more cheers. The conference
then began with the national anthem. Everyone, it seemed, knew the
words.

1932 Remembered

Eleven days after the press conference the Popular Organizations staged the biggest mass demonstration El Salvador had ever

Photo 5.2   January 22, 1980, demonstration.

seen. According to OP leaders, the demonstration had three objectives: to "pay homage to the *compañeros* who had died in the 1932
uprising"; to "celebrate the unity" of the Popular Organizations; and to
"demonstrate the capacity of the OPs to organize and mobilize the people."†

   At least 200,000 people gathered in the capital from all over the
country in a show of power that was characterized by extraordinary
discipline, order, and patience. What began as a peaceful march
ended in chaos as the demonstrators were fired on along the line of
march by National Guardsmen and National Police, ANTEL security
guards, and men in civilian clothes. When the shooting was over,
forty-nine were dead and hundreds injured. The government
disclaimed all responsibility, asserting that all security forces had
been confined to barracks for the day and that "armed leftists" had
started the trouble. Eyewitnesses interviewed on the day of the march
and later, however, unanimously agreed that shooting had come from
the roofs of at least fourteen public and private buildings in the center
of the city. Subsequently, a well-placed army officer confirmed in an
interview that there had been a conspiracy among Minister of Defense
José Guillermo García, his subsecretary, Nicolás Carranza, and cer-

Photo 5.3 On January 22, 1980, a peaceful
demonstration of 200,000 people was fired on
by Salvadorean security forces, killing forty-
nine and wounding hundreds. One of the
wounded was carried into the cathedral, where
this picture was taken on January 23. "Revolu-
ción o Muerte" (Revolution or Death) is written
in the slain person's blood.

tain members of the oligarchy to disrupt the march and provoke the
left into a confrontation.† But the Popular Organizations refused to be
provoked.

CONSOLIDATION OF THE OPPOSITION

By killing Roque Dalton, the ERP became the outcast among the
OP-Ms, and there were questions whether the breach would ever
heal. The ERP was conspicuously absent when the other three OP-Ms
created a coordinated command in December 1979. Although negotia-

tions were going on at the time and continued into the new year, only with the formation of the Unified Revolutionary Direction (DRU) on May 22, 1980, did the prodigal return to the fold.

The formation of the DRU, with three commanders from each of the organizations, represented a step forward in the development of a unified military apparatus. In principle, the DRU provided the structural means for the various OP-Ms to create a unified command. The DRU was, in other words, a joint chiefs of staff. That unified command, however, would not become a procedural reality for more than a year.

Lingering Discord

The creation of the DRU did not mean an end to ideological problems among its constituents. A decade-old debate over how to prosecute the struggle continued into 1981. On one side, the largest of the OP-Ms, the FPL, had long insisted on *la guerra popular prolongada* (prolonged popular war-GPP), a strategy of wearing down the existing regime through hit-and-run military assault, sabotage, and similar tactics. The other OP-Ms favored the strategy of popular insurrection. The FPL lost this debate, and plans were made for a general offensive in early 1981. When that offensive failed to produce a victory the OP-Ms had little choice but to fall back and regroup. At this point the FPL insisted on adhering to the GPP strategy; the other four OP-Ms adhered to a strategy that combined revolutionary war with popular insurrection.

Another example of the divisions among the organizations occurred in early September 1980, when the RN walked out of the DRU in a dispute over policy and organization. One policy difference, for example, concerned efforts by the RN to exploit a crisis within the Salvadorean army officer corps. It was noted earlier that the RN had a long-standing policy of developing allies within the officer corps. It for many months had been holding secret conversations with various officers. In early September a large number of young officers who were allied with junta member Colonel Adolfo Majano were transferred by Defense Minister García and junta member Gutierrez, thereby isolating Majano and dispersing his supporters. The RN saw in this maneuver an opportunity to gain some more allies within the army. Other DRU members thought the RN efforts too zealous and criticized it sharply for its activities.

That alone would not have been sufficient to cause the RN to leave the DRU. At the same time, however, a major organizational dispute erupted within the DRU over the adoption of the Leninist principle of democratic centralism[10] and the formation of a unified revolutionary (vanguard) party. Until this time the DRU had operated by consensus or unanimity. But the FPL, ERP, and PCS wanted to adopt democratic centralism as an operating principle. The RN argued that "it is inadmissible, we said 1001 times, to pretend to apply a Leninist criterion of organization to a coordinator of organizations in which every component organ continues existing individually." The RN maintained that first it was necessary to create a revolutionary party and then apply "not only one but all the Leninist principles of organization."[11] When it was overruled, the RN withdrew, although it remained in contact with the other groups.

It can be argued that the RN was logically correct but tactically wrong, given the momentum that was building after the general strike in August (see below), to deliberately throw the revolutionary movement into disarray. In addition, the RN lost far more than it gained, for when it returned to the fold on November 8, it was forced to accept a series of decisions that had been made in its absence – including the formation of the Farabundo Martí Front for National Liberation (FMLN) on October 10 and the adoption of democratic centralism.

The persistence of these and other differences into 1981 not only indicated the extent to which political maturation was needed by all parties; it also reemphasized an ancient lesson of politics – that unity is not an absolute end, but a process.

Once the movement toward unity began in early 1980 a certain momentum was achieved, helped along by the unfolding political events within El Salvador. The growing and uncontrolled repression in the countryside and the inability of the junta to control the security forces led to the resignation of Christian Democrat Héctor Dada Hirezi from the junta on March 3. Three days later the first stage of an agrarian reform was promulgated, followed a day later by seminationalization of the country's largely de-capitalized banking system. Along with these two reforms the government instituted a state of siege, ostensibly to facilitate the occupation of the nationalized *haciendas*. In fact, it provided a cover for greatly increased repression, which began on the day the agrarian reform was announced.

One measure of the repression was that four days after that announcement, *campesinos* began streaming into the Arzobispado in San Salvador seeking refuge. Conversations with these people produced a host of horror stories: security forces or men in civilian clothes driving into the middle of a village and opening fire in all directions; women and girls being raped, then killed; houses being searched, ransacked, and burned; animals destroyed; women and children shot while sleeping; young people being taken off and "disappearing." As most of the refugees were women and children, they were asked where the men were. There was one answer: "They've gone to the mountains"—that is, they had gone to join the guerrillas.[12]

The Christian Democratic Party Splits

The resignation of Dada and the murder of Mario Zamora (see Chapter 6) precipitated an open split in the Christian Democratic Party that had been festering for two months. José Napoleón Duarte, the titular head of the party, engineered a national convention called on March 9 to elect a new member of the junta. Duarte and his followers hand-picked most of the delegates, thus ensuring his own selection to fill Dada's place. This was achieved over the unanimous opposition of all the Christian Democratic ministers in the government and the most progressive wing of the party. Duarte won the election, but the progressives walked out and almost immediately reconstituted themselves as the Popular Social Christian Movement (MPSC).[13]

The assassination of Archbishop Oscar Romero two weeks later was a further impetus toward unity of the center-left, social democratic political groups and the CRM. On April 11 a coalition of political parties, professionals and technicians, small business organizations, the National University, six unions and union federations, and a student association, with the UCA and the Catholic Church as observers, announced the formation of the Democratic Front (FD). Five days later this alliance joined the CRM in creating the Democratic Revolutionary Front (FDR), thus unifying all the opposition forces from the center-left to left of the political spectrum.

A week after its formation the FDR held a general assembly to elect the Executive Committee. That committee was composed of eight members, five from the organizations making up the CRM and one each from the MNR, MPSC, and MIPTES (Independent Movement of Professionals and Technicians of El Salvador). Enrique Alvarez Córdova, who had twice been minister of agriculture, was elected president of the FDR. According to Alvarez, the FDR operated by consensus, not majority vote. "When there is dissent," he said in an interview, "we continue talking until the differences are resolved."

Throughout the spring and summer delegations from the FDR toured Europe and Latin America in a fairly successful effort to gain international support. Four European countries declared their support for the FDR, and the Socialist International, at its June 1980 meeting

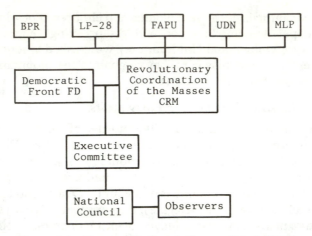

Figure 5.1   Democratic Revolutionary Front (FDR)

in Oslo, voted to support it. In Latin America, the strongest early support came from Mexico's President José López Portillo, who permitted the FDR to establish political offices in that country.

THE STRATEGY FOR AN INSURRECTION

Within El Salvador the FDR changed tactics, abandoning mass demonstrations in favor of general strikes. On June 24–25 a general strike shut down the country for forty-eight hours. Another strike two weeks later was called off at the last minute because of a lack of coordination between the FDR and the DRU. The strike was rescheduled for August 13–15, and the FDR announced that the DRU for the first time would be "taking appropriate actions" during the period. That strike was widely reported as a failure in the U.S. press. On the contrary, it revealed an advance in the organization of the people from the block level to the guerrillas, and it represented a new form of general strike.

The June strike had been a classic example of the traditional Latin American strike: Workers occupied their factories and shut them down, *campesinos* sat down on the farms, and office employees stayed home. The objective was to demonstrate broad popular support for the FDR, and with 90 percent of the country's work force out, the FDR succeeded in doing just that. The August strike, although it included these traditional actions, was in other respects a first for Latin America. Called by FDR leaders an insurrectional strike, its goal was to test an organizational structure that would be employed in a general insurrection.[14] The structure had three main elements—the

Photo 5.4 A contingent of children from Zacatecoluca, departmental capital of La Paz.

guerrillas, the militia, and the popular neighborhood committees.

The Guerrillas. Each unit, organized in squads of three to eleven individuals, platoons of twenty to thirty, and large units, were capable of functioning on two levels: first, as traditional guerrilla forces operating in both city and countryside, whose primary objective in the pre-insurrectionary period was training and obtaining arms and munitions from government troops and garrisons; who carried out, during the 1970s, kidnappings of oligarchs and officials of transnational corporations for ransom; and who selectively killed members of right-wing paramilitary groups such as ORDEN; and second, as a regular army, with a military structure and strategy, a war plan, base camps, and uniforms. By mid-1981 this organization had a name: the Revolutionary Popular Army (EPR). Fermán Cienfuegos, one of five members of the FMLN General Command, explained in a 1981 interview that the FMLN had "combined guerrilla war with the war of movements" (traditional war) and that, "depending on the situation, we use a regular or irregular structure."[15]

The Militia. Composed of peasants and workers with some military training and minimally armed, the militia until late 1980 had the primary role of harassing government troops and protecting unions and their leadership. As the FMLN began to occupy zones of the country for increasingly extended periods of time, the tasks of the militia became more complex. According to Commander Jacinto Sánchez, a member of the DRU located in Los Cerros de San Pedro in the Department of San Vicente, "The militias are organized by brigades for different tasks: production, self-defense, securing the periphery of towns, vigilance in the areas controlled by us, and at times extending into the territory where the enemy is located." They work, Sánchez continued, "in military engineering constructing places of refuge and underground tunnels for storage and protection from air attacks."[16]

Popular Neighborhood Committees. These committees, which were also organized at the block and zone levels, had responsibility for stockpiling food, water, medicines, and "popular arms." They provided logistical support for the military units by erecting barricades and digging ditches. Political education was also conducted through these committees by means of neighborhood study groups. As the FMLN began serious preparations for a popular insurrection in 1981, these committees assumed responsibility for self-defense preparations in their respective neighborhoods.

During the August 13–15 strike all three levels of this revolutionary organization were mobilized for the first time. The results were not inconsiderable: 445 different operations were conducted by

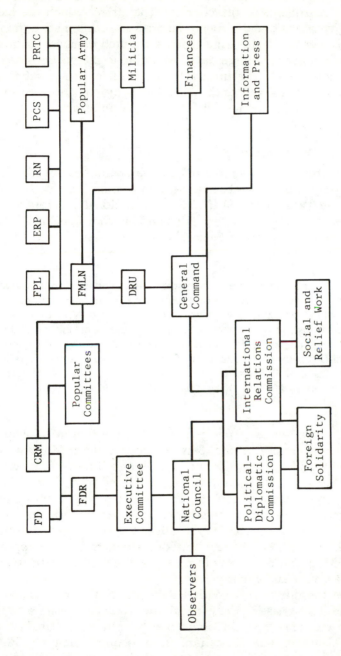

Figure 5.2 Revolutionary Organizations of El Salvador

the DRU and FDR in eighty-four different locations throughout the fourteen departments of the country. The strike, which the Salvadorean government and private enterprise proclaimed a failure, engaged 70 percent of the armed forces; resulted in an economic loss of $60 million over the three days, according to the business sector's own estimate; led to the militarization of all electric, water, and telephone plants, as well as the Port Authority; and resulted in the proscription of the militant electrical workers' union and to the jailing of four of its leaders.

The January Offensive

With the creation of the FMLN, preparations for the long-awaited general offensive began. At 6:30 P.M. on January 10, 1981, units of the Farabundo Martí Front for National Liberation commandeered radio stations in San Salvador. Salvador Cayetano Carpio, now a member of the FMLN General Command, issued the call to battle:

> The hour to initiate the decisive military and insurrectional battles for the taking of power by the people and for the constitution of the democratic revolutionary government has arrived. We call on all the people to rise up as one person, with all the means of combat, under the orders of their immediate leaders on all war fronts and throughout the national territory. . . . The hour of revolution, the hour of liberation is here. The definitive triumph is in the hands of this heroic people. . . . *Revolución o Muerte. ¡Venceremos!* [Revolution or Death. We will triumph!][17]

In the first hours of the general offensive the FMLN had the Salvadorean army on the run. San Francisco Gotera, Morazán, fell. Two officers and eighty soldiers in the Second Brigade at Santa Ana revolted, burned a large part of the garrison, and went over to the insurgents; for a time the FMLN flag flew over that city. Towns around the country and suburbs on the northern and eastern periphery of San Salvador, where the Popular Organizations had spent years organizing the people, rose up in insurrection. For forty-eight hours it appeared that the FMLN was on its way to repeating the Sandinista triumph in Nicaragua a year and a half before.

Then the tide turned. Within days, the FMLN announced the end of the "first phase of the general offensive" and began a tactical retreat to its home bases in Chalatenango, Morazán, Cabañas, San Vicente, Usulután, and Cuscatlán. In subsequent analyses, FMLN commanders were candid in reviewing their errors. There had been no unified war plan; there had been little coordination among the commanders, a problem that was exacerbated by a lack of radio-communications equipment; there had been many tactical errors, such as the failure to cut the supply lines of the Salvadorean army.[18]

One FMLN leader noted that they had commandeered the radio stations for a second time on January 11 to tell workers to prepare for a general strike, but they were unable to take the stations a third time to announce the beginning of the strike.† This situation was compounded by the fact that, although the suburbs of San Salvador were well organized and many were in FMLN hands within twenty-four hours after the offensive began, the city of San Salvador itself was not well organized. Thus the Salvadorean armed forces were able to militarize public transportation, factories, and services. The result was that the strike as a tool of insurrection was even less successful than the August strike.

Another major error lay in the way the FMLN laid siege to garrisons in a number of towns. FMLN forces were able to prevent the exit of those inside, but the insurgents did not have enough firepower to force the soldiers to leave the garrison, nor did they have enough forces to simply starve out the garrisons. So, ultimately, the FMLN had to withdraw. This error "was rectified" when orders were given "to concentrate the effort on ambushing enemy forces."[19]

But for all the FMLN's errors, the Salvadorean army was little better. A senior official of the FMLN commented several months later that "if the enemy had been well prepared, efficient, and coordinated, we would have been annihilated."† Nevertheless, Minister of Defense García announced that the FMLN had been routed, that the Salvadorean army had won a great victory and was in control of the entire country, and that the threat of revolution was past in El Salvador. The U.S. government concurred in this assessment, then rushed in $10 million in military assistance and nineteen military instructors and maintenance personnel just to make sure.[20] Sources in Washington, D.C., asserted that the Reagan administration scenario for El Salvador included a "military victory" over the FMLN in sixty to ninety days.† In March the administration sent another $25 million in emergency aid and raised the number of U.S. military advisers to fifty-six. By early summer, however, after a period of analysis, self-criticism, and regrouping, not only had the FMLN not been defeated, it was once again inflicting large numbers of casualties on government forces.[21] Guerrilla leaders insisted that they controlled more territory after the offensive than before.[22] At the very least, in mid-1981, there was a military stalemate in El Salvador.

THE POLITICAL SIDE OF THE REVOLUTION

Four days after the general offensive began, the FDR and FMLN called a press conference in Mexico City to announce the formation of a Political-Diplomatic Commission (CPD). The body was composed of seven members, one from each of the OP-Ms and two from the FDR. Guillermo Manuel Ungo, who had been José Napoleón Duarte's running mate in 1972, had served on the first junta after the October coup, and had been elected president of the FDR following the assassination of Enrique Alvarez Córdova and five other members of the FDR Executive Committee the previous November, stated that the purpose of the CPD was to represent the FDR/FMLN in the international arena. In the following months, the CPD acquired the character of a foreign ministry. Its seven members began traveling around the world in search of support from governments, political parties, and international organizations. Ungo, with his strong ties to the Socialist International, was particularly effective in garnering support in Europe. Meanwhile, the FDR/FMLN sent official representatives – the equivalent of ambassadors – to thirty-three countries. An FMLN leader commented that this was "not only more missions than the Salvadorean government has embassies," but that the representatives "exercise a stronger presence."† In other words, the FDR/FMLN was aggressively seeking out government ministers and legislators as well as talking to the media and citizens' groups on a daily basis. This effort paid off when, on August 28, 1981, the governments of France and Mexico issued a joint declaration recognizing the FDR/FMLN as a "representative political force" that should be directly involved in any political settlement.

In addition to the CPD, the FDR/FMLN created two other joint organs with similar membership (see Figure 5.2). One was the International Relations Commission, which was responsible for developing international solidarity among the citizenry of various countries and for overseeing social and relief work connected with the hundreds of thousands of Salvadoreans who, beginning in early 1980, were fleeing their own country and seeking refuge in countries from the United States to Panama. The second was the Commission on Information, which was responsible for the production of several publications, news bulletins, posters, and so on.

In addition to these overtly political structures, there was also a series of professional working groups created in health, education, agrarian reform, the economy, and other areas. These groups were offshoots of "professional groups" that the BPR and FAPU had put

Photo 5.5 Political-Diplomatic Commission of the FDR/FMLN announces its formation. From left: Rubén Zamora (MPSC), José Rodríguez Ruiz (RN), Guillermo Manuel Ungo (MNR), Salvador Samoyoa (FPL); moderator (unidentified); Ana Guadalupe Martinez (ERP); and Mario Aguiñada (PCS). Not in picture: Fabio Castillo (PRTC).

together in 1979 to analyze the country's socioeconomic problems and needs and to develop national plans to be implemented once the Democratic Revolutionary Government (GDR) came to power. By early 1982, these groups of economists, doctors, agricultural technicians, teachers, and others were well advanced in their planning for a new government. One source in the FDR said that by late 1981 the groups in health and education had virtually completed their work.†

The development of the joint commissions and the working groups implied several things. First, and most important, it emphasized that in a revolutionary process the political dimension is as important as the military. Second, it demonstrated that, in addition to the guerrillas, several thousand people were working full time in the struggle. Third, it suggested that revolution was an expensive activity, running into millions of dollars annually. Fourth, it underlined a point members of the FDR/FMLN made frequently: That through working together day in and day out, they were achieving unity not in theory but in practice.

While the FMLN operated on the basis of democratic centralism, the FDR continued to operate on the basis of consensus, as did the joint commissions. By late 1981 mechanisms of coordination between the FMLN and the FDR were such that all important decisions could be made together. One example of this coordination, and of the balance between the political and the military dimensions, was the decision to destroy the Puente de Oro on October 15, 1981. This decision was not an exclusively military one. First there was an extended discussion of both the internal and the external political dimensions and potential costs as well as the economic cost ($10 million) to the government of destroying the bridge. Once the political decision was made, the military planning became exclusively the domain of the FMLN. When the action was carried out, on the second anniversary of the October coup, units from the four organizations with bases in the area participated. One set the explosives; another, assisted by militia, evacuated the thousand people living under each end of the bridge; meanwhile, the others distracted the guard posts at each approach and at nearby garrisons.†[23]

THE MOUNTAIN IS THE PEOPLE

The fact that the FMLN could evacuate, under the noses of the National Guard, more than a thousand people in the dead of night, is one small indication of the extent of popular support for the revolutionary organizations among the Salvadorean people. The question of support has been much in dispute. The U.S. and Salvadorean governments maintained that the FDR/FMLN had little popular support. It is true that the situation in El Salvador was historically different and far more complex than that in Nicaragua, where an entire population rose up against a hated dictator.

First, the regime did not provide the population with one figure, like Somoza, whom everyone loved to hate. The problem in El Salvador was an economic and political system, a far more amorphous enemy. Second, the system of repression in El Salvador was more pervasive and more consistent, spanning a half century. A third factor was size. The Sandinistas could always retreat to the Segovia Mountains in north central Nicaragua, where they were virtually untouchable by Somoza's National Guard. The Salvadorean revolutionaries, in contrast, have had to live and work among the people; there are almost no uninhabited areas of the country.[24] Fourth, most of the Salvadorean revolutionaries had learned an important lesson from Che Guevara's disastrous experience in Bolivia. Guevara and his band of followers made little or no effort to build support among the population. Thus when U.S. Special Forces went looking for Che in the jungle there was no network to warn him and no one to hide him.

In El Salvador, from the first days of the FPL and the ERP, the guerrillas lived among the people; they helped plow land and harvest crops; they provided medical care and other forms of assistance; they taught the peasants how to protect themselves. For example, a woman from Sensuntepeque, Cabañas, said that the FPL taught her fellow villagers to put a lookout on a small hill below her hamlet and to fire a flare if they saw the army or security forces coming. When the army moved in on June 1, 1980, after six months of rumors, the flare went off and all the men ran to the mountains. No one died that day, although one old man who remained behind was tortured.[25]

Others who have visited guerrilla camps tell of walking for several kilometers with their escorts and passing seemingly innocent women, children, and old people. All of them, however, were part of a vast security network that extended several kilometers in all directions from the camp. Via whistles and other prearranged signals, the word could be passed quickly if troops were moving in. The guerrilla forces could not have survived in the mountains for a decade if they had not had popular support. They depended on the people for food, shelter, and protection. And they got it.

Juan José Martell, the MPSC representative on the seven-person FDR Executive Committee, addressed the issue of popular support in an October 1981 interview:

> The armed struggle in El Salvador is characterized by an incorporation of the population, or by its support for the guerrilla. El Salvador has 21,000 km². It is possible to cross the length of the country, by car, in three and a half hours; in one morning one can reach whatever point in the country. It has an enormous density of population which means that there virtually does not exist a truly rural zone. The armed forces have 28,000 troops.
>
> In this context it is impossible, militarily, for a guerrilla movement to survive, even for a few weeks, if it does not have the massive support of the population. We can ask ourselves who gives food to the guerrilla? Who advises them of the army's movements? To where does the population run when it is attacked by the army — because the army attacks the population as it does the guerrilla?
>
> Evidently, it is not the Russians, nor the Cubans, nor the Nicaraguans who daily send tons of food for thousands of guerrillas to

eat; tons of clothes to wear; and such exact information of the movements of the enemy. It is the people who do all this, who sow the basic
grains, prepare the food, and make the clothes.

> El Salvador has no mountains, but the mountains of the guerrillas
are their people.[26]

There is little question that the continuing violence was ex-
hausting the Salvadorean population, but it is important not to confuse
that exhaustion with absence of support for the FDR/FMLN or, con-
versely, with support for the military-civilian regime. A subtle indication of support was that in personal conversations with hundreds of
peasants they never used words like "terrorists" and "subversives" to
describe the revolutionary organizations. They talked about "the Bloc"
(BPR), "the Leagues" (LP-28), the "Popular Organizations," and "the
Front" (FMLN). They referred to the guerrillas most often as *"los compañeros"* and occasionally as *"los muchachos"* (the boys). The first four
terms are neutral, the last two are positive, and *"muchachos"* is a term
of affection.[27]

Size and Strength of the FMLN

The size of the revolutionary army was disputed, with Salvadorean government sources tending to downplay its numbers and re-
jecting the FMLN estimates. In a mid-1981 interview, Commander
Fermán Cienfuegos said that the FMLN had "4,000 guerrillas in arms"
and "more than 5,000 militia."[28] These figures were very close to
estimates by various observers. Nevertheless, by January 1982 FMLN
leaders were complaining in interviews that the problem was not
combatants, the problem was arms. One FMLN leader said in a
February 1982 interview that "we have more people than arms." As a
result, for example, in a platoon of twenty-one combatants, there was
a rotation system so that everyone could rest; five would receive
"three-to-five-day passes," and their places would be taken by others
who did not have their own arms.†

This view was endorsed by Roberto Roca, a member of the
FMLN General Command. "We don't need the support of combatants
from other countries. There are really more than enough combatants
in the Salvadorean revolutionary force. Perhaps there are too many
combatants and too few arms." These words tended to belie the efforts
of the Reagan administration to portray the guerrilla force as armed to
the teeth by Vietnam, the Soviet Union, and Cuba. Roca spoke to this
point as well: "We do not discard the possibility that, in the face of
[direct] intervention, we will not only solicit [help] openly and pub-

licly, but that we want to count on the certainty that the people of the world and some governments will have courage sufficient to give us arms that we have lacked in order to impede the massacre of our people. The moment we need arms we are not going to deny it, we will solicit openly because it will be after open intervention."[29]

The FMLN had four primary sources of arms. The first two were the international arms market and corrupt army officers in the region who sold the FMLN arms. The money for these purchases came primarily from ransom money received from the kidnapping in the late 1970s of ten Salvadorean oligarchs and several other foreign businessmen, most of whom were released. Estimates of the amount of money acquired by this means varied wildly, from $40 million to $170 million. The most likely figure was in the neighborhood of $65 million.† By 1981 the FMLN was also receiving voluntary contributions from around the world. The people of West Germany, for example, contributed more than $1 million during 1981 in an "Arms for El Salvador" campaign.

A third source of arms was manufacture by the FMLN itself. The group became adept at making its own weapons, and there were at least two villages in zones under FMLN control where many of the residents were, according to visiting journalists, voluntarily working full-time making hand grenades and land mines. The fourth source, which became increasingly important by late 1981, was the more direct and increasingly successful method of attacking the armed forces in their barracks or ambushing them on patrol to obtain weapons. One guerrilla commander told a visiting journalist that the more arms the United States sent, the more the FMLN recovered. "We want to thank the United States government," the commander said, "for sending us so many weapons."[30]

The Rationale Behind Kidnappings. The kidnappings have been internationally condemned as wanton acts of terrorism. Without in any way attempting to justify these acts, we should try to understand the rationale behind them. As we saw in earlier chapters, the Salvadorean oligarchy had amassed large fortunes while extending its control over the national economy. At the same time the vast majority of the Salvadorean people continued to live in abject poverty, with no hope of improving their lot. The revolutionary organizations of El Salvador, in the words of one RN leader, viewed the kidnappings as a means of "recouping some of this wealth for the people, to shape and develop the political struggle for their liberation. It is mistaken to say," he continued, "that all this money is used to buy arms; much of it has been used to build the Popular Organizations. The armed struggle is

Photo 5.6 An FMLN arms factory in one of the zones under control. Here men are making *abanicos,* a type of mortar that fires rockets in three directions at once. Credit: COLCOM-HM

necessarily a part of the struggle," he concluded, "not because we would have chosen that path but because there is no other way to wrest political and economic power from the dominant forces and change the structures to a more just and humane system."†

OUTLINES OF A REVOLUTIONARY SOCIETY

By 1981 it was possible to discern the shape and character of the revolutionary society in El Salvador from the organizations that already existed, from the forms of governance that operated in areas of the country under FMLN control, and from the ideology of the revolution as manifested in everyday practice.

The Political Program of the FDR/FMLN

A month after the January 22, 1980, demonstration, the CRM published its Platform for a Democratic Revolutionary Government. Asserting that "this revolution . . . is not nor can it be the work of a group of conspirators," but "is the fruit of the struggle of an entire people," the CRM appealed to "all social classes disposed to . . . serve the interests of the people." It then outlined a series of "immediate political measures," including adherence to the U.N. Declaration of Human Rights and due punishment for those responsible for the "disappeared," the tortured, and the murdered; the decentralization of power to municipalities; a foreign policy of nonalignment; and the development of a popular army, incorporating honest, patriotic troops and officers of the present army.

Under "structural changes," it proposed nationalization of the banks, external commerce in major exports, the entire energy system, and "monopolistic enterprises in industry, commerce, and services." It promised extensive agrarian and urban reform but pledged to honor the holdings of small and medium-sized property owners. It committed the GDR to an extensive tax reform and to the establishment of effective mechanisms of credit, especially for small and medium-sized businesses. Finally, in the area of "social measures," the GDR proposed to reduce unemployment by creating jobs and to implement massive projects in housing, health, education, and culture.[31]

More than a year later, on August 7, 1981, the General Command of the FMLN issued a declaration in which it listed seven points that would guide the implementation of the GDR. Those seven points, which remained the most recent statement as of early 1982, include the following:

> 1. The Democratic Revolutionary Government will be implemented with the participation of all popular democratic and revolutionary sectors that have contributed to the defeat of the genocidal dictatorship and have been opposed to the intervention of imperialism or its minions in our country.
> 2. The GDR will guarantee national independence, will assure and defend the self-determination of the Salvadorean people.
> 3. The GDR will guarantee to the Salvadorean people peace, liberty, welfare and progress by implementing social, economic and political changes that ensure a just distribution of the wealth, the enjoyment of culture and health, and the effective exercise of democratic rights of the great majorities.
> 4. The GDR will facilitate the integration of the Popular Revolutionary Army and the patriotic and democratic sector of the army of the dictatorship, in an army of a new type, faithful to the Salvadorean people and its interests, faithful to its mission to safeguard the peace, independence and sovereignty of the nation (Patria) and to secure the

political social and economic transformation that the revolution will put into effect.

5. The GDR will guarantee the freedom of belief and the free exercise of all religious denominations.

6. The GDR will support all private businesses that are opposed to genocide, the imperialist intervention, who cooperate with the implementation of its program and who contribute to the functioning and development of the national economy.

7. The GDR will apply an international policy of peace and nonalignment.[32]

These documents, along with that read by Nicaraguan Commander of the Revolution Daniel Ortega before the United Nations on October 7, 1981, reflect the progressive political maturation of the Salvadorean revolutionary organizations as well as their growing self-confidence. The clearest example of this is the changing position of the FMLN on the question of a new army. The three key passages are as follows:

> [The GDR will] fortify and develop the Popular Army, in which will be incorporated those elements of the troops, non-commissioned officers, officers and commanders of the present Army who maintain "clean conduct," reject foreign intervention against the revolutionary process and support the liberating struggle of our people.

> GDR Program, February 1980

> The GDR will carry out the integration of the Popular Revolutionary Army and the patriotic and democratic sector of the army . . . in an army of a new type. . . .

> – FMLN General Command Declaration, August 1981

> The . . . Armed Forces [will be restructured], based on the officers and troops of the present Army who are not responsible for crimes and genocide against the people, and . . . the commanders and troops of the FMLN [will be integrated into it].

> – FDR/FMLN Declaration before the
> United Nations, October 1981

The evolution of this position regarding the formation of a new army can be attributed to at least three factors. First, the FMLN experienced a growing military confidence and capability during this period. Between August and October 1981, for example, it carried out an enormously successful offensive against the Salvadorean army. Second, the recognition by France and Mexico of the FDR/FMLN as a "representative political force" that should be taken into account in any political settlement in El Salvador implied the necessity for an increasingly mature response from the FDR/FMLN, which was reflected in the declaration before the UN. Third, there was a growing unwillingness to prolong the war unnecessarily (thereby increasing the bloodshed) by holding out for an absolute military victory such as the Sandinista National Liberation Front had achieved in Nicaragua in 1979.

By October 1981 the FMLN was strong enough to militarily defeat the Salvadorean army. But U.S. intervention (see Chapter 6) guaranteed that the war would continue indefinitely.

New Political Structures

In urban areas the Popular Committees, as the basic unit of political organization, could be expected to continue providing political education as well as helping resolve day-to-day problems of the neighborhood. In the countryside, by early 1981 forms of direct participatory democracy were already developing in zones under FMLN control. In El Jícaro, Chalatenango, for example, virtually all 2,000 inhabitants were involved in making daily decisions that affected their lives.[33]

With much of the province of Chalatenango under FMLN control, other indications of what life would be like in revolutionary El Salvador emerged. The guerrillas organized collective farms; they introduced compulsory education; they instituted medical care in an area where most people had never seen a doctor; and they initiated a literacy campaign for villagers as well as for unschooled guerrillas. By 1981 the FMLN had produced workbooks and teachers' guides for literacy campaigns.[34] When journalist Alex Drehsler asked a peasant on one of the collective farms if he missed having his own small plot of land, the answer was unequivocal. "Before the government drove me out . . . I was always struggling to grow enough food for my family," the middle-aged man replied. "Often we went hungry. Now, we all work the same land and all of us have food. We don't go hungry. Do I miss having my own land? No. This way my children get enough to eat. I can't feed them a handful of earth."[35]

Civil Administration in the Zones Under FMLN Control. These developments in Chalatenango were repeated and expanded in other zones under FMLN control in the Departments of Morazán, Cuscatlán, San Vicente, and Usulután. By early 1982, the FMLN had

Photo 5.7 A literacy class for FMLN combatants being conducted in a war front in El Salvador. The writing on the "blackboard" reads: "Oscar A. Romero" literacy school of the E. Che Guevara *destacamento* (a military unit larger than a platoon). Credit: COLCOM-HM

established Consejos Farabundistas (administrative councils) throughout these zones. The councils were subdivided into four sections, with the leaders of the first three sections elected by the people living in the area. The four sections were as follows:

1. *Civil registrar.* This office corresponded to the mayor's office; registrars were responsible for day-to-day civil procedures, as well as for taking and maintaining a census of the population, including statistics on births, deaths, marriages, and divorces.

2. *Representative for the religious sector.* This person, in the absence of a priest, was responsible for promoting the religious life of the community and for helping the people, through courses and talks, to relate their faith to the revolutionary process. The representative could be a catechist, a delegate of the Word, or simply a member of the community.

3. *Economy.* This section was responsible for agricultural and other production and for the distribution of the produce.

4. *Self-Defense.* In this section the militia had primary respon-

sibility for teaching the people what to do during an invasion by government forces. What could be called "popular military engineering" became a skill born of necessity, as the militia, for example, working with the people, constructed *tatus* in nearby hills. *Tatus,* a device borrowed from Vietnam, are elaborate tunnel systems constructed inside hills or mountains where people can hide and be protected from bombardment.

According to Commander Jacinto Sánchez, a member of the DRU located in the Cerros de San Pedro, the principal task of the Consejos Farabundistas was "the leadership of the population to normalize civic life and control and administrate resources and collective production."[36] María Caminos, a member of the FMLN who works in information and political education, elaborated. "There is the construction of *tatus,* as well as literacy campaigns and the making of clothes. There are councils of elders who know all about popular or traditional medicines," she continued, "and who are teaching the doctors who studied in the university how to cure certain illnesses. This," she noted, "is one example of how the revolution recovers the values of the people." There is also a campaign called "a glass of milk," which is intended to give every child under the age of seven in the zones under control one glass of milk per day. This, Caminos said, "has never been done in El Salvador."[37]

The Role of Women. Fifty percent of the OP rank and file, 30 percent of the FMLN combatants, and 40 percent of the revolutionary leadership are women—an extraordinarily high figure in a society with a particularly strong (even by Latin American standards) cultural trait of protecting females. According to Marisol Galindo, who was a guerrilla for three years before moving into political work, a majority of the women in the FDR/FMLN are mothers. Galindo herself is the mother of three.

Behind the statistics is a revolution in attitudes. One guerrilla said in an interview that the "process of coming to see women as *compañeras* and not as sex objects" was one he and his fellow guerrillas had had to go through in the mountains. In his particular unit two-thirds of the combatants were women. "There is a great concern," he said, "to destroy *machismo.*"† Alex Drehsler encountered similar attitudes in Chalatenango. Said a male guerrilla commander, "We are trying to teach the women that they do not have to accept only the traditional roles for women, that they should try to examine their potentialities. We have some peasant women who join us as cooks. Soon they realize that they have opportunities to do other things. They become combatants, medics, or leaders."[38]

Photo 5.8 The combat units of the FMLN include both women and men. Credit: COLCOM-HM

Ideology and Practice

The presence of women, of Christians, of the "democratic" – as distinguished from "revolutionary" – sectors of Salvadorean society within the FDR/FMLN, as well as different political tendencies among the revolutionaries themselves, all contributed to a vigorous dialectical process of thought and action that gave the Salvadorean revolutionary process its own unique characteristics.

Liberation. The central concept in this process was that of liberation. The term was common to the discourse not only of the revolutionaries but also of the church (see Chapter 4). In El Salvador and among the refugees in other countries of Central America, the people who were members of Christian Base Communities spoke most frequently of "liberation" rather than of "revolution." Personal interviews with dozens of refugees from Mexico to Costa Rica over a period of two years showed that the concept of liberation had a very concrete meaning; it meant they would no longer be hungry, illiterate, sick, forced to live in housing of cardboard, sticks, and dirt floors. For FDR/FMLN leaders it also meant something more; María Caminos explained that "the people are struggling . . . to expel foreign dominance

Photo 5.9 BPR organizer Elsa Cásera, from Usulután, said she "works in the cotton harvest when [she] can." Apart from the six weeks of the harvest, she said during the January 22, 1980, demonstration, there was no other work available.

Photo 5.10 Commandante Ana Guadalupe Martinez
on her return to El Salvador from exile in Mexico,
November 1979.

and a small, dominant class that has kept the people subjugated for
many decades."[39] This is what the FDR/FMLN meant by an "anti-
oligarchical" and "anti-imperialist" struggle.

In addition, the concept of national liberation includes both
women's and men's liberation. Norma Guevara, who was a member of
the FDR/FMLN Commission on Information, said that "the resources
for which we are struggling belong to all so that the possibility of
resolving the problems of women and children exists only in the con-

Photo 5.11 The Mothers' Committee of the Disappeared holds a press conference. Women whose children had "disappeared" organized this committee in order to pressure the government for information about them. As time passed these women became progressively radicalized and militant.

text of a project that takes account of all the social, political, and economic problems of our country."[40] "It isn't possible to liberate women outside the process of national liberation in El Salvador," added Caminos.[41]

Pluralism. In Norma Guevara's view, pluralism "is directly associated with the concept of liberation" because it reflects "the breadth of the social forces in the struggle." She defined pluralism as the integrated, coordinated action of different political forces. The strength with which various sectors participate is important, not where they are on the political spectrum," Guevara emphasized.[42] María Caminos added that pluralism means that these different sectors, "while still having some ideological differences, agree on the principal points of the struggle." These points include national independence, the right to self-determination, a more just distribution of the wealth, and the necessity for structural changes that will permit social progress.[43]

Both Guevara and Caminos were members of organizations that make up the FMLN. Rubén Zamora was secretary general of the MPSC and a member of the CPD. In his view, pluralism is necessary in the Salvadorean revolutionary process for three reasons. First, it guarantees a spirit of self-criticism, without which "the revolution will become asphyxiated and bureaucratized." Second, the character of this revolution is such that "there has been an historic demand by the people for democracy and pluralism." Third is a tactical reason: "A young revolutionary process has to deal with the hostility of imperialism. At the present time imperialism acts through sectors within the society; therefore, social sectors not incorporated into or neutralized by the revolution will fall into the hands of imperialism."[44]

A common charge of U.S. officials was that the pluralism reflected in the composition of the FDR was merely a facade for the "hard-line Marxists-Leninists" of the FMLN who after victory would shove all the "democrats" aside and seize total control of the state. Several dozen interviews with members of both organizations produced the same response: "rubbish." María Caminos gave one of the most incisive answers:

> That charge is a maneuver of imperialism to deny the authenticity of our revolutionary process and to sow divisions among the revolutionary forces. It is also an effort to present our struggle as a struggle for communism manipulated from the outside. I believe that the democratic sectors can never be isolated from the process because they represent the aspirations of the people; as long as they do that, they will be present.[45]

Juan José Martell discussed what this meant for the MPSC and other organizations of the FDR:

> Our organizations have a great input into the decisions that are made. Actions are not taken behind our backs. Not only are we consulted, but we are actively involved in the making and execution of all

[political] decisions, a fact that will be much more important after taking power.

The MPSC has the support and sympathy of large sectors of the population. All the strength that the PDC had during the 1970s, that permitted it to become the primary political power in the country, is now with us. The PDC has been converted into a shell of its former self, sustained by a handful of corrupt leaders, without any popular support. That enormous support of the population for us is our best guarantee, now and after the taking of power.[46]

It is clear from these comments, as well as from the type of structures developed in the zones under control, that a revolutionary political system would create democratic structures different from those traditionally associated with liberal democracy. Essentially, liberal or Western-style political systems are organized around parties, running candidates for public office, and winning elections. Such political systems work on the republican principle of representative government. In revolutionary El Salvador one could expect a deliberate effort to ensure that all sectors of society, from the local to the national level, have a voice in governance, especially those sectors that traditionally have been excluded – that is to say, the majority of the population.

The Popular Organizations of El Salvador have had a concept of political mobilization quite different from that of liberal democracies, which emphasize turning out the vote. In El Salvador a process of political education oriented to preparing citizens to participate directly in making decisions that affect their daily lives and to working together toward common goals has been under way since the early 1970s. It is a process that has been reinforced by the Christian Base Communities. This concept of participatory democracy is one to which citizens of the United States have had little exposure.

While these developments were taking place inside and outside El Salvador during 1980 and 1981 a series of tangential events were occurring within the Salvadorean government, military, and oligarchy. In addition the United States became more involved in defending what it insisted on calling a "moderate, reformist government." It is to these developments that we turn our attention in the last chapter.

6
Descent into Anarchy 1980–1982

"Now there is only the law of the jungle. There is no law." The oligarch pulled out a very large gun and placed it on the table. Pointing to it, he said, "Today El Salvador, this is the Constitution." Then he pulled out two loaded clips and placed them beside the gun. "These," he added, "are the amendments."†

THE PROCESS OF *DERECHIZACIÓN*

"Whenever the Army feels threatened as an institution," a U.S. Embassy official long acquainted with the Salvadorean military observed in early 1980, "it joins together and moves to the right."† That rightward movement, or *"derechización,"* occurred following progressive victories in 1944, 1948, 1960, 1972, and 1979. The latter case, however, offered one new twist to the old pattern: The process began, as Chapter 1 illustrated, even before the October 15 coup. It accelerated with the passing weeks. It was strengthened by the governmental crisis that occurred in late December 1979 – a crisis that was inevitable, given the integrity and commitment to reform of the men and women who staffed the government. Their resignations signaled the reconsolidation of power in the hands of the most conservative elements of the army.

This is not to say that Minister of Defense García and his colleagues enjoyed carte blanche, for some limitations were imposed on their actions from two sources. One was within the army itself. Majano and his followers (the *majanistas*) – or the October 15 Movement – continued to support the reforms to which they had committed themselves in the Proclama. The problem, in the words of a former Christian Democrat who served in the governments of the first and second juntas, was that "the Young Military don't have political experience; they are not well educated. They are too sentimental, idealistic in a bad way. They are not scientific. There are very good people there, but without a project, program, or links to the popular movement. Without these the High Command could and did exploit their weakness."†

The real wishes of the *majanistas*, who included in varying degrees of commitment a majority of the officer corps, became clear when in a January 15, 1980, meeting about 75 percent of those present voted to demand the resignations of Minister of Defense García and Subsecretary Carranza. That same day identical letters, addressed to Majano, Gutierrez, and the civilian members of the junta, circulated in the fourteen departmental garrisons and other army centers, such as the Military Academy and the Military Hospital. The letters read, in part:

> The representatives of the Young Military, conscious that the objectives of our Proclama, which reveals our concerns and wishes in support of the people, the real cause of our October 15 Movement . . . along with our institutional existence and considering that such programs that have since been initiated, have been obstructed by irrational actions motivated by personal interests of our defense officials . . .
> DEMAND THE IMMEDIATE DISMISSAL OF THE MINISTER AND SUBSECRETARY OF DEFENSE.†[1]

The letters were signed by 186 officers. All 74 officers in the garrisons of San Carlos, El Zapote, the Military Hospital, and the Military Academy (all located in San Salvador) signed. This letter precipitated the most serious crisis within the Salvadorean military since the October coup. When it was given to Majano and Gutierrez, they apprised García and Carranza of its contents—and then did nothing. Meanwhile, however, García and Carranza began to rally their supporters. The showdown, when it came, ended in a standoff; that is to say, García and Carranza won.

Two months later, when an officer showed me the original letters, I asked why the Young Military had not forced the issue. "We are still waiting for the junta to act," he replied. Héctor Dada Hirezi later said in an interview that he and the other civilian members of the junta had never seen the letter; they had never been informed of the crisis.[2]

This story not only illustrates the paradox of political division coupled with clannishness within the army, it also reveals the marginalization of the Christian Democrats in the government and confirms where the real power in El Salvador lay in January 1980.

The Christian Democrats Join The Government

The facade of a civilian/military coalition was maintained by the PDC, which appeared to come galloping out of the sunset to save the day when the government of the first junta retired. In fact, some members of the party were negotiating conditions for the formation of a new government with elements in the army while the crisis between government ministers and COPEFA was erupting in late December. By playing both ends against the middle, the PDC effectively undercut any possibility that the mediation effort of Archbishop Romero to resolve the crisis would succeed.†

Three days after the government resigned, the PDC nominated José Antonio Morales Erlich, a former mayor of San Salvador and vice-presidential candidate in 1977, and Héctor Dada Hirezi, a former member of the National Assembly and immediate past foreign minister, to replace Guillermo Manuel Ungo and Román Mayorga on the junta.[3] The party also laid down conditions under which it would participate in the government. The most important of these were that the army publicly commit itself to a program of economic reforms, including agrarian reform and nationalization of the banks; that the repression cease; that the army commit itself to open a dialogue with the Popular Organizations; and that no representatives of business organizations, such as ANEP, be appointed to the junta or the cabinet.†[4]

The army accepted these conditions. On January 9 Morales Erlich, Dada, and José Ramón Avalos, a political independent who happened to be Gutierrez's personal physician, were sworn in as the new civilian members of the junta. Putting together a cabinet proved to be more difficult. Almost no one who resigned on January 3 was willing to return to the government. Many others were unwilling to associate themselves with it. By the time the cabinet was completed in late January it was common knowledge in San Salvador that most of the appointees were second and third choices.

Betrayal

The last of the new ministers were sworn in on January 17, in the midst of the crisis in the army. Five days later the largest demonstration in Salvadorean history was deliberately fired on by security forces, giving the lie to assurances by Minister of Defense García that "all troops were confined to barracks for the day." That night the commander of the San Carlos garrison, Colonel Daniel Bustamante y Caballero, ordered units from San Carlos to surround the National

Photo 6.1 The second junta. From the left: Colonel Adolfo Majano; Christian Democrat José Antonio Morales Erlich; Dr. José Ramon Avalos, an independent; and Christian Democrat Héctor Dada Hirezi. Not in picture: Colonel Jaime Abdul Gutierrez.

University, where 25,000 *campesinos* had taken refuge after the demonstration was broken up. Bustamante acted with the approval of Majano, in order to prevent the National Guard and National Police from storming the campus.†

At 8:30 the next morning the junta met with the army High Command, including the directors and other officers of the security forces. The latter wanted to invade the university. When the junta refused to give its permission, Major Roberto Staben from the National Police and Captain Arnoldo Pozo of the Treasury Police announced they would invade the university with or without orders. Héctor Dada demanded that Minister of Defense García discipline these officers for insulting the junta and for insubordination. García responded that he did not have the power or authority to control the security forces.†[5]

Occupation of the PDC Headquarters. One week later another crisis descended when LP-28 occupied the building in which the Christian Democrats had their offices and held several hostages, including the daughter of Morales Erlich. LP-28 demanded the release of political prisoners taken in recent weeks and said that "the occupation is for the repression against the people and to denounce the counterrevolutionary character of Christian Democracy at the national and international level."[6]

Several days later LP-28 and the PDC quietly negotiated a peaceful settlement in which the junta concurred. But, according to a Christian Democrat who was then a member of the government, the "armed forces broke the agreement."† LP-28 had agreed to release the hostages in return for safe conduct away from the building. But the security forces stormed the building, lined everyone up, and forced them to identify themselves. Those who identified themselves as Christian Democrats were ushered out of the building. Five members of LP-28 were then shot. Twenty-three were captured and "disappeared." The remaining LP-28 members escaped by lying about their identities.

As the attack began Rubén Zamora, who had been one of the negotiators for the PDC, called Morales Erlich at the Casa Presidencial and told him the security forces were going in. Morales said he would call García immediately. García's response was, roughly, "Yes, Doctor, nothing happened; all is calm." Morales called Zamora back and reported García's comments. Zamora by that time was screaming into the telephone. "I have a radio. Don't you hear the shots?" Ten minutes later García called Morales and told him that everything was under control; that the party's headquarters and his daughter were safe.†[7]

Political Intervention by the United States

These events took place as the Department of State was reviewing U.S. policy toward El Salvador. Frank Devine had retired as ambassador, and Robert White, the new appointee, was being subjected to rigorous review by conservatives on the Senate Foreign Relations Committee. The resignation of the first junta had caused "consternation," according to one embassy official; this same official subsequently admitted that the United States should have "made it clear what our policy was" with regard to supporting the reforms and the junta but that "we were trying to play the game very openly and honestly – to avoid the appearance of intervention."†

Mixed Signals. But even at the time that the United States was supposedly clarifying its policy, Assistant Secretary of State William Bowdler visited El Salvador on January 22–24. In two meetings, one with Archbishop Romero, the other with ANEP, Bowdler, accompanied by Devine, continued the contradictory policy line. According to an individual present at the meeting with Romero, the conversation began with Bowdler telling the prelate, "We don't want to continue talking in favor of urgent changes but for the future."

Romero: Those who want the changes are the people.

Devine: The popular groups want power, not changes.

Romero: The people want the changes quickly and the more rapidly they come, the less violence there will be.

Devine: International Communism is exacerbating these problems.

During the conversation, Bowdler tried to get the archbishop to endorse the Christian Democratic–military government "for the good of the church." Romero rejected the request. (He consistently took the position that it was not the business of the church to endorse specific governments.) Finally, when the U.S. diplomats realized that they had come up against a wall in Romero, Devine said, "We'll support the changes."†

In a subsequent meeting with the National Association of Private Enterprise, Bowdler, according to an official of that organization, said he was aware of the communist infiltration in El Salvador and that the communists were very active. It was better, he continued, to have the present government than what could come afterward. Bowdler also noted that the specter of an extreme-right military coup was real – as was the possibility of civil war. Given these alternatives, the assistant secretary suggested it was best to keep the Christian Democrats in power. But Bowdler did not conclude there. The ANEP official reported that the diplomat asserted, "We've got to move the Christian Democrats to the center and get them to act less demagogically than they are acting." The United States was not interested, he continued, in seeing the Christian Democrats go to the extreme left and behave like the extreme left. The most important thing to do, Bowdler concluded, was reestablish law and order.†

An embassy official denied that different messages had been given to the church and to ANEP. He insisted that the same message had been given to both: support for the government and the changes it was proposing. But it is clear that certain elements among the oligarchy, bourgeoisie, and military *received* a different message.

"Clean, Counter-Insurgency War." Another indication that the United States was more concerned with order than with reform came in a meeting of the Christian Democratic members of the government with James Cheek, the chargé d'affairs, in late February. The principal theme of this meeting, according to Christian Democrats present,[8] was Cheek's insistence on the need to create "adequate conditions" for

a "clean, counter-insurgency war." Cheek suggested reforming the Salvadorean penal code in order to permit the armed forces to retain prisoners for an indefinite period of time.[9] He also proposed a training program for the Salvadorean army, presumably to be conducted by U.S. military advisers. Another individual present in the meeting reported that Mario Zamora, Rubén's brother and the *procurador general de los pobres* (a combination of public defender and family court lawyer), answered Cheek by saying that "sufficiently repressive laws" already existed in El Salvador.†

James Cheek remembered the meeting somewhat differently.[10] Cheek said that he opened the session by reviewing a meeting he had with the High Command in which he had talked with them about undertaking a "clean campaign" against the left and the right. The military's response was that the laws did not permit the kind of operations Cheek was proposing. Cheek then said that the civilians had a responsibility in this matter, that they should cooperate with the military by revising the law. As an example, Cheek mentioned in the interview the arrest of the then secretary general of the BPR, Juan Chacón, and his release by a civilian judge for lack of evidence three days later. The arrest of Chacón was a result of pressure from the U.S. Embassy to "use means other than military to combat subversion."† In the meeting with the Christian Democrats, then, Cheek was trying to convince them of the necessity to reform the penal code so that persons like Chacón could be held for trial with the goal of obtaining conviction. But, Cheek asserted in his interview, "Héctor Dada and Rubén Zamora did not agree with that."

This incident, with its conflicting versions, illustrates the problems with U.S. policy in early 1980. Cheek felt that the Christian Democrats did not understand him. But Rubén Zamora insisted that the Salvadoreans understood Cheek perfectly. They also understood, according to Zamora, that in the Salvadorean context, Cheek's desire for a "clean war" was impossible.[11]

The Aborted Coup. In late February rumors of an imminent rightwing coup began circulating in San Salvador. The existence of a written plan for such a coup was confirmed. Its leaders were Minister of Defense García, Subsecretary Carranza, and the head of the Joint Chiefs of Staff (Estado Mayor).[12] As of March 1, however, the country was still waiting.

There were two reasons for this nonevent. First, the army was divided. San Carlos and El Zapote garrisons were firmly in the hands of the Young Military. Carrying out a successful coup would have meant the difficult task of subduing both these barracks. The written plan took account of this division and, unlike the coup of October, counted on the participation of the National Guard.

The second reason the coup did not take place was the extraordinary pressure the United States placed on the military and the oligarchy. From both Washington and San Salvador the word went out by a variety of means that a coup engineered by the right was wholly unacceptable to U.S. interests and would be opposed both during and after the fact. The military High Command was called and members of the oligarchy were invited to the embassy to hear this message. The United States also turned on the pressure in Miami, sending an envoy to inform members of the oligarchy residing there that their residence visas would be revoked if the coup were carried out. In Florida there were references to *"la cosa Somoza"*† –recalling the U.S. threat to expel Anastacio Somoza when Nicaragua's interim President Urcuyo announced the day after Somoza's resignation that he intended to continue in office until 1981, instead of the seventy-two hours agreed upon prior to Somoza's departure.

The situation in which the United States found itself in the last week of February was one it had helped create. By pushing a "law and order" line with the Salvadorean military, U.S. officials were encouraging the most conservative elements within the armed forces in their own policy of repression. At the same time the military was under pressure from right-wing elements within El Salvador who were complaining that the civil unrest was adversely affecting their economic interests and that the "international communist threat" had to be stopped.

The reaction from the right to this U.S. intervention was predictable. One member of the bourgeoisie raised the rhetorical question, "When the United States finds itself in a hole, what does it do?" His answer: "You behave like a real great power, showing how *macho* you are [and saying] 'Uh-uh, you are not going to do that.'" Another commented that the United States needed to communicate more "without prejudice" and that it needed to remember its own Bill of Rights. "We have the right also to determine our way of living without taking *patrones extranjeros* [foreign bosses]," he concluded.

The United States, as it turned out, succeeded only in postponing another coup attempt. A second effort was made on April 30–May 1. According to official reports, the attempt was made by ex-Major Roberto D'Aubuisson, the head of the White Warriors Union, a terrorist organization.[13] The second attempt suggested that the right in El Salvador was sufficiently desperate to ignore the threats of the United States because, from its perspective, in the long run U.S. aid was not that central to its interests. What it wanted was the reimposition of law and order, an end to the threat from the left, and the freedom to create its own economic miracle in El Salvador. A right-wing coup, followed by the murder of about 100,000 people, would, the right believed, enable it to pursue its economic interests with little interference.[14]

Assassination and Resignation. During the turmoil of late February six masked men, armed with G-3 and M-16 rifles (both standard issue of the Salvadorean armed forces), broke into the home of Mario Zamora during a midnight meeting of leading Christian Democrats. After forcing those present to identify themselves, they took Zamora into another room and, using guns with silencers, shot him ten times.[15] A leading member of the government subsequently said in an interview that within two days the junta had "concrete proof" implicating Subsecretary of Defense Nicolás Carranza in the assassination.† But once again, no charges were brought.

A week later Héctor Dada resigned from the junta. In his letter of resignation he charged that "we have not been able to stop the repression, and those committing acts of repression irrespective of the authority of the Junta go unpunished; the promised dialogue with the popular organizations fails to materialize; the chances for producing reforms with the support of the people are receding beyond reach."[16]

The Christian Democratic convention on March 9 to choose Dada's successor split the party wide open. A majority of the delegates were hand-picked by José Napoleón Duarte and his supporters rather than elected in departmental conventions. Duarte and his son lobbied hard for Duarte's election. On the other side, all Christian Democratic ministers opposed Duarte's election. Colonel Majano called Duarte personally and told him the Young Military did not want him on the junta. During the convention Morales Erlich spoke twice in opposition to Duarte.[17]

There was a move in the convention to resign from the government en masse. Duarte and San Salvador Mayor Adolfo Rey Prendes opposed this, arguing, "We have fought twenty years for [the agrarian reform and nationalization of banks that had been promulgated three days earlier] and now that we have them you want us to resign."† By the time the convention ended that day, Duarte was the new member of the junta and the left-of-center wing of the PDC had walked out. This group officially resigned from the party on March 10, charging that

the maintenance of repression and complacency in the face of foreign interventionist plans [a reference to a U.S. offer to send military aid and thirty-six advisers] constitutes the gravest accusations of behavior absolutely contradictory with the posture our Party has maintained throughout twenty years of struggle on behalf of the Salvadorean people. To accept this course of action in return for a share of the power—more formal than real—constitutes an unacceptable crippling which allows the governmental process to degenerate into something neither democratic nor Christian.[18]

By November 1981 at least 60 percent of the party had resigned; most of them became members of the MPSC.

Reform and Repression

The agrarian reform and bank nationalization, which Duarte defended, and the accompanying repression, which the departing Christian Democrats condemned, were the result of extreme pressure from the United States for the reforms on the one hand and a quid pro quo within the Salvadorean army on the other. The quid pro quo was simply that the Young Military got their reforms and García got carte blanche to implement a systematic policy of repression against the people, particularly those who lived in the countryside.[19] On the day the agrarian reform was promulgated, a state of siege was imposed. It was still in effect two years later.

The agrarian reform was to be implemented in three stages. Phase I, promulgated on March 6, nationalized 376 farms of more than 500 hectares. The 244 former proprietors were compensated with thirty-year bonds. Phase II, which would affect about 2,00 farms of between 100 and 500 hectares, was announced and promptly postponed for an indefinite period. Under continuing pressure from the United States, the government promulgated Phase III on April 27.

Phase I farms were largely pastureland or cotton or diversified crop farms. Phase II included most of the coffee *fincas*; therefore its postponement signaled once again that El Salvador's first source of wealth would continue untouched. Phase III (Decree 207), called "land to the tiller," mandated that all rented land now belonged to those who cultivated it. This phase was widely touted as "self-implementing." That proved, however, to be an overstatement. According to published reports, the junta implemented Phase III on the recommendation of the American Institute for Free Labor Development[20] without consulting the ministers of agriculture or planning. Both men promptly resigned in protest over having been excluded from the policymaking process and then expected to implement a fait accompli. One of them, Jorge Villacorta, subsequently became the FDR/FMLN representative in Costa Rica.

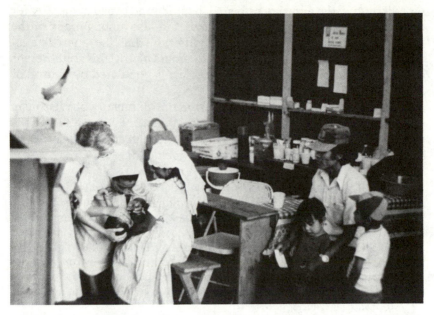

Photo 6.2 Four days after the agrarian reform was promulgated on March 6, 1980, refugees began streaming into the Arzobispado in San Salvador to escape the repression that had been unleashed against them. An infirmary was set up and staffed by nuns. This family is Protestant. They can be identified by the white scarf and the simple, early-twentieth-century-style dress the mother is wearing. Women and girls belonging to several Protestant sects in El Salvador wear such head coverings.

U.S. and AIFLD officials consistently maintained that the reform was working, was a success, and was draining off support from the left.[21] Yet a lengthy report, written by Norman Chapin, an AID official who spent five weeks in May and June 1980 visiting numerous nationalized farms, presented a very different perspective.[22] Chapin found that although a small minority of the farms were working as planned, most suffered from a shortage of credit, seed, fertilizer, and technical assistance. There were an insufficient number of agricultural technicians, and dozens of those working in the program were killed by security forces or death squads in the months following institution of the reform. Many others left the program or the country. The results in terms of production were that production of maize, a staple of the Salvadorean diet, increased in 1980–1981, but the amount of crops produced for export declined.†[23]

In spite of widespread reports from official sources that the left was disrupting the agrarian reform, Chapin found broad sympathy for the OPs, not only among the *campesinos*, but also among many of the agrarian technicians. There is little question that the guerrillas attacked farms that had been given to members of ORDEN; but there is a remarkable shortage of evidence that farms populated by neutral or sympathetic peasants were attacked.[24]

A July 18, 1980, memorandum from the University of Wisconsin Land Tenure Center to AID official Tom Mehen analyzed at length the problems with Decree 207. After running through a list of forty-seven separate criticisms, the memorandum concluded:

> In general, this is a very hastily and poorly drafted law. There are huge gaps and questions left unanswered. It is full of loopholes, contradictions, and ambiguous, imprecise language, which is likely to result in time-consuming litigation. Substantively, the law is very paternalistic. It sets the stage for a top-down land reform process tightly controlled by government, with no significant participation by *campesinos* at any level. Also, it creates a cumbersome two-tier bureaucratic structure for acquiring and distributing land, which is very inefficient and likely to lead to large inequities.[25]

As the memorandum anticipated, Decree 207 led to the formation of FINATA, the National Financial Institution for Agricultural Lands, which was specifically charged with processing the applications from the new landholders for titles. It was estimated that there were 150,000 titles to be processed in a multistage procedure that began with forms to be completed by claimants and landowners for a "pre-preliminary title."

By mid-1981, according to a Department of State official, 6,000 pre-application forms had been filed by claimants and only 7 by owners. A total of 345 *provisional* titles had been granted. Furthermore, violence toward these new "landowners" by the security forces was the subject of cable traffic between the U.S. Embassy in San Salvador and the Department of State.†

In January 1981 the head of the Salvadorean Institute of Agrarian Transformation (ISTA), Rodolfo Viera, and two U.S. AIFLD advisers were gunned down in a restaurant of the Hotel Sheraton in San Salvador by masked gunmen who then walked calmly out of the hotel and disappeared into the night.[26] Six months later the UCS branches in Ahuachapán, Sonsonate, and Santa Ana threatened to pull out of the agrarian reform program because of the official repression. Relations between the UCS and the regime further deteriorated in June with the murder by the Treasury Police of a UCS leader in Morazán,

Mariano Arevalo, and his son. Then, in December, the UCS direc-torate completed a report requested by José Napoleón Duarte, which said that "the failure of the agrarian reform process is an immediate and imminent danger." The report charged that "at least ninety [UCS] officials" and "a large number of beneficiaries" of the agrarian reform "have died during 1981 at the hands of ex-landlords and their allies, who are often members of the local security forces." It also charged that more than 25,000 former *aparceros* had been evicted from their *milpas*, or farms, "in the majority of cases with the assistance of members of the military forces," before they could obtain provisional titles.[27]

CONCURRENT DEVELOPMENTS

The regime's policy of reform with repression on one side and the growing pressure from the revolutionary organizations on the other created a socio-politico-economic context of virtual anarchy by late 1980. Visitors to San Salvador reported that during the day the city seemed remarkably normal. As soon as dark fell, however, one could hear the shooting begin. In the countryside, entire villages were being destroyed by government forces in a Salvadorean version of the pacification program in Vietnam a decade earlier.[28] In this setting various institutions of Salvadorean society were coping in different ways.

Collapse of the Economy

According to the Inter-American Development Bank, the economic performance of El Salvador in 1979 "was adversely affected by prolonged strikes in industry, interruptions in the harvesting of certain crops and an extraordinary flight of private capital due to the political developments during the year."[29] One of those political developments was the deliberate policy of both the revolutionary organizations and right-wing elements to paralyze or destroy the economy.[30]

This led to a decrease in the real gross domestic product of 1.5 percent, as compared with an increase of 4.8 percent in 1978 and an average annual growth of 5.2 percent during 1975–1977. Gross domestic investment declined 20.18 percent in 1979 and 62 percent in 1980. Meanwhile, the consumer price index (CPI) rose 17.2 percent in 1980 (compared with 15.9 percent in 1979, 13.2 percent in 1978, and an annual average of 12.7 percent during the mid-1970s).[31]

Capital flight took on the characteristics of a stampede as

members of the oligarchy sent their money to Miami and other safe havens. The Inter-American Development Bank reported that the net outflow of private capital was estimated at $176 million for 1979, compared with a net inflow of $159 million in 1978. But in January 1980 the assistant manager of the Central Bank reported that in the preceding two years $1 *billion* had left El Salvador through the black market.[32] As the fear of impending bank nationalization grew, savings banks suffered. By late January 1980, $800,000 per day was being withdrawn from savings accounts.[33] By May 1981, only four banks remained solvent. The Central Bank was not among them.

Employment in the industrial sector dropped sharply. By early 1980 all the industries located in an area known as the *Zona Franca* (free zone) in eastern San Salvador had closed.[34] A January 12 story in San Salvador's *Prensa Gráfica* reported that twenty businesses employing 8,200 workers had ceased operations in the preceding months. Two weeks later the paper reported that another 7,000 workers had been laid off. This was in a country where the total number of full-time industrial employees in the late 1970s barely exceeded 35,000 (see Table 3.4.).[35]

By late 1980 the Salvadorean government was almost wholly dependent on the United States to remain solvent. A State Department source admitted that without continuing U.S. and multilateral assistance from such institutions as the International Monetary Fund the Salvadorean government would be bankrupt within days.†

Never Say Die

Angered by the refusal of the Christian Democrats to permit participation of the private sector in the government of the second junta, ANEP withdrew all its members from various governmental agencies in the capital and around the country.[36] After José Napoleón Duarte replaced Héctor Dada on the junta in early March, conversations resumed between the ANEP and the government. In an effort to gain support for their position, especially in the United States, the oligarchy and elements of the bourgeoisie, through ANEP, created the Productive Alliance in mid-1980. The alliance was, by its own description, "a broadly based association of businessmen's groups and professionals" committed to continuing to work in El Salvador and "not to stop its own productive processes."

In its initial position paper the organization said its constituent members had "come to the decision that the country's economy can only be saved through the collaboration of both the productive sector and the government." The alliance maintained that it was "not trying

Figure 6.1 The engine (Salvadorean free enterprise) is pulling (from the first car back) the public treasury, schools, public works, the government, hospitals, employment, and the universities.

to overthrow or destabilize the Junta, but [was] trying to restore, in a short period of time, [El Salvador's] economic situation."[37] In June it sent a delegation to Washington, D.C., to call "the attention of the U.S. government to the importance of private sector cooperation in achieving a climate of tranquility in El Salvador and reducing unemployment."[38]

In Miami, where between 150 and 300 families from the oligarchy had taken up residence by mid-1980, the El Salvador Freedom Foundation was established. The 250 members of the group hired a Washington, D.C., lobbyist for $7,500 per month to introduce them to friendly legislators like North Carolina's Senator Jesse Helms and to help them counter critical press stories. "We are not oligarchs in the sense of exploiters," asserted Alfonso Salaverría, a scion of one of the largest landowning families prior to the 1980 agrarian reform. "We developed our country, we penetrated its jungles, and planted coffee. We are like the pioneers of the United States. We don't want unjust privileges. We just want our country to return to a democratic regime."[39]

The Church After Romero

The nomination of Arturo Rivera Damas as apostolic administrator following the assassination of Archbishop Oscar Romero was greeted with joy and relief throughout the archdiocese and the progressive sector of the Catholic Church. Rivera, after all, had been the first choice of this sector to succeed the aged Luís Chávez back in 1977.

Rivera began with a pledge to continue in the pastoral line of Romero, and it appeared for a time that he would indeed do so. But Rivera was a different personality with a different background. Romero, although his homilies were models of clarity, was first and foremost a pastor. Rivera, a canon lawyer by training, did not convey the personal warmth that Romero had projected. More important, Rivera immediately came under strong pressure from Rome to heal the rift in the hierarchy—which inevitably meant being more cautious about what he said. The fact that he had been named administrator rather than archbishop meant that he was forced to operate under constraints with which Romero had not been saddled.

Romero and Rivera had been close friends; indeed, Rivera was the only supporter the archbishop had among the five Salvadorean bishops. They had together written a pastoral letter after Rivera became bishop of Santiago de María, "The Church and the Popular

Political Organizations." In it they had taken the position, following Medellín, that the people had a right to form their own political organizations and that the church had a responsibility to "accompany" the people as they engaged in that activity. The two bishops had also addressed the question of violence and condemned what they termed "institutionalized violence," the repressive violence of the state, spontaneous violence, and seditious or terrorist violence, which they specifically distinguished from "revolutionary" violence. They praised the doctrine of nonviolence as the highest form of morality but then argued that under certain specified conditions violence as "legitimate defence" was justified.[40]

In early 1980 it was clear from listening to Monseñor Romero's homilies Sunday after Sunday that he was moving toward a position of ultimately supporting the right of the Salvadorean people to insurrection. This was a position the archbishop of Managua, Miguel Obando y Bravo, had taken prior to the final insurrection in Nicaragua in 1979.[41] The reasoning in both cases was that the evil confronting the people was greater than the evil of insurrection and war.

But Rivera backed away from that position. There were several reasons for this. First, the Vatican made it clear that it wanted Rivera to heal the breach in the Episcopal Conference (CEDES) that had opened up as a result of Archbishop Romero's vigorous positions. The Vatican also kept Rivera on a short leash by refusing to name him archbishop. (In contrast, Poland had a new archbishop within three weeks after the death of Cardinal Wiszinski.) Third, Rivera was a close personal friend of José Napoleón Duarte. Fourth, Rivera knew what had happened to Monseñor Romero.

There was another factor as well. The public pronouncements of Rivera between April 1980 and January 1982 regarding the character of a resolution of the political conflict in El Salvador mirrored the fortunes of the left. That is, during the periods when the FDR/FMLN showed political and military strength, Rivera's pronouncements favored its inclusion in a political settlement. When the fortunes of the left waned, however, Rivera demonstrated a reluctance to argue that it should be included. Rivera admitted as much in a March 1981 interview. "These are very different moments," he said, referring to a period just weeks after the January 1981 offensive, when many thought the FMLN was finished. "In those years that Romero lived, there was hope in the liberation movements. There was a great sympathy on the part of the people. Later these movements were losing credibility and popular support. I don't think they lost it only because of government repression. They've lost this support because the people saw that they tended toward the conquest of power for its own sake and not toward satisfying the hopes of the people."[42]

Six months later, however, after the FMLN had initiated, without fanfare as in January, an extremely successful offensive, and after the Franco-Mexican recognition of the FDR/FMLN as a "representative political force," Rivera parted company with his fellow bishops, saying that "we have spoken of the necessity for dialogue and for seeking a political solution to our situation"; therefore if the Franco-Mexican declaration "signifies the call to dialogue in order to find a peaceful solution, we would not find it inconvenient to accept."[43] The other bishops issued a statement in CEDES's name that condemned the "intervention" of Mexico and France and added that the FDR/FMLN was not representative of the people, "has lost its popular support and is dedicated to sowing terror among the population."[44]

By November 1981 Rivera was saying that elections for a constituent assembly, scheduled for March 1982, could not be carried out without "previous understanding among the parties most involved in the conflict."[45] Less than three weeks later he declared that the elections "are not the solution to the Salvadorean conflict."[46]

All of this is not to say that Rivera ignored the excesses of the government. On the contrary. Following the general strike in August 1980 he sharply criticized the regime for militarizing all public services and demanded that the junta lift the five-month-old state of siege. In an April 6, 1981, letter to Vice-President George Bush, Rivera bluntly told him that "the 'right' in our country believes you do support them. . . . The provision of military assistance at this moment in our country's history simply strengthens the military and increases the attitude of 'triumphalism' among them."[47]

Following the murder of four U.S. missionaries in December, Rivera joined the priests and nuns of the archdiocese in the most strongly worded condemnation of official repression to be expressed by the church since the assassination of Romero. "We hold the Security Forces and ultra-rightist groups responsible for the persecution against the Church and specifically for the assassination of priests and lay pastoral workers. We therefore also hold responsible the Government Junta, which given its ultimate authority over the Armed Forces is responsible for actions by members of the military."[48]

Meanwhile, the formation of the National Conference of the Popular Church (CONIP), an organization of priests, nuns, and Christian communities, caused further tensions as CONIP took the position that the FDR/FMLN constituted, for political purposes, the "authentic representatives" of the Salvadorean people.[49] A number of priests—perhaps as many as seven—joined the FMLN as combatants. At least one was a commander. Other priests and nuns, however, while eschewing arms, moved to controlled zones to continue their pastoral work or began working for the FDR/FMLN outside the country.

DERECHIZACIÓN CONTINUES

A second attempt at a coup from the right occurred on April 30. This time, however, Colonel Majano did not sit back. He ordered the arrest of Roberto D'Aubuisson and dispatched a contingent from San Carlos to bring him in. D'Aubuisson was caught with a suitcase full of incriminating documents and was promptly arraigned. Three days later a judge, under pressure from Defense Minister García, found there was insufficient evidence to hold D'Aubuisson for trial, and he was released. Majano was then stripped of his position as commander-in-chief of the armed forces, a position that was given to Colonel Gutierrez. Majano threatened to resign from the junta but was talked out of it by a worried U.S. Ambassador Robert White.†

Majano's position was further eroded when the Order of the Month, which lists all new assignments, transfers, and so on, was issued September 1. All the *majanistas* were transferred to insignificant posts within El Salvador or out of the country. The new commanding officers of the garrisons in San Salvador were García's men. In November Majano narrowly escaped death when a bomb intended to explode beneath his car missed. The December 1 Order of the Month named the colonel as ambassador to Spain. He refused to go and went into hiding. He charged in several clandestine press conferences that the government was supporting the death squads. García issued a warrant for Majano's arrest, but he was not found until February 20, 1981. The army threatened to court-martial Majano for refusing an order. After a month in custody, with the regime under extreme pressure from Panama's General Omar Torrijos, Majano was put on a plane and shipped into exile.[50]

With the removal of Majano in December a shuffling of positions occurred in the Salvadorean government. Duarte became president of the junta and Gutierrez was named vice-president. José Antonio Morales Erlich became head of the agrarian reform program. Nothing more was heard from Dr. Avalos. This shake-up was heralded in Washington as a sign that the influence of Duarte was increasing, with the implication that civilian control over the military was emerging. Nothing could have been further from the truth. As the progressive isolation of Majano during 1980 demonstrated, the real power in El Salvador lay in the hands of the minister of defense and his minions, of whom Duarte became one. Kowtowing to García was the only way to survive in El Salvador by the end of 1980.

Beyond this, Duarte was useful. His continuing presence in the government assured the continuing support of the Christian Democrat–led Venezuelan and Costa Rican governments. With Duarte gone, the Salvadorean regime would have had almost no support outside the United States, Guatemala, and Honduras. The United States needed Duarte to justify its policy of support for a "moderate, reformist, civilian/military government." An unanswered question was what would happen when Duarte, Morales, and the other Christian Democrats in the government were no longer considered indispensable.

The Derechización of U.S. Policy

With the arrival of Robert White in early March 1980 as the new U.S. ambassador the one thing that could be said about U.S. policy was that it was being forcefully enunciated for a change. White managed to alienate both the left and the right within three weeks of assuming the post. He infuriated the CRM by announcing (erroneously) the death of BPR Secretary-General Juan Chacón and then accusing the OPs of causing the violence at Archbishop Romero's funeral. He enraged members of the business community by telling them they shared responsibility for the current situation in El Salvador through their greed and lack of a social conscience.[51] White insisted that El Salvador had a "revolutionary government" that had implemented the "most sweeping land reform since the Mexican Revolution." He defended Duarte as a champion of democracy. Most of all, he insisted that the Christian Democratic–military junta headed a "moderate, reformist" government caught between two warring extremes of left and right. White was the first U.S. official to openly acknowledge that some elements of the security forces were implicated in much of the violence. He maintained that the greatest danger in El Salvador came not from the left but from the right.

White sailed along until Ronald Reagan was elected president in November 1980. Shortly thereafter a "hit list" of ambassadors to be replaced, prepared by a Reagan transition team, surfaced. White's name was on it. He stormed into Washington charging that his authority had been undermined. He was correct, but his outburst did little to endear him to the emerging powers in the Reagan foreign policy camp.

With the assassination of three U.S. nuns and a lay missioner on December 2 the Carter administration had suspended the balance of the $5.7 million in "nonlethal" military aid that had been reprogrammed by Congress shortly after Archbishop Romero's death.[52] The administration had also suspended economic assistance but reinstated it two weeks later because the Salvadorean economy was on the verge of collapse. The suspension of military aid remained in effect until three days before Carter left office – and a week after the beginning of the FMLN's general offensive. "We must support the Salvadorean government in its struggle against left-wing terrorism supported covertly with arms, ammunition, training, and political and military advice by Cuba and other Communist nations," the State Department announced.[53]

White at first supported and then opposed the resumption of military assistance in general and the authorization of an additional $5 million in lethal weapons in particular. Furthermore, he went public with his opposition. As a result, White was recalled to Washington ten days after the inauguration and told he would not be returning to El Salvador.[54] When he declined to accept a make-work job in the foreign service inspector general's office he was automatically retired ninety days later.

The White Paper. A month after Ronald Reagan occupied the White House the Department of State issued a document, "Communist Interference in El Salvador." The "White Paper" claimed, in the words of its anonymous authors, that it offered "definitive evidence of the clandestine military support given by the Soviet Union, Cuba, and their Communist allies to Marxist-Leninist guerrillas now fighting to overthrow the established government of El Salvador" and that "the insurgency in El Salvador has been progressively transformed into another case of indirect armed aggression against a small Third World country by Communist powers acting through Cuba."[55] With the report and supporting documents in hand, U.S. officials launched a diplomatic blitz throughout Western Europe and Latin America in an effort to win support for the Reagan administration view that the Soviet Union was extending its tentacles into Central America. A media assault was simultaneously launched in the United States. El Salvador, the message went, was the place the United States would make its stand against International Communism.

Unfortunately for the Reagan administration there were three problems. The first was that the "supporting documents" did not support the extravagant claims of arms shipments to the FMLN or of Soviet or Cuban control of the revolutionary forces.[56] The second problem was that most U.S. allies did not believe the "evidence," did not view El Salvador in such cataclysmic terms, or had been supporting the FDR/FMLN and would continue to do so. Countries like Austria, Mexico, and Ecuador fell into the latter category; Brazil, West Germany, and Sweden into one of the first two. The third problem was that both the Senate Committee on Foreign Relations and the House Committee on Foreign Affairs refused to be railroaded. On April 29 the latter voted twenty-six to seven to bar all military assistance and advisers unless President Reagan certified that the Salvadorean government had met six conditions designed to prevent human rights violations and promote democratic reforms.[57] Shortly thereafter the Senate committee passed a similar measure.

Undeterred, the administration announced days after the White Paper's release new increases in military assistance totaling $25 million. By late March fifty-six military advisers and instructors, including twelve Green Berets, were in El Salvador "to train Salvadorean personnel in communications, intelligence, logistics, and in other professional skills designed to improve their capabilities to interdict infiltration and to respond to terrorist attacks."[58]

Sources within the administration privately revealed that the game plan was to "win a military victory in sixty to ninety days."† By July 1981, however, the new U.S. ambassador, Deane Hinton, was sending cables to the Department of State acknowledging that the Salvadorean military was not winning the war; that there was a military stand-off; that the armed forces were losing. He began asking for massive amounts of additional military assistance and an increased number of military advisers.†

The political game plan called for electing, on March 28, 1982, a constituent assembly that would write yet another constitution. Duarte in El Salvador and U.S. State Department spokespeople maintained that the Salvadorean government was merely "transitional" and that free elections would set the country once and for all on the road to democracy.

The Resurgence of the FMLN

In late July, after six months of analysis, self-criticism, and reorganization, the FMLN, unannounced, launched its second offensive of the year. The offensive went virtually unnoticed for the first few days, until August 10, when the insurgents captured Perquín Morazán, 203 kilometers northeast of San Salvador, after a two-day battle. The FMLN destroyed the National Guard garrison, killed at least six guardsmen, and for the first time, took prisoners of war. Sixteen guardsmen and twenty-four members of paramilitary units were captured. The FMLN announced that the Geneva Conventions regarding prisoners of war would be observed and asked the International Red Cross to assume responsibility for them. Twelve of the prisoners declined the offer and joined the insurgents. The FMLN also acquired at least thirty-six rifles, one M-60 machine gun, and 8,000 rounds of ammunition.[59]

Then, at 8:12 P.M. on August 12, a subsergeant in the National Police, Jacinto Mendoza, drove his car into the parking lot of the police headquarters in downtown San Salvador. He parked beside an armored personnel carrier, got out, removed a package that he shoved under the personnel carrier, and walked away. At 8:15 P.M. two explosions destroyed the car, the personnel carrier, and an unknown number of other vehicles. It also ignited the gasoline tanks of the filling station in the parking lot. The police acknowledged eleven injuries, but sealed off the area and refused to give out any additional information. The FMLN, however, was less reticent. It announced that Mendoza had been one of its own since 1975, having joined the guerrillas after his brother was killed by the police.[60]

During the fall the FMLN maintained pressure on the army throughout the eastern two-thirds of El Salvador. By blowing up telephone centrals, electric towers, and bridges, especially the strategic Puente de Oro on October 15, the FMLN progressively isolated this region, making it increasingly accessible only by air. Meanwhile, between May and December the army averaged three offensives per month against the insurgents, sending in from 1,500 to 4,500 troops in each drive. Guazapa Volcano, 26 kilometers north of San Salvador between Suchitoto and Aguilares, had been an FMLN stronghold since 1980. The FMLN had several base camps around the skirts of the volcano and had dug an elaborate tunnel system into the mountain. The Salvadorean army attempted eight times during this period to dislodge the guerrillas from Guazapa. Once the army overran one of the several camps. As of mid-April 1982 the FMLN was still entrenched on Guazapa, which covers an area of about 600 square kilometers, as well as in every one of the other eight zones under FMLN control. The army also carried out five offensives each in Chalatenango and Morazán; four against the Chinchontepec (San Vicente) Volcano, 57 kilometers east of the capital; and three in the Cerros de San Pedro. Said a senior FMLN official in January 1982, "The army has not achieved even one objective."† All the independent information out of El Salvador tended to confirm his assessment.

The army's biggest offensive against the insurgents, as of early

Photo 6.3 The FMLN has a policy of evacuating civilians from battle zones. In the December 1981 offensive in Morazán, the FMLN evacuated approximately 3,000 civilians from the area. Credit: COLCOM-HM

1982, came in early December in Morazán. There 4,500 troops, acting in coordination with the Honduran army, attempted to trap the FMLN between Salvadorean government forces, which moved in from the south, and Honduran troops, massed just across the frontier to prevent either guerrillas or civilians from seeking refuge in that neighboring country. A major government objective was to destroy the FMLN's Radio Venceremos, which had been broadcasting by shortwave uninterrupted for almost a year. This "hammer and anvil" strategy, which had been employed in the other border departments of Cabañas and Chalatenango, failed once again. The government announced on December 14 that Radio Venceremos had been destroyed; but the station once again began regular broadcasts on December 26.[61]

There was a darker side to the Morazán offensive, however. The FMLN, with advance notice of the offensive, began advising the people to move out and seek safety in the other areas. The FMLN itself moved several thousand people out of a large area that had long been under its control. None of these people died during the offensive. But many people did not heed the warnings. There were two reasons for this. One was that these people, who were largely Protestant, were not organized politically and believed that, because they were Protestant, the army would not bother them. The second reason was that the army had swept through the area in an October offensive and had not harmed them. But in December, the people guessed wrong. As the army moved through El Mozote, Cerro Pando, and Poza Honda, three small towns in central Morazán, it destroyed everything in sight. In El Mozote alone, 480 bodies were found after the army left.[62]

Then, in January 1982 the FMLN, again without fanfare, opened up yet another offensive. On the night of January 27 FMLN commandos slipped into the Ilopango air force base, on the eastern side of San Salvador, and placed forty-two packages of dynamite under the airplanes and helicopters. The explosions destroyed 70 percent of the air force, including helicopters, bombers, and troop transport carriers. Minister of Defense García, who had recently promoted himself to general, along with Gutierrez and Vides Casanova, arrived to personally direct the firefighters—which prompted Radio Venceremos to begin calling him "the firechief."

The insurgents immediately followed the attack on Ilopango with an attack in broad daylight on Usulután, El Salvador's fourth largest city. For almost a week the FMLN dug into the periphery of the city, forcing the army and security forces to seek refuge in the Usulután army garrison. During this period the revolutionary forces sealed off all points of entry to the city and extended their control over the Litoral and Pan-American highways. They opened up attacks in San Miguel and laid siege to San Francisco Gotera, the capital of Morazán. They also, increasingly, brought the war to San Salvador.[63] Meanwhile, for the first time in a year, FMLN forces began staging large attacks in the western third of the country. This zone had been relatively quiet since the January 1980 offensive for two reasons. First, it is the area where the 1932 peasant uprising occurred; as a result it has always had a strong concentration of security forces who worked hand in glove with the oligarchy. This enabled the government to maintain tighter control over the peasantry and made it more difficult for the FMLN to operate. Second, the entire FMLN General Command for that zone had been killed during the offensive, along with several dozen combatants. Thus it took the FMLN a year to rebuild the command structure and its units in the area.[64]

A senior FMLN official said in February 1982 that "after the December 1981 offensive in Morazán, the FMLN moved into a military campaign" and as of the moment was "still on the offensive." It appeared to be the intention of the FMLN to continue the offensive indefinitely. When Rubén Zamora was asked in an interview with journalists what the FDR/FMLN's response was to the March elections, he said,

> The war has its own logic. The elections are a thing apart and have nothing to do with the prosecution of the war. The FDR/FMLN is not fighting to support or impede the March elections, but to secure the liberation of our people.[65]

A New Political Offensive

While preparations were under way for the March elections, the Reagan administration attempted to recover the public relations initiative. Having failed to convince many people with the White Paper in February 1981, it tried in October with José Napoleón Duarte in person. In bringing Duarte to the United States for thirteen days, the administration had two objectives. One was to try to influence both U.S. public opinion and the Congress. The other was to send a message to the extreme-right elements in El Salvador that the United States was firmly behind Duarte. The visit, however, was a disaster for the governments of both countries. In the midst of Duarte's visit and in the face of public opposition by both Duarte and Reagan, the Senate approved, in two successive votes, the imposition of conditions for U.S. aid to El Salvador. President Reagan would have to certify, in writing, within 30 days, that the Salvadorean government was making progress toward controlling the security forces "in order to end the torture and indiscriminate assassinations against Salvadorean citizens."[66] When the president did certify in a letter in late January 1982 that the government had indeed made progress, the public outcry was immediate. The *New York Times*, for example, was moved to comment that "the Reagan Administration has clearly failed to restrain the murderous armies. Congress tried to give it new leverage by tying American aid to respect for human rights. The leverage has not been well used."[67]

But the administration appeared determined that a military victory over the insurgents should be achieved. It studiously ignored repeated declarations by the FDR/FMLN that the revolutionary forces were prepared to negotiate. One of the two most significant efforts in this regard was the speech by the Nicaraguan leader Daniel Ortega Saavedra before the United Nations on October 10. In it he read a "Proposal for Peace" prepared by the DRU and the FDR Executive Committee, which called for negotiations with an open agenda and without prior conditions. Said a senior FMLN official of the U.N. speech, "That was the moment to be absolutely serious about negotiations."† The other appeal was directed to President Reagan in a January 18, 1982, letter, signed by all five members of the General Command.

Instead of responding politically to these initiatives, the administration sponsored two new regional alliances that were obviously designed to encircle El Salvador and to isolate Nicaragua. The first was the "Triangle of the North," a military alliance among Guatemala, Honduras, and El Salvador. The second, created in January 1982, was the Central American Democratic Community, composed of Costa Rica, Honduras and El Salvador. A senior U.S. diplomat in the region asserted in the fall of 1981 that "the administration has said that we will not permit the insurrection to win in El Salvador. I think that the administration will do everything to prevent it, but I also think actions will be taken before it gets to that point." The diplomat insisted that the Reagan administration knows that "change is inevitable and necessary," but that "insurrectionists' methods are not the way to go. We don't want another communist government in the region."†

Elections

The way to go, the Carter and the Reagan administrations decided, was elections that would legitimate junta president Duarte and the Christian Democratic party. The plan was to elect a constituent assembly in 1982 and a president and national assembly in 1983. By the fall of 1981 seven parties had registered for the elections. All were located on the right of the political spectrum. Three of them, with virtually no political base, could be easily dismissed.[68] The other parties began slugging it out in the fall through the Central Elections Council that had been created to conduct the proceedings.

The four major parties in the campaign were the following:

1. *The Christian Democrats.* José Napoleón Duarte, still the titular head of the PDC, completed the *derechización* of the party by purging its list of potential candidates of all members known to have sympathies for the MPSC.

2. *The Nationalist Republican Alliance.* ARENA was formed in November 1981 by Roberto D'Aubuisson, who, among other things, had been responsible for S-2, the National Guard's intelligence service between 1970 and 1979. With the coup he was cashiered from the guard but left the country only briefly. ARENA's campaign slogan was "El Salvador will be the tomb of the reds," and D'Aubuisson promised that if his party won, the FMLN would be annihilated within three months.

3. *The Party of National Conciliation.* The PCN had the distinction

in Salvadorean history of being the only official party to survive a coup d'etat. In the past, Pro-Patria had gone out of existence with Martínez; the PRUD, created in 1949, had vanished with the 1960 coup. But the PCN lived on, yet another reflection of the extent to which the old order had not changed at all. The PCN was initially considered the PDC's strongest competition, although that began to change with the murder of the PCN secretary general, Rodríguez González, on January 27, 1982, in front of the PCN headquarters. No one even accused the FMLN of carrying out the assassination, and it was widely assumed that it had been done on orders from someone further to the right.

4. *The Democratic Action Party.* The AD was also created in November 1981 and quickly became known in San Salvador as the "Rotary Club" of the oligarchy's lawyers. Its political base was broader than that, including owners of medium-size farms and businesses, middle-level business managers, and professionals. It was ideologically closer to the Christian Democrats than were any of the other parties, in that it supported the first phase of the agrarian reform. On the other hand, the AD opposed further nationalization of land and advocated the return of the banks and external commerce to their original owners—the oligarchy. The AD was also noted for trying to cloak its rightist leanings in technocratic language.

The MNR (social democrats) and the MPSC were invited to leave the FDR and participate in the elections. They were told that they could campaign by long distance (for example, by television from Guatemala) if they were afraid to campaign openly inside El Salvador. Apart from the fact that this represented a transparent attempt to split the FDR, MNR and MPSC members had good reason to be afraid; sixty Christian Democratic mayors and other officials had been assassinated by death squads in the previous year. If the government could not guarantee the safety of members of the party in government, it could hardly offer guarantees to parties in open opposition. In September 1981 the president of the CCE, Jorge Bustamante, publicly recognized the FDR as a representative political force but refused to do the same for the FMLN, arguing that it was a group that sowed terror, hatred, and violence.[69]

The FMLN took the position that (1) it was not opposed to elections; (2) elections must be in the context of a total political solution to the crisis in El Salvador; (3) the setting in El Salvador made it impossible for elections to be held; and (4) with the election as projected, the war would continue to worsen. The General Command's January

18, 1982, letter to President Reagan stated:

> To pretend that the solution to the Salvadorean conflict is the March elections, is . . . outside reality. How can a democratic process be guaranteed in the context of indiscriminate repression? If you can decide the destiny of the United States, it is because you hold your office by virtue of free elections. North Americans went to elections in peace and this is the indisputable condition in order for a people to elect their governors.[70]

In late fall, Duarte narrowly survived a maneuver by Robert D'Aubuisson to demand his resignation from the junta. That came in a meeting of all the political parties with the CCE to discuss the election law. Duarte was saved by the vote of General José Alberto Medrano, who had long been known for his idiosyncrasies. On several other occasions D'Aubuisson moved to have the PDC representatives expelled from the CCE but failed in those efforts as well. By February 1982 ARENA was gaining strength on the extreme right, and there was speculation that the extreme-right parties would win a majority in the assembly. There was little question that if that happened, Duarte would be invited to leave the junta. In an interview with journalist Yan Verbeek in late January, Juan Vicente Maldonado, the president of ANEP, said that his organization would exert pressure to form a junta composed solely of military officers and businessmen. In Maldonado's view, that was the only way to end the war and rescue the economy from complete disaster.[71]

The Results. The U.S. Embassy was initially euphoric about the outcome of the elections (see Table 6.1). Voter turnout, as reported by the government, was high (75 percent), and the Christian Democrats gained a plurality.[72] But with only 35 percent of the vote, Duarte's party was unable to contemplate forming a controlling majority in the assembly with the party closest to it ideologically, Democratic Action. Furthermore, ARENA, with one-quarter of the votes, immediately began pressing, as it had long promised, to throw the Christian Democrats out. Within two days all the extreme-right parties, including Democratic Action, announced that they had signed an agreement to form a majority coalition in the assembly.

Meanwhile, however, the U.S. government began putting extreme pressure on these parties to keep Duarte and the Christian Democrats in the government. D'Aubuisson, who had promised during the campaign to try Duarte and company for treason, said no. But

TABLE 6.1

ELECTION RETURNS, 1982

Political Parties	Votes	Percentage of total ballots cast	Assembly seats
Christian Democratic party	526,890	35.5	24
Nationalist Republican Alliance	383,632	25.8	19
National Conciliation party	248,964	16.8	14
Democratic Action	98,364	6.6	2
Popular Salvadorean party	38,504	2.6	1
Popular Orientation party	12,151	0.8	0
Null ballots	127,442	8.6	
Blank ballots	49,238	3.3	

Total ballots cast: 1,485,185

SOURCE: Foreign Broadcast Information Service (FBIS), April 2, 1982.

continuing pressure from Ambassador Deane R. Hinton and later a congressional delegation produced a tentative willingness to compromise. Other parties, such as the PCN and AD, began suggesting that some Christian Democrats could remain but that Duarte would have to go. As Duarte and his party had formed the centerpiece of U.S. policy toward El Salvador since January 1980, the desperation of the Reagan administration to keep them in the government was easy to understand. But D'Aubuisson and company took the position that they had won the right to form a government and that if the United States did not approve and decided to cut off aid, El Salvador had other supporters, such as Argentina, to turn to.

The Meaning of the Elections. The Reagan administration sponsored the elections in El Salvador in order to legitimate Duarte and the Christian Democrats. The elections had the effect, however, of legitimating Roberto D'Aubuisson and his fascist ARENA party. Within days, the initial euphoria over the large number of voters gave way to a desperate search for a means of keeping Duarte and the PDC in the government. This maneuvering served to confirm once again that the cornerstone of U.S. policy since January 1980 had been the continued presence of the Christian Democrats in the government. It also confirmed that the rationale that undergirded the policy lay in shambles.

The triumph of the extreme right emboldened the army's most repressive officers and gave new hope to the Salvadorean oligarchy that the old order could once again be restored. This was not a vain hope, as all the parties to the right of the PDC had pledged to denationalize the banks and external commerce and to either halt the partially implemented agrarian reform or reverse it completely. Meanwhile, the possibility of Duarte's departure and the emergence of an extremist government increased the likelihood that President Reagan would find it difficult to secure congressional approval for his proposed $225 million in additional economic and military assistance to the regime. The shape of the final coalition remained unclear two weeks after the election, but it was obvious that although El Salvador might eventually have what U.S. officials had often called a "legitimate government," it would hardly be "moderate and reformist." Indeed, the election simply conferred a new legitimacy on the system of military dictatorship that had been in place for half a century.

Legitimating the status quo ante had two effects. It completely polarized the political situation in El Salvador. No longer could there be even a pretense of a "moderate center." And it demonstrated the futility of conducting an exercise in procedural democracy when there was no hope that that outcome could materially affect the root causes of the crisis.

INTERVENTION OR NEGOTIATION?

The electoral results and the growing strength of the FMLN by the spring of 1982 meant that the Reagan administration was faced with a rapidly diminishing array of policy options. There was a growing internal debate between, on the one hand, a coalition of liberal Democrats and the bulk of U.S. public opinion, which was increasingly edgy, and, on the other, the new cold warriors, who insisted that El Salvador was no more than a pawn in the East-West struggle. Most of the options were not mutually exclusive, but all carried price tags. The price of increased military involvement, up to and including the dispatch of troops, was growing opposition, both domestically and internationally. Direct intervention by U.S. troops would also cost the Reagan administration its domestic program. That was not an inconsiderable cost, given that Ronald Reagan came to the White House with one overriding objective: to reshape U.S. society and turn it away from the direction established in the New Deal years of Franklin D. Roosevelt. Direct intervention would rapidly put thousands of people in the streets of the United States and other cities around the world. It would outrage U.S. allies in Europe and elsewhere. Intervention by U.S. or foreign troops would also instantly regionalize the war. The revolutionary struggle in Guatemala was sufficiently advanced that an intervention in El Salvador would necessarily spill over to its northern neighbor and into Honduras as well.

On the other hand, maintaining the current level of advisers and aid or the cessation of that assistance would guarantee the military victory of the FMLN in either the very short or medium term; that is, within a few months. Negotiations, could they be initiated, would also carry a price; as the object of negotiations would be to find a means of incorporating the FDR/FMLN into a new government, the United States would have to learn how to live with yet another leftist government in Central America, with the prospect of a third (Guatemala) looming on the horizon. The electoral result virtually precluded this option, at least in the short term.

The question was whether or not the administration would be prepared to pay the cost of preventing an FMLN victory in one form or another. To put the dilemma for the administration another way, what would the U.S. government choose to do when the Salvadorean army began to collapse?

In April 1982 that was the key question. The Salvadorean armed forces had 17,500 men and no possibility of increasing in size. There were no reserves, no pool of potential recruits. The smooth success of the attack on Ilopango suggested inside assistance, and indeed thirty people were arrested on suspicion of having collaborated with the insurgents. An army that was carrying out systematic massacres like that which occurred in Morazán in December 1981 was an army in trouble. The contradictions within the officer corps were increasing. The proof of that lay in rebellions inside the army garrisons of San Carlos and in San Miguel and Santa Ana in late January and early February 1982. All were put down, but they portended more problems in the future. A lieutenant killed five of his soldiers in early February in Usulután when they refused to fire on civilians.

Ultimately, the choice for the United States would come down to two options: invade or negotiate. It was not clear in April of 1982 which road the Reagan administration would choose.

Prognosis

El Salvador by early 1982 was a living disaster area. Its economy was in shambles; its law was the law of the gun; peace was too often that of the grave. More than 30,000 Salvadoreans had died since October 15, 1979 – the overwhelming majority of them by the guns of the Salvadorean armed forces, provided by the government of the United States. More than 400,000 Salvadoreans were in exile, half of them refugees in other countries of Central America and in Mexico.

The United States had decreed that an indigenous revolutionary movement, created in desperation a dozen years earlier and with roots deep in Salvadorean history, was the puppet of Moscow. Determined not to permit a "second Nicaragua" or a "third Cuba," the Reagan administration – in spite of vehement denials – appeared headed toward a second Vietnam.

Yet, the forces weighing in against the Reagan policy in El Salvador by early 1982 were increasingly strong and vocal. Within the government, the Department of Defense, in particular the Joint Chiefs of Staff, under no circumstances wanted to get involved in another Vietnam-like quagmire. The White House domestic policy staff saw their grand plan for restructuring U.S. society placed in jeopardy by the civil war in El Salvador. The Congress was divided. Republicans in both the House of Representatives and the Senate had been expressing opposition for months. Cracks in the Republican rank and file began to show when Senator Larry Pressler expressed scepticism publicly and noted that his conservative constituents in South Dakota did not want to get involved in another Vietnam.

Public opinion in the United States galvanized in opposition to the Reagan policy. Six weeks after the White Paper was issued in February 1981, 29 percent of the U.S. public told a Gallup poll that they thought the United States should "stay completely out of the situation."[73] A year later that figure had grown to 54 percent.[74] Congressional mail was regularly running ten to one against U.S. policy; at one point in the spring of 1981 a White House press spokesperson admitted that its mail was twenty-five to one against. At the international level, the governments of France and Mexico were the leaders of an increasingly vocal group of U.S. allies that opposed U.S. policy and called for negotiations.

The reaction of the business community in the United States was a big question. There were indications that big business was more and more nervous about the Reagan administration's intentions in Central

America. How much they were saying and how strongly they were saying it to President Reagan was the question. This was critical, because it was only when the U.S. economic elite divided over the war in Vietnam that the United States began to disengage itself from that quagmire.

On the other side, the forces supporting U.S. policy were extremely vocal. Within the government those forces included top Reagan foreign policy appointees and the far right, both inside and outside Congress. At the international level, only the conservative-to-reactionary regimes of the hemisphere, including Guatemala, Honduras, Argentina, Chile, Uruguay, Paraguay, and Bolivia, joined by Great Britain and Israel, gave verbal support to U.S. policy or material support to the Salvadorean government.

On balance, it seemed that when decision-making time came, the preponderance of forces would oppose direct intervention and favor negotiations. Would President Reagan listen? Whatever else one could say about the president, one had to acknowledge that he was a consummate politician. Given that, it seemed likely that political instincts would, in the end, win out over ideological purity. In other words, when the crunch came, the balance of forces seemed to dictate that the direction of U.S. policy would be toward some form of negotiated settlement.

The question that remains, however, is whether there are two parties to conduct negotiations. Roberto D'Aubuisson had pledged during the campaign to exterminate the guerrillas within three months, using all available means, including napalm. The FDR/FMLN, for its part, said that it would not negotiate with the extreme right. At the same time the revolutionary organizations reaffirmed their commitment to the principle of a negotiated settlement with centrist elements in El Salvador but asserted that it was not possible to negotiate with "democratic fascists."[75]

The Repeating Cycle[76]

The triumph of the extreme right in the March elections brought full circle the political cycle that had begun with the October 1979 coup d'etat. Once again the most conservative political forces in El Salvador were openly in control of the country. Once again, as in 1960–1961, the hand of the United States could be seen attempting to guide events. Unlike the countercoup of January 1961, however, in which the objective was to restore the most conservative elements of the military to power, the United States sought in 1982 to preserve the so-called moderate center. The irony was that this time the extreme right beat the United States at its own game by using the sacred rite of elections to restore the status quo ante. Contemplation of Salvadorean history shows the similarity with other, now ancient patterns. The weekly toll of innocent civilians recalls the massacre of 1932 and earlier, less well-remembered punitive campaigns dating back to the sixteenth century. The free-enterprise rhetoric of the various right-wing parties with their new-found legitimacy and their obstreperous campaign against the limited economic and agrarian reforms brings to mind the age-old greed and arrogance of the oligarchy. In the spring of 1982 El Salvador was reliving its own history.

There are only two distinctly new elements on the domestic scene: the role of the church as an agent of social change and the stubborn ability of the revolutionary organizations to survive. Meanwhile, U.S. preoccupation with events in El Salvador is exercising an influence as never before. Previous administrations generally allowed the Salvadoreans to fight out their bloody class struggle in unmarked obscurity. By the 1980s resurgence of the same struggle was imbued with a vast East-West significance. Washington's feverish perceptions of the Salvadorean reality had become as important as that reality itself.

Whatever the U.S. government decides to do, one conclusion can be stated with some certainty: No lasting, viable political solution is possible in El Salvador without the participation of the Democratic Revolutionary Front and the Farabundo Martí Front for National Liberation. The remaining question is how much more blood will be spilled before the government of the United States accepts that basic fact.

April 1982

Notes

CHAPTER 1. THE COUP OF OCTOBER

1. All information on the coup d'etat of October 15, 1979, unless otherwise noted, comes from interviews with eight individuals who had first-hand knowledge of this event, including René and Rodrigo Guerra y Guerra.

2. Alan Riding, "Militants in El Salvador Undeterred by the Death of 22," *New York Times*, May 10, 1979; "Salvador: Murder at the Cathedral," *Newsweek*, May 21, 1979, pp. 47–49; "Salvadoran Police Fire into Crowds; 8 Reported Killed," *Washington Post*, May 9, 1979.

3. For a study of the Nicaraguan National Guard, see Richard Millett, *Guardians of the Dynasty* (Maryknoll, N.Y.: Orbis Books, 1978).

4. The committee was composed of one colonel (Gutierrez), one lieutenant colonel (Guerra), one major, and two captains.

5. René Guerra was one of the best-educated and brightest officers in the Salvadorean army. On one occasion President Romero, on whose staff Guerra reluctantly served for a time, told a mutual friend that he did not know what to do with Guerra because he was "too sharp."

6. While arrests were being made within the barracks, calls occasionally had to be made to San Salvador to confirm that a certain senior officer was a "good guy." Because there was absolutely no communication between the lower-level officers and their superiors, the lieutenant or major with principal responsibility in each barracks had no idea whom the Coordinating Committee had recruited among the senior officers.

7. It would later become known that Gutierrez was in close contact with Colonels José Guillermo García, Nicolás Carranza, and Eduardo Vides Casanova, a fact that would have profound implications for the coup. This contact was not a coincidence, as all of them had worked together from 1974 to 1977 in ANTEL, the government-owned National Telecommunications Company.

8. Maybe. There were, in fact, three coups in the making: one from the extreme right, led by Colonel Ramón Alfredo Alvarengo, a known accomplice of the CIA, who felt President Romero was not tough enough; a palace coup, led by Colonel José Eduardo Iraheta, whose object was to simply get rid of

Romero, the symbol of all the problems the government was having with the United States; and that of the Young Military. Many Salvadoreans with whom I talked felt that the United States was closer to and had more control over the first two than the third. But whatever efforts the United States was making failed as the October 15 Movement grew.

9. Captain Francisco Mena Sandoval was also involved in calling the second meeting and supporting Gutierrez. (There is an unconfirmed story, from a reliable source, that Mena Sandoval was the person who tipped off Gutierrez about the coup plot in August.) In the ensuing months, however, Mena Sandoval became progressively disillusioned. When the Farabundo Martí Front for National Liberation (FMLN) called the general offensive on January 10, 1981, he and another officer, along with eighty of their men, joined the insurgents. See Alberto Pipino, "En cuatro puntos clave de Santa Ana ondea la bandera roja del Frente Farabundo Martí"[In four key points of Santa Ana the red flag of the Farabundo Martí Front waves], *Uno Más Uno* (Mexico City), January 12, 1980, p. 9. Many people in and out of El Salvador have written that the United States was involved in the coup. See, for example, Carolyn Forché, "The Road to Reaction in El Salvador," *Nation*, June 14, 1980, pp. 712–716. Far from providing evidence, however, these individuals have generally asserted what needs to be proven on the implicit and questionable assumption that the *golpistas* could not have succeeded without U.S. assistance. Apart from the fact that this assumption belittles the intelligence and competence of the 15th of October Movement, it gives the U.S. Embassy far more credit than it deserves. I may, at some future date, have to eat my words, but all the evidence is that the U.S. role was one of neutrality.

An unanswered question is whether or not the U.S. Embassy encouraged Gutierrez and García to call the meeting that deposed René Guerra from the junta and installed Gutierrez in his place. Guerra has said that he has no evidence of U.S. involvement in this regard, but that after the coup, in several meetings with U.S. Ambassador Devine, the latter "insisted on supporting García." Interview with René Guerra, June 22, 1981.

On the other hand, it is very likely that the "ANTEL Mafia," as García, Gutierrez, and Carranza were known, had intimate relations with the Central Intelligence Agency (CIA). (It is widely documented in studies of the CIA that "the Company" makes strong efforts to establish ties with the telecommunications system in each country – an obvious objective for any intelligence-gathering organization. See, for example, Philip Agee, *Inside the Company: CIA Diary* [New York: Simon & Schuster, 1975].) Thus it is possible that the second meeting was suggested and/or supported by the CIA out of fear that the Young Officers would go too far in their zeal for reform.

10. Román Mayorga, *La universidad para el cambio social* [The university for social change] (San Salvador: UCA Editores, 1978).

11. Several months later Gutierrez wrote René Guerra out of the history of the coup in an interview with El Salvador's English-language newspaper, the *News-Gazette*. The interviewer, editor Mario Rosenthal, wrote: "It is well-known, and something which has not been denied that the anti–General

Romero coup was organized by Colonel Gutierrez and planned by him and Colonel José Guillermo García and Colonel Carlos E. Vides Casanova, who now heads the National Guard."

Then Rosenthal quoted Gutierrez:

> The planning began a long time ago. We were concerned about the situation. The actual strategy took between four and six months. I was commanding the National Armory at that time and from there I proceeded to take over the First Brigade [San Carlos]. I called Gen. Romero and told him that he had a military uprising on his hands under my command. I advised him since some barracks had not yet made up their minds, the best thing for him to do, to avoid bloodshed, was to leave the country, and I gave him three hours to leave the country. When the time was almost up he called me on the telephone.
>
> He asked me to go to Casa Presidencial to talk things over. He naturally wanted to win me over. I refused. Then I got a call from Colonel Iraheta, who commanded the Air Force, and he said that he would never surrender. That I would have to take him out of his barracks dead.
>
> Gen. Romero spoke to me and sent an emissary to ask me to extend the time limit until 5:00. I accepted this with the condition that the chiefs of the security forces resigned and turned their responsibility over to their subordinates; that Col. Iraheta leave the Air Force base and go to the Casa Presidencial, and that telephone communications, which had been cut by ANTEL [the telephone company] be reconnected. This would be a sign that they were not setting a trap or gaining time for some maneuver. There was no trick; communications were restored immediately.
>
> Later, at 5:00, Gen. Romero called me again and told me that the airplane had arrived and that he would go to his house to collect his personal effects and would then leave the country. He asked that security for himself and his family be guaranteed and I guaranteed it.

According to Rosenthal, Gutierrez confirmed that the Central American University had nothing to do with the coup. "Some officers had contact with UCA [the Colonel said]. But I told them that we must not speak with anyone outside the army. One of the conditions for being part of the movement was that the officers have no contact with civilians, with priests, with no one who could destroy the movement. Once we had triumphed, naturally, since we wanted a government with broad participation we were in contact with the universities." Rosenthal wrote that Gutierrez was "emphatic" in denying that there had been contacts outside the army before the coup. "I had no contact with Luís de Sebastian, [vice-rector of UCA], [Ignacio] Ellacuría [rector of UCA], nor with Archbishop Romero" (News-Gazette, March 16–22, 1980, pp. 1,2, 10). It is true that Gutierrez had no contact with the universities or the church in the months leading up to the coup, but he did meet with Román Mayorga on October 13, two days before the coup.

12. Interview with René Guerra, June 21, 1981. Guerra also said that García was already calling back some of ex-President Romero's closest aides. René Guerra, García, Gutierrez, and Majano met with Archbishop Romero on October 17. During that meeting Romero accused García of human rights violations in San Vicente during his tenure as commander of the local garrison.

13. "Disappeared" has come to be used as a noun with increasing frequency in Latin America to refer to people who simply vanish without a trace, often while in official custody.

14. See the "Informe de la Comisión Especial Investigadora de Reos y Desaparecidos Políticos" [Report of the Special Investigative Commission on Political Prisoners and Disappeared], *Estudios Centroamericanos (ECA)*, Vol. 35, No. 375-376 (January-February 1980):136–139.

15. Between January 1 and October 15, 1979, 475 people died at the hands of security forces and ORDEN. Between October 15 and November 3, 105 died under similar circumstances. Figures are from the Commission on Human Rights of El Salvador. It should be noted that, according to both human rights and church organizations, 80 percent of the more than 10,000 deaths in the country during 1980 were caused by government forces, ORDEN, or right-wing death squads.

16. El Salvador has had four security forces in addition to the army. They are the National Guard (4,000 men), National Police (2,500), Treasury Police (2,000), and Customs Police (500). According to both the Central Intelligence Agency (CIA) and the Democratic Revolutionary Front, El Salvador's opposition coalition, army strength in 1980 was about 8,000 soldiers and 500 officers.

17. COPEFA's statement appeared in all newspapers in Sal Salvador on January 3, 1980.

18. "Mons. Romero intenta mediar para resolver crisis gubernamental" [Mons. Romero intends to mediate in order to resolve the governmental crisis], *El Independiente*, January 3, 1980. Romero gave an account of this effort in his homily on January 6, 1980. See *Orientación*, January 13, 1980.

19. Accounts of the crisis may be found in *Prensa Gráfica, El Independiente, Diario de Hoy, El Mundo*, and *La Crónica*, January 3-6, 1980. Archbishop Romero, in his homily on January 6, called on Minister of Defense García to resign. García declined, explaining that as a military officer he was under different orders that could be changed only by the military. "Ministro de Defensa explica razones para no renunciar" [Minister of defense explains reasons for not resigning], *El Mundo*, January 10, 1980.

CHAPTER 2. THE ROOTS OF REVOLUTION

1. Melvin Burke, "El sistema de plantación y la proletarización del trabajo agrícola en El Salvador" [The plantation system and the proletarianization of agricultural labor in El Salvador], *Estudios Centroamericanos (ECA)*, Vol. 31,

No. 335-336 (September-October 1976):476-479.

2. Ibid., p. 473.

3. Ibid., p. 479.

4. The limitations of these data are that the three easternmost departments of the country are excluded and that farms of 11-99 hectares are not counted. Yet the data are consistent with other accounts. See, for example, ibid., p. 474; Eduardo Colindres, *Fundamentos económicos de la burguesia salvadoreña* [Economic fundamentals of the Salvadorean bourgeoisie] (San Salvador: UCA Editores, 1977), p. 468; and Alastair White, *El Salvador* (London: Ernest Benn; Boulder, Colo.: Westview Press, 1973), pp. 113-134. At the same time these data have the advantage of being the most recent available, and they are broken down in terms of property owners rather than number of plots. The latter can be somewhat misleading because one proprietor often owns more than one parcel of land. This is particularly true in the case of large landholders.

5. Burke, "El sistema de plantación," pp. 479-481; see also *Development Assistance Program Central America*, Book 2 (Washington, D.C.: Agency for International Development, 1973), Chapter 7, "El Salvador."

6. These data are from the Ministry of Agriculture, San Salvador, 1979; Dirección General de Estadística y Censos, May 1978; United States Agency for International Development, "Agricultural Sector Assessment," August 1977, pp. 19-27; United Nations, *Indicators of Economic and Social Development in Latin America* (New York: U.N. Social and Economic Council [CEPAL], 1976).

7. Santiago Barbarena, *Historia de El Salvador* [History of El Salvador] (San Salvador: n.p., 1914-1917), quoted in Roque Dalton, *El Salvador (Monografía).* [El Salvador (Monograph)] (San Salvador: Editorial Universitario, 1979). Information on the colonial period is also drawn from Colindres, *Fundamentos económicos;* John Baily, et al., *El Salvador de 1840 a 1935* [El Salvador from 1840 to 1935] (San Salvador: UCA Editores, 1978); White, *El Salvador;* and David Browning, *El Salvador: Landscape and Society* (Oxford: Clarendon Press, 1971).

8. Murdo J. MacLeod, *Spanish Central America: A Socioeconomic History 1520-1720* (Berkeley: University of California Press, 1973), p. 49. The concept of a repeating economic cycle is drawn from MacLeod, as is much of the information in this section.

9. Ibid., p. 91.

10. Ibid., pp. 170-173.

11. Ibid., pp. 221-223, 381; Browning, *El Salvador*, pp. 260-261.

12. MacLeod, *Spanish Central America*, p. 385.

13. Blacks have been officially barred from living in El Salvador for many years. Nonetheless, the Black heritage of many Salvadoreans is apparent in a stroll down any city street, especially in the capital. There seems to be no discrimination because of this. By 1980 El Salvador was an almost completely *mestizo* nation and what discrimination existed was much more because of class than because of ethnic background. For example, in conversations with

members of the oligarchy, they regularly disparaged the peasants as having "no culture," and in 1980 a government official associated with the land reform program referred to them as *"los monos"* (monkeys).† The complete syllogism was that therefore, the peasants were incapable of rational political participation.

14. Colindres, *Fundamentos económicos*, p. 24.

15. Liberals and conservatives in Latin America bear little resemblance to liberals and conservatives in the Anglo-American political tradition. Conservatives were aristocrats and monarchists who wished to keep church and state tied closely together and who were dedicated to preserving the church's wealth and privileges. Liberals were profoundly anticlerical and often antireligion. They were inclined to support free trade while conservatives preferred to erect tariff barriers to protect local textile production. Within El Salvador the differences were not so great as in other countries because the church did not have much wealth that could be confiscated. The liberals therefore succeeded in abolishing monastic orders, establishing civil marriage, and taking some initial steps toward removing education from control by the clergy and creating a state education system.

16. White, *El Salvador*, pp. 72–73.

17. Ibid., pp. 72–74; Dalton, *El Salvador*, pp. 71–73.

18. Unlike in Guatemala and other Latin American countries, which attracted large numbers of European immigrants during this period, there were only about twelve families from a half dozen countries who came to El Salvador, became large landowners, and became completely assimilated into the existing elite (White, *El Salvador*, pp. 79, 85).

19. Abelardo Torres, "More from the Land: Agrarian Reform in El Salvador," *Americas*, Vol. 14, No. 8 (1962):6–12.

20. White, *El Salvador*, pp. 86–87; Browning, *El Salvador*, p. 217; Colindres, *Fundamentos económicos*, p. 29.

21. Robert Varney Elam, "Appeal to Arms: The Army and Politics in El Salvador 1931–1964," Ph.D. dissertation, University of New Mexico, 1968, p. 9; Colindres, *Fundamentos económicos*, p. 302; White, *El Salvador*, p. 120.

22. In Spanish the concept of *"illegitimacy"* does not exist; one speaks of *"niños naturales,"* never of *"niños ilegítimos."*

23. Everett Alan Wilson, "The Crisis of National Integration in El Salvador 1919–1935," Ph.D. dissertation, Stanford University, 1968, pp. 32–33.

24. Ibid., p. 47; Browning, *El Salvador*, pp. 229–231.

25. All three banks, several of whose owners were major growers, profited from coffee. For example, the Guirola family, which was – and remained in the late twentieth century – one of the largest landowners in El Salvador, with the Trigueros family controlled one-half the total stock of the Banco Salvadoreño in 1919. In the 1970s these families, plus the Quiñonez, Meza Ayau, Hill, and Regalado Dueñas families, all of whom were major landholders, continued to control this bank. Wilson, "Crisis of National Integration," p. 61; Colindres, *Fundamentos económicos*, pp. 400–424.

26. Belarmino Suarez, *Pláticas populares* [Popular talks] (San Salvador: n.p., 1921), p. 147. (Translations from the Spanish by the author.)

27. Emilio Villacorta, *Por la patria y su gobierno* [For the homeland and its government] (San Salvador: n.p., 1919), pp. 25–29.

28. "El Banco del Pueblo" [The People's Bank], *Patria*, December 22, 1928.

29. Max P. Brannon, *El Salvador: Esquema estadística de la vida nacional* [Statistical outline of national life] (San Salvador: n.p., 1936), pp. 22–24. The amount of land planted in coffee kept growing. In 1950 it was 115,429 hectares, or 75 percent of the total land under cultivation; in 1961, 139,000 hectares, or 87 percent of the total. Colindres, *Fundamentos económicos*, p. 72.

30. "La crisis del maíz" [The maize crisis], *Patria*, January 18, 1929.

31. *Patria*, January 4, 1929.

32. "Sobre la carestía periódica del maíz en El Salvador" [About the periodic scarcity of maize in El Salvador], *Patria*, April 4, 1929, p. 5.

33. Wilson, "Crisis of National Integration," p. 114.

34. "Como anda la justicia en esta San Salvador" [How justice operates in this San Salvador], *Patria*, November 30, 1928.

35. Arthur Ruhl, *The Central Americans* (New York: n.p., 1927), p. 206.

36. Wilson, "Crisis of National Integration," pp. 51–52.

37. Alejandro Bermudez, *Salvador al Vuelo* [El Salvador: An Overview] (San Salvador: n.p., 1917), pp. 171–172, Carlos Urrutia Glamenco, *La Ciudad de San Salvador* [The city of San Salvador] (San Salvador: n.p., 1924), p. 208. Thomas Anderson's assertion in *Matanza* [Massacre] ([Lincoln: University of Nebraska Press, 1971], p. 23) that "the first labor unions got started in 1923" and Alastair White's statement (*El Salvador*, p. 94) that "in 1923 the first permanent trade unions were founded" are incorrect. See also Arístides Augusto Larín, "Historia del movimiento sindical de El Salvador" [History of the union movement in El Salvador], *La Universidad*, Vol. 96, No. 4 (July–August 1971):136–137.

38. Wilson, "Crisis of National Integration," p. 53.

39. Ibid., p. 54; Arias Gomez, "Augustín Farabundo Martí (Esbozo Biográfico)" [Augustín Farabundo Martí (biographical sketch)], *La Universidad*, Vol. 96, No. 4 (July–August 1971), p. 211; interview, Miguel Mármol, October 1981.

40. Wilson, "Crisis of National Integration," p. 97.

41. It is doubtful that any sort of conspiracy existed between the oligarchy and the military in carrying out the coup. Rather, it is more likely that the young officers were aware of the oligarchy's sentiments and shared their fear of anything that smacked of "socialism"—which was how some of Araujo's policies were perceived. For a fuller discussion of this point, see Anderson, *Matanza*, pp. 55–56.

42. For the fullest treatment of this wrenching event see Anderson, *Matanza*. Much of the material in this section is drawn from this book as well as Arias Gomez, "Farabundo Martí," and Wilson, "Crisis of National Integration," pp. 218–232. Anderson's book is an excellent historical study of an extremely complex period, but I believe he erred in his basic premise, as reflected in the subtitle "El Salvador's Communist Revolt of 1932." Obviously

Martí and certain other leaders of the insurrection were members of the PCS and the movement had received limited funds and a great deal of printed material from New York. But Anderson himself made a strong case that beyond the leadership few communists were involved in the uprising. The vast majority of the Indians and *campesinos* who participated in the revolt were acting not out of ideological commitment but out of genuine social, political, and (especially) economic grievances. As the revolt a hundred years earlier had demonstrated, the *campesinos* did not need a sophisticated political ideology to help them understand exploitation or poverty.

43. February 1931 letter to the Uruguayan poet Blanca Luz Brum, quoted in Anderson, *Matanza*, pp. 38–39.

44. Ibid., pp. 40–41; Arias Gomez, "Farabundo Martí," pp. 201–202.

45. Anderson, *Matanza*, pp. 93–97.

46. Arias Gomez, "Farabundo Martí," p. 230.

CHAPTER 3. THE STATE: A DIVISION OF LABOR 1932-1979

1. Rubén Zamora has suggested that *"compadrazgo"* may be likened to Mayor Richard Daley's Chicago political machine with its system of rewards for the faithful and exclusion (or worse) for the rebellious.

2. Interview with Rubén Zamora, August 1980, Mexico City.

3. Elam, "Appeal to Arms," p. 55, passim; Wilson, "Crisis of National Integration," p. 262. For latter-day methods, see Ana Guadalupe Martinez, *Las carceles clandestinas de El Salvador: Libertad por el secuestro de un oligarca* [The clandestine prisons of El Salvador: Liberty for the kidnapping of an oligarch] (n.p., 1978).

4. Elam, "Appeal to Arms," pp. 46–47. It should be noted, however, that individuals from the economic elite continued to serve in various government posts, in particular agriculture and economy. Indeed, this was inevitable, as the oligarchy contained most of the educated elite of the country. In addition, coffee was not even under the Ministry of Agriculture (White, *El Salvador*, p. 103).

5. Wilson, "Crisis of National Integration," p. 258.

6. White, *El Salvador*, p. 114, n. 51. Miguel Mármol confirmed this in an interview, October 1981. Mármol, who was born in 1905, was one of the founding members of the Communist Party of El Salvador and the only leader to survive the 1932 massacre. He, along with several other leaders, was shot by a firing squad. Their bodies were dumped in a ravine outside San Salvador, but Mármol, who had received relatively minor wounds, was spirited away by comrades who came looking for the bodies in order to bury them. In 1981 and 1982 Mármol, then 76, ever the revolutionary, was touring many countries on behalf of the Farabundo Martí Front for National Liberation.

7. Indeed, this is what ultimately happened. Prior to the arrival in the 1950s of the ADOC shoe factory, which was jointly owned by six oligarchic

families, there were several thousand shoemakers and assistants in El Salvador. ADOC created several hundred industrial jobs, but it put most of the shoemakers out of business. The families are Palomo, Simán, Dueñas, Hill, Alvarez Meza, and Meza Ayau (Colindres, *Fundamentos económicos*, pp. 131, 400–428).

8. Wilson, "Crisis of National Integration," pp. 250–254; Elam, "Appeal to Arms," pp. 56–57.

9. Wilson, "Crisis of National Integration," p. 255–256.

10. *Anuario Estadístico de El Salvador, 1935* [Statistical annual of El Salvador, 1935] (San Salvador: Imprenta Nacional, 1936), p. 58; Elam, "Appeal to Arms," p. 54.

11. Elam, "Appeal to Arms," p. 48.

12. Ibid., pp. 48–49; *New York Times*, June 15, 1940.

13. Elam, "Appeal to Arms," p. 48.

14. Ibid., p. 50. Martínez's flirtation with the Axis, the presence of Axis officers in El Salvador during the 1930s, and the training of Salvadorean officers in Germany and Italy raise the question of the extent to which fascist ideology had permeated the army officer corps and continued to be an element long after Martínez switched sides.

15. Ibid., pp. 50–51.

16. Ibid., pp. 60–67; White, *El Salvador*, p. 103.

17. Elam, "Appeal to Arms," p. 68.

18. Martínez was encouraged in his course of action by, among others, the U.S. ambassador to El Salvador (White, *El Salvador*, p. 103). Common wisdom has it that the rebels of April 2 assumed that diplomats in San Salvador, including the U.S. ambassador, would encourage Martínez to depart quietly. But David Luna, who has written a detailed account of the revolt, related that after U.S. Ambassador Walter Thurston exchanged coded cables with Washington early in the morning of April 3 from a telegraph office controlled by the *golpistas*, his attitude toward them chilled. Later that day, as the revolt collapsed, one of its leaders sought asylum in the U.S. Embassy—and was turned away by the ambassador. Colonel Tito Tomás Calvo was subsequently shot during Martínez's "reign of terror" ["Analisis de una dictadura fascista latinoamericana, Maximiliano Hernandez Martínez 1931–44" (Analysis of a Latin American fascist dictatorship, Maximiliano Hernandez Martínez 1931–44), *La Universidad*, Vol. 94, No. 5 (September-October 1969):106–126].

19. Elam, "Appeal to Arms," pp. 74–75.

20. For a first-hand account of this period, with a focus on political mobilization, see Francisco Morán, *Las jornadas cívicas de abril y mayo de 1944* [The civil marches of April and May 1944] (San Salvador: Editorial Universitaria, 1979).

21. Elam, "Appeal to Arms," pp. 95–105. A final attempt by the liberals to seize power took the form of an invasion planned by several hundred army officers and armed civilians and launched from Guatemala through Ahuachapán. Supposedly, the commander of the army barracks in

Ahuachapán was one of the conspirators, but when they arrived the commander engaged the rebels in battle and defeated them (White, *El Salvador*, p. 104). Interestingly, one of the leaders of the Jornada de Ahuachapán, as the invasion came to be known, was Julio Adalberto Rivera, who would lead a counter-coup from the right in 1961 (to be discussed later in this chapter).

22. Henry C. Wallich and John N. Adler, *Public Finance in a Developing Country, El Salvador—A Case Study* (Cambridge, Mass.: Harvard University Press, 1951); Elam, "Appeal to Arms," p. 122.

23. "Sin comentarios a la conciencia ciudadana" [To the citizen's conscience, without commentary], circulated by the Social Democratic party in September 1948; "El Ministerio de Defensa: ¿Comite político?" [The ministry of Defense: Political committee?], unsigned and circulated October 1948; "Hoja suelta de la Directiva Suprema del Partido Democrática Republicano" [Leaflet from the Supreme Directorate of the Republican Democratic party], circulated November 1948; Elam, "Appeal to Arms," p. 127.

24. Elam, "Appeal to Arms," pp. 129–130.

25. Ibid., pp. 131–132; White, *El Salvador*, p. 105.

26. Elam, "Appeal to Arms," p. 144.

27. Ibid., p. 147.

28. José María Lemus, *Entrevistas y opiniones* [Interviews and opinions] (San Salvador: Imprenta Nacional, 1955), p. 29.

29. White, *El Salvador*, p. 105.

30. Production increased from 57.7 million short tons in 1945 to 65.9 million in 1951, a 14 percent increase. The value of the total crop, however, increased 406 percent, from $18.7 million to $76 million. Héctor Dada Hirezi, *La economia de El Salvador y la integración centroamericana 1945–1960* [The economy of El Salvador and Central American integration 1945–1960] (San Salvador: UCA Editores, 1978), p. 29.

31. *NACLA Report on the Americas*, Vol. 14, No. 2 (March-April 1980):7; Browning, *El Salvador*, pp. 230–231.

32. Browning, *El Salvador*, pp. 232, 234–235, 240. By the mid-1970s cotton production had rebounded to levels exceeding those of 1960.

33. Ibid., pp. 240–241. Another cost, for which there is apparently no scientific data available, is the effect on the health of the Salvadoreans who live in the cotton-growing area. On January 22, 1980, I was present at the largest demonstration in Salvadorean history (see Chapter 5). I was in a section of the demonstration with people from Usulután, a department in the southeastern part of the country in the heart of the cotton-growing region. Low-flying planes passed directly overhead and sprayed the crowd. The spray did not affect me in any way, but dozens of people around me were affected severely. Their eyes turned red and began tearing heavily, a reaction that lasted for at least thirty minutes. Clearly, these people had developed an allergy to the material with which we had been sprayed. They had undoubtedly been caught many times before in the spray from a crop-dusting plane, although perhaps not deliberately as on this day.

34. White, *El Salvador*, p. 131.

35. William Durham, *Scarcity and Survival in Central America: Ecological Origins of the Soccer War* (Stanford, Calif.: Stanford University Press, 1979), p. 36. In the years between 1970 and 1974 coffee's contribution to the total value of Salvadorean exports averaged 42.5 percent, that of cotton, 10.3 percent, and that of sugar cane, 6 percent. These three crops together, then, accounted for 58.8 percent of El Salvador's total exports – twenty-five years after the great commitment to industrialization (Inter-American Development Bank, *Economic and Social Progress in Latin America,* 1979 Report [Washington, D.C.: IDB, 1980], p. 452).

36. Elam, "Appeal to Arms," p. 149.

37. Thorsten V. Kalijarvi, *Central America: Land of Lords and Lizards* (Princeton, N.J.: Van Nostrand Co., 1962), p. 84. Kalijarvi served as U.S. ambassador in El Salvador during the last years of the Eisenhower administration. He left El Salvador in late 1960.

38. Ibid., pp. 151–153.

39. *New York Times,* December 19, 1959.

40. The repression and the methods of torture are recounted in painful detail by Salvador Cayetano Carpio, *Secuestro y capucha en un país del "mundo libre"* [Kidnapping and hooding in a country of the "free world"] (San José, Costa Rica: EDUCA, 1979). This book was originally written in 1954.

41. Elam, "Appeal to Arms," pp. 153–155.

42. Stephen Webre, *José Napoleón Duarte and the Christian Democratic Party in Salvadoran Politics 1960–1972* (Baton Rouge: Louisiana State University Press, 1979), p. 28.

43. Ibid., pp. 28–29.

44. U.S., Congress, House, "Human Rights in Nicaragua, Guatemala and El Salvador: Implications for U.S. Policy," Hearings before the Subcommittee on International Organizations of the Committee on International Relations, 94th Congress, 2nd session, June 8 and 9, 1976, p. 47.

45. Elam, "Appeal to Arms," pp. 156–157; Webre, *Duarte,* p. 35.

46. Webre, *Duarte,* p. 37.

47. U.S., Congress, House, "Human Rights," pp. 47–48.

48. Elam, "Appeal to Arms," pp. 162–163. Alastair White (*El Salvador,* p. 193) reported that Rivera and other leaders of the 1961 coup approached the recently formed Christian Democratic party (PDC) and offered to make it the official party. The price was that a military officer would continue to occupy the presidency. According to Rubén Zamora, who was a member of the PDC until his resignation in March 1980, there was a conservative faction within the party that wanted to accept Rivera's offer. When the PDC decided not to, that faction left and formed the PCN (interview, June 28, 1981).

49. Webre, *Duarte,* p. 47. AGEUS said it was "the only candidate worthy to compete against officialism" (AGEUS, "El pueblo tiene una cita" [The people have an appointment], *Diario de Hoy* [San Salvador], April 16, 1962).

50. The information in this section, unless otherwise noted, is derived from four interviews with members of the PDC and with Dr. Edgar Jiménez Cabrera of the Ibero-American University in Mexico City.

51. See Webre, *Duarte*, pp. 49–68, for a full discussion of the ideology and progress of the Salvadorean PDC.

52. First Meeting of the Committee of Economic Cooperation of the Central American Isthmus (CCE), Resolution 2, August 27, 1952, cited in Dada Hirezi, *La economia de El Salvador*, p. 88, 96; *NACLA Report*, p. 11.

53. "Central American Patterns of Regional Economic Integration," *Bank of London and South America Review*, June 1979, pp. 340–342; *NACLA Report*, p. 11.

54. Carmen Sermeño Zelidon, "Las nuevas formas de dominación política en El Salvador 1972–1977" [The new forms of political domination in El Salvador], Thesis for the *Licenciatura* in sociology, University of Costa Rica, 1979, p. 65.

55. Francisco Chavarría Kleinhenm, "Fundamentos Políticos, económicos, y sociales de la evolución y desarrollo del movimiento sindical en El Salvador" [Political, economic, and social fundamentals of the evolution and development of the union movement in El Salvador], Thesis for the *Licenciatura* in sociology, University of Costa Rica, 1977, p. 451.

56. Rafael Menjivar, *Crisis del desarrollismo: Caso El Salvador* [The crisis of development: The case of El Salvador] (San José, Costa Rica: EDUCA, 1977), pp. 70–71.

57. White, *El Salvador*, pp. 227–228, 249.

58. Burke, "El sistema de plantación," p. 476. A fraction of this increase was due to the influx of thousands of Salvadoreans expelled from Honduras in 1969. If one assumes an average rural family of six children, then by 1975 more than 1 million people, or 25 percent of the population, had no means of gainful employment or regular income.

59. For a fuller discussion of the war and its causes, see Durham, *Scarcity and Survival in Central America*. See also White, *El Salvador*, pp. 183–190; and Webre, *Duarte*, pp. 106–121.

60. Frank T. Bachmura, "Toward Economic Reconciliation in Central America," *World Affairs* Vol. 133, No. 4 (1971):286.

61. Webre, *Duarte*, pp. 93, 97.

62. *Diario de Hoy*, January 15, 1967.

63. In fact the Catholic Church had moved away from that position during the Second Vatican Council, which ended in 1965, but the Salvadorean bishops had not yet gotten the message. As we will see in the next chapter, however, things began to change soon thereafter.

64. White, *El Salvador*, p. 203. Immediately after the election the PAR was outlawed.

65. Webre, *Duarte*, p. 106.

66. Ibid., p. 119.

67. Casa Presidencial Press Release, in *Prensa Gráfica*, August 15, 1969.

68. Alvarez was the first and only member of the Salvadorean oligarchy to give his *hacienda* to the *colonos* who worked it as a cooperative—an act that earned him the eternal contempt of his fellow oligarchs. He began the process in 1972, but the workers did not receive title for five years because there was

no Salvadorean law under which such transfer could occur. Meanwhile, Alvarez simply drew a salary as the farm administrator and devoted those years to training the workers to run the farm themselves.

69. "Resoluciones y recomendaciones del Primer Congreso Nacional de Reforma Agraria" [Resolutions and recommendations of the First National Congress of Agrarian Reform], *Economía Salvadoreña*, Vol. 28 (1969):109.

70. Ibid., p. 114.

71. Webre, *Duarte*, p. 105.

72. Webre erred when he wrote that the UDN was a "quasi-personalist vehicle organized and led by former vice-president Francisco Roberto Lima" (p. 136).

73. "Manifiesto al pueblo salvadoreño" [Public declaration to the Salvadorean people], *Prensa Gráfica*, September 3, 1971, quoted (in translation) in Webre, *Duarte*, p. 158.

74. "Programa de gobierno de UNO" (UNO's program of government], *Prensa Gráfica*, January 17, 1972.

75. Estimates on membership in ORDEN ranged from 50,000 to 150,000. The most commonly accepted figure in El Salvador was about 100,000 card-carrying members. It is important to understand, however, that most ORDEN members belonged as a means of self-protection. If they were stopped for any reason by the security forces and could produce an ORDEN card, they were assured that nothing would happen to them. Without the card, they were at the mercy of their captors. My informants in El Salvador estimated that only 5 to 10 percent of ORDEN members actually functioned as vigilantes and *orejas* (informers) for the government.

76. UNO figures were: Duarte, 326,968; Molina, 317,535. The CCE figures on February 21 were Molina, 314,748; Duarte, 292,621.

77. Webre, *Duarte*, p. 177.

78. The U.S. Embassy and government remained silent throughout this period. All the 1960s rhetoric about finding a democratic "third way" between military dictatorship and communism were lost in the realpolitik world of Richard Nixon and Henry Kissinger. The U.S. ambassador, Henry Catto, never breathed a public word of condemnation of the blatant electoral manipulations. The United States did provide Molina, who was visiting Taiwan at the time, with a military aircraft to fly him directly back to El Salvador.

79. Webre, *Duarte*, p. 181.

80. This assertion was indirectly confirmed when I asked then junta member Colonel Adolfo Majano about corruption in the officer corps. Majano, who was widely regarded on all sides as incorruptible, said he did not have any first-hand knowledge. He may well have been telling the truth, because he had always been a barracks officer.

81. White, *El Salvador*, p. 95.

82. Latin American universities, unless they are private, by tradition are completely autonomous institutions, although much of their funding comes from government sources. This was true of the UES.

83. Webre, *Duarte*, p. 185; Mario Flores Macal, "Historia de la Univer-

sidad El Salvador" [History of the University of El Salvador], Vol. 2 (1976):13–35.

84. The actual amount expended was kept secret, but the figure of $30 million is generally agreed upon by knowledgeable sources. The pageant itself was strictly for the elite. Tickets were sold by invitation only, and only the oligarchy and government officials were permitted to purchase them.

85. The director of the National Guard, Colonel Mario Rosales, had been ordered not to let the march leave the UES campus. But Rosales had his own game plan. According to sources within the officer corps, he was trying to set up the conditions for a coup from the right, so he let the demonstrators leave the university and set up a trap.†

86. U.S., Congress, House, "Human Rights," pp. 40–41; Webre, *Duarte*, p. 188.

87. FALANGE is the acronym for Anticommunist Wars of Elimination Liberation Armed Forces. Other groups were the White Warriors Union; the White Hand; the Anticommunist Front of Central American Liberation (FALCA), which made its appearance claiming responsibility for bombing on at least two different occasions the radio transmitter of the archdiocesan radio station in San Salvador in 1980; and the Death Squad.

88. These sources are both civilian and military. The first official admission of record that security forces moonlight as death squads came from junta President José Napoleón Duarte following the murder by security forces of four U.S. missionaries in December 1980.

89. *Pronunciamientos de ANEP*, Nos. 1, 2, and 3, reprinted in *Estudios Centroamericanos* (*ECA*), Vol. 31, No. 335-336 (September-October 1976):611–615. This issue of *ECA* is devoted to the question of agrarian transformation.

90. Webre, *Duarte*, pp. 193–195; interview with Luís de Sebastian, December 13, 1979.

91. Sermeño Zelidon, "Nuevas formas," p. 87; Colindres, *Fundamentos económicos*, p. 140; White, *El Salvador*, p. 173.

92. Sermeño Zelidon, "Nuevas formas," p. 74. A good example of this phenomenon was the shoemaking industry.

93. Ibid., p. 69. See also Oscar Cuellar Zaavedra, "Las tendencias de cambio en Centroamerica y el caso de El Salvador: El período 1960–1975" [Tendencies for change in Central America and the case of El Salvador: The period 1960-1975], UCA, 1977 (mimeo), pp. 17, 22–23.

94. Webre, *Duarte*, p. 197.

95. *Central American Report* (Guatemala City), March 7, 1977; Webre, *Duarte*, pp. 197–198.

CHAPTER 4. THE CHURCH

1. This account is taken from interviews with Arturo Rivera Damas, Ricardo Urioste, and José Alas. For an extended discussion of the Agrarian

Reform Congress, see Webre, *Duarte*, pp. 126–130. Webre erred when he said, "The abduction of a young priest in San Salvador during the congress may have been entirely unrelated to this issue [of the Church's support for agrarian reform]." On the contrary, Alas's abduction was directly related to the church's position and to the fact that Alas presented it.

2. The social doctrine of the church is dated generally from Pope Leo XIII's encyclical, *Rerum Novarum*, in 1891. In it he recognized exploitation of workers by callous employers through unrestrained competition, and while he rejected socialism, he criticized capitalism. *Quadragesimo Anno*, issued by Pope Pius XI in 1930, reiterated the themes of *Rerum Novarum* in a new social situation; it was more critical of the right of private property and distinguished between "communism," which it rejected, and "mitigated socialism," which, Pius affirmed, had some affinity with Christian principles. Pius also asserted that sin is collectivized in modern life, an idea that prefigured the contemporary notion of "institutionalized sin." In *Mater et Magistra*, John XXIII brought a global perspective, announced the need for economic assistance to the Third World to help surmount inequality, and reminded the well-nourished to provide the malnourished without "imperialistic aggrandizement."

3. Penny Lernoux, *Cry of the People* (New York: Doubleday, 1980), pp. 36–41.

4. *The Church in the Present Day Transformation of Latin America in the Light of the Council* (Washington, D.C.: U.S. Catholic Conference, 1970), pp. 80–82.

5. Michael Dodson has discussed the concept of a prophetic church at length in "Prophetic Politics and Political Theory," *Polity*, Vol. 12, No. 3 (Spring 1980):388–408. T. S. Montgomery reviewed contemporary ferment in Latin American Protestantism in "Latin American Evangelicals: Oaxtepec and Beyond," in Daniel Levine, ed., *Churches and Politics in Latin America* (Beverly Hills, Calif.: Sage Publications, 1980), pp. 87–107.

6. Thomas Quigley of the U.S. National Catholic Conference's Office of Justice and Peace coined this phrase.

7. The four were the bishops of Santa Ana (Marco René Revelo), San Vicente (Pedro Aparicio), and San Miguel (José Eduardo Alvarez); and the president of the Episcopal Conference, Freddy Delgado. The previous bishop of Santa Ana, Benjamin Barrera, was also among this group. He retired in early 1981.

8. Interview, December 14, 1979.

9. This phrase came out of the Third Conference of Latin American Bishops (CELAM III), which met in Puebla, Mexico, in January 1979. In El Salvador it appears on posters with pictures of the six priests who were assassinated between March 1977 and August 1979.

10. This chapter deals only with the Catholic Church because, with only one exception, the Protestant churches in El Salvador have historically been either politically conservative or simply apolitical. One Baptist church, the Iglesia Emanuel in San Salvador, went through a process similar to that

described in this chapter with the development of Christian Base Communities. This one church has produced at least a half dozen leaders of the revolutionary organizations, the best known of whom was Augusto Cotto, its minister for several years. At the time of his death in an accidental plane crash off the coast of Panama in September 1980, Cotto was one of the top twenty leaders of the National Resistance.

On the other side, an alliance of sorts was struck between the Salvadorean government and several Protestant leaders (most of whom were from the United States). In August 1980, for example, photos appeared in the newspapers of San Salvador showing two visiting U.S. ministers holding hands with the members of the junta. The caption said that they were "praying for justice and peace in El Salvador."

In the countryside, the National Guard found yet another means of intimidating the peasantry. A refugee from the Department of Cabañas told me in Nicaragua in February 1980 that the commander of the local garrison went around to all the Catholics in her village, most of whom were members of CEBs, and told them that the "true Christians" were going to the Protestant church and that anyone who went to the Catholic church was a "communist" or a "subversive."

11. As a result, much of the discussion in this chapter about the "church" is about the archdiocese.

12. Interview, Arturo Rivera Damas, January 25, 1980, Santiago de María, Usulután.

13. *Rutilio Grande: Martir de la evangelización rural en El Salvador* [Rutilio Grande: Martyr of rural evangelization in El Salvador] (San Salvador: UCA Editores, 1978), p. 38.

14. By 1981 that ratio had leapt to about 1 : 17,000, after the assassination of a dozen priests and the exile or expulsion of another sixty.

15. Interview, Mexico City, February 7, 1981.

16. Interview, Maryknoll, N.Y., February 22, 1981.

17. One priest took responsibility for the CEBs in the city while the others worked in the countryside, but they were all assisted by twenty "collaborators," who were Jesuit, university, and seminary students.

18. *Rutilio Grande*, pp. 68–75. Other indicators of success were that in the first nine months there were 700 baptisms, each after approximately four preparatory sessions; the Men's Association of the Holy Sacrament developed, with more than 300 members; novenas were celebrated for the feast days of the patron saints of Aguilares and El Paisnal, the other major town in the parish, and audiovisual presentations of the Word of God were given in the various neighborhoods; and Holy Week was celebrated in eight different locations in the parish (*Rutilio Grande*, p. 72). These details were important because they reveal the extent of the emphasis on religious education and training and on the sacraments.

19. See also, for example, "The Rich Man and Lazarus" (Luke 16:19–31), "The Last Judgment" (Matt. 25:31–46), and "The Rich Fool" (Luke 12:13–21).

20. *Conciencia mágica* is a state of mind that attributes to human events a "superior power that dominates them from outside and to which it is

necessary to submit docilely. This type of consciousness is dominated by fatalism" (*Rutilio Grande*, p. 72).

21. Ibid., pp. 83–85.

22. *Grupos fantasmas* are phantom organizations created by various individuals on the political right that take responsibility for paid political advertisements, flyers, and the like and that attack proposed reforms or individuals that their sponsors consider "subversive" or "communist."

23. This and the quotations in the remainder of the paragraph are from Lernoux, *Cry of the People*, p. 68. Aparicio, in the late 1970s, became more concerned with the threat of International Communism than with the problems of poverty and injustice in his diocese. Owner of a large *hacienda*, a gift from President Molina, Aparicio's sympathies tended more and more toward his fellow proprietors. On at least three occasions he suspended a diocesan priest, Father David Rodriguez, who was trying to carry out pastoral work similar to that of Rutilio Grande. Suspended in the fall of 1979, Rodriguez was forbidden to say mass or conduct courses in his own parishes; further, Aparicio threatened to suspend any priest who invited Rodriguez into his parish. As a bishop's authority extends only to the boundaries of his diocese, Rodriguez at the invitation of Archbishop Romero simply spent a great deal of time in the archdiocese doing all the things he was forbidden to do in San Vicente. But he continued to live in his parish, to be near his people, commuting into San Salvador when necessary. Rodriguez, by 1979, was one of many priests on right-wing death lists.

24. White, *El Salvador*, pp. 238–239.

25. See *Estudios Centroamericanos (ECA)*, Vol. 31, No. 335-336 (September-October 1976). The entire issue is devoted to a political and economic analysis of the proposed reform and includes various manifestos of interested groups, from ANEP, political parties, and the Popular Organizations.

26. Ibid., Vol. 31, No. 337 (November 1976):637–643. The title is a play on words. The Spanish equivalent of "Aye, aye sir" is "A sus ordenes, mi capitan"—idiomatically, "At your service, my captain."

27. Lernoux, *Cry of the People*, pp. 73–76; *Rutilio Grande*, pp. 106–118. In a homily a month earlier, Grande anticipated his own martyrdom: "In Christianity it is necessary to be willing to give one's life in service for a just order, to save the rest, for the values of the Gospel" ("Homilia de Apopa," February 13, 1977).

The campaign against the church included widespread attacks in the newspapers. Between November 29, 1976, and May 31, 1977, for example, sixty-three *campos pagados* appeared in Salvadorean newspapers. In the same period, there were thirty-two editorials against the church, and only two in favor. In May 1977 alone, there appeared a series of fourteen articles under the same name. See *Persecución de la iglesia en El Salvador* [Persecution of the church in El Salvador] (San Salvador: Secretariado Social Interdiocesano, 1977), passim. A similar, although slightly less intense, campaign ensued in December 1979 (ibid., pp. 19–20).

28. Interview, December 14, 1979.

29. Philip Land, "Military Aid to El Salvador," *America*, March 22, 1980, p. 245.

30. See any homily reprinted (in part before December 16, 1979, and in full thereafter) in *Orientación*, the archdiocesan newspaper.

31. Lernoux, *Cry of the People*, p. 79. It should also be added that right-wing terrorist groups always took responsibility for these attacks. When the transmitter was blown up in January 1980, the archdiocese asked other stations in San Salvador to broadcast the mass, but all declined. Then a 50,000-watt station in Costa Rica volunteered air time, and the homily was transmitted live via telephone every Sunday morning for several weeks. Subsequently, it was reported that the Costa Rican station had been bombed for its efforts.

32. Personal statements from Sister Nicolasa Ramírez Contreras, San Salvador, January 17, 1980; *Orientación*, July 27, 1980, p. 7.

33. Jack Anderson, "Of Arabs, Weapons, and Peanuts," *Washington Post*, July 10, 1980, p. D.C.9. I learned through other sources that the documents that came into Anderson's possession were found in a suitcase of Roberto D'Aubuisson at the time he was arrested for attempting a right-wing coup in early May 1980.

When Colonel Adolfo Majano was sent into exile in March 1980 (see Chapter 6) he took with him documents implicating members of the Salvadorean Army High Command in the assassination of Romero. Majano gave copies of these documents to the State Department, but the first mention of these from any U.S. official came when former ambassador Robert White testified before the U.S. Senate during the spring of 1980. This new information was almost totally ignored in the U.S. press.

34. All information in this section, unless otherwise noted, comes from interviews with José Inocencio Alas in April and July 1980 in Washington, D.C.

35. *Persecución de la iglesia*, p. 20. José Alas and his brother Higinio would be slandered, threatened, and forced into exile three years later during the right-wing campaign against all activist priests. In May 1977 Monseñor Chávez would go to Suchitoto the day after the Alas brothers departed to prevent a massacre by the government's security forces, as had happened in Aguilares following the assassination of Rutilio Grande. Chávez reasoned (correctly) that the government would not chance injuring or killing the recently retired archbishop.

CHAPTER 5. THE REVOLUTIONARIES

1. "Declaración del CC del PCS en ocasión del 50 aniversario del levantamiento armado de 1932" [Declaration of the Central Committee of the Salvadorean Communist Party on the 50th anniversary of the 1932 armed uprising], El Salvador, January 1982.

2. Carpio, *Secuestro y capucha*.

3. Mario Menéndez, "Salvador Cayetano Carpio: Top Leader of the

Farabundo Martí FPL" (written for *Prensa Latina*), February 1980 (mimeo).

4. "Declaración del CC."

5. Menéndez, "Salvador Cayetano Carpio."

6. This intransigence cost them dearly during the January 1981 offensive.

7. Augusto Cotto, one of the top twenty leaders of the RN until his death in September 1980, confirmed in an interview in August 1980 that this work had been going on. Cotto said Alas did not know the leftists were working with the *campesinos*. The following month I asked Alas if he had known, and he said that he had not, until that moment.

8. For a discussion of ORDEN, see Chapter 4.

9. About 60 percent of the UCS was in the first group, 40 percent in the second.†

10. Democratic centralism is the procedural principle of binding all members of a political party or organization to a decision that has been approved by the majority. The procedure assumes that until the vote is taken all opinions may be freely expressed and debated; once the majority has spoken, however, all members of the party are expected to adhere to that decision, whether or not they agree.

11. "Comunicado de las Fuerzas Armadas de la Resistencia Nacional (FARN)" [Communique of the FARN], September 15, 1980, in *ECA* Vol. 35, No. 383 (September 1980):921–922.

12. This information comes from interviews I conducted with several dozen refugees on March 15, 1980, at the Arzobispado. The people were not only from the archdiocese of San Salvador but from the diocese of San Vicente as well. As time passed, they began coming in from as far away as Morazán and San Miguel.

13. This information is from three Christian Democrats present at the convention.

14. Adolfo Gilly, "Experiencias y conquistas de una huelga límite" [Experiences and conquests of a limited strike], *Uno más Uno*, August 21, 1980.

15. "Entrevista con el Comandante Fermán Cienfuegos" [Interview with Commander Fermán Cienfuegos], *Pensamiento Revolucionario* [Revolutionary thought] (Centro de Documentación e Información C.D.I. of the FMLN), No. 11 (1981):11. Cienfuegos was the RN commander on the General Command.

16. "En los Cerros de San Pedro el FMLN construye el poder popular" [In los Cerros de San Pedro the FMLN constructs popular power], *Venceremos*, Vol. 1, No. 2 (January 1982):8. *Venceremos* is the official newspaper of the FMLN.

17. Press Release, SALPRESS, Mexico City, January 12, 1981.

18. "Entrevista con Cienfuegos," p. 10; Joaquin Villalobos, "Acerca de la situación militar en El Salvador" [About the military situation in El Salvador] (n.p.: July 1981), passim. Villalobos was the ERP commander on the General Command.

19. "Entrevista con Cienfuegos," p. 10.

20. Cynthia Arnson, "Background Information on El Salvador and U.S. Military Assistance to Central America," Update #4, Institute for Policy

Studies, Washington, D.C., April 1981 (mimeo).

21. Alex Drehsler, "Revolution or Death!" *San Diego Union*, March 1, 1981. Journalist Drehsler accompanied a contingent of eighty-five guerrillas in an attack on the village of San Antonio de la Cruz, Chalatenango, on the night of February 19–20, 1981. There were, according to the FMLN, between fifty and seventy soldiers in the hamlet. The battle began at 11:30 P.M. and lasted four hours. When it was over there were eighteen dead soldiers, five prisoners of war, and one wounded guerrilla. A similar ratio is reflected in many reports of similar attacks by guerrillas throughout the country.

22. Reports from various journalists who have been in FMLN-controlled areas tend to confirm this.

23. Miguel Angel Guardado Rivas, "Así fue la voladura del Puente de Oro" [That's how the Puente de Oro was blown up], *Barricada* (Managua), November 23, 1981.

24. The FSLN also had Costa Rica to flee into; the FMLN was surrounded by hostile forces in Honduras and Guatemala. See Thomas W. Walker, *Nicaragua: The Land of Sandino* (Boulder, Colo.: Westview Press, 1981).

25. The soldiers told him they would spare him if he gave them $200. He offered them a cow; they took it and let him live. My informant said the army returned the next day and a man who had come back was killed. At the time of this interview the woman was in a refugee camp in Chinandega, Nicaragua. She said she and her family had been members of a CEB for two years. One son was a member of the FMLN, but she, eight other children, and her husband had fled to Nicaragua on December 28, 1980.

26. Martell, born in 1955, was a member of the FDR Executive Committee from its inception. During the 1970s he was secretary general of Christian Democratic Youth for the Department of Santa Ana and a member of the departmental directorate. He, along with other Christian Democrats, resigned from the party in March 1980. At the time Martell was secretary general of the Santa Ana departmental directorate, as well as a member of the PDC national Executive Committee, among other party posts.

On November 27, 1980, security forces surrounded a Catholic school in which the FDR Executive Committee was to hold a press conference. Men in civilian clothes entered the school and forced the six committee members who had already arrived to go with them. Hours later the bodies of the six, including FDR President Enrique Alvarez Córdova, BPR Secretary General Juan Chacón, and UDN Secretary General Manuel Franco, were found along roads near San Salvador. At a press conference commemorating the first anniversary of the assassinations, Martell related that he had avoided being a seventh victim by sheer luck; he was late, and as he approached the school he could see the troops. So he immediately went to a safe house where he remained for some time.

A growing number of journalistic reports from early 1981 and 1982 served to confirm Martell's analysis. See, for example, Alex Drehsler, "Guerrillas Use Guns to Forge Marxist Society," *San Diego Union*, March 2, 1981;

Bob Rivard, "A Journey into the 'Liberated Zone,'" *Dallas Times Herald*, January 18, 1982; Raymond Bonner, "With Salvador's Rebels in Combat Zone," *New York Times*, January 26, 1982, and "In a Salvador Classroom, Rebels Study Marx," *New York Times*, January 28, 1982; John Dinges, "Salvadorean Rebels Hold Base," *Washington Post*, January 22, 1982.

27. In my interviews with Salvadorean refugees who were fleeing government repression following promulgation of the agrarian reform in March 1980 and with refugees in Mexico and Nicaragua in August 1980 and January–February 1981, every single one supported the FDR/FMLN. Many other investigators have had the same experience. Alex Drehsler related in a conversation an identical experience in the refugee camps of Honduras; U.S. Representatives Barbara Mikulski and Gerry Studds reported the same following their trip to Central America. See Barbara Mikulski, "An American Tragedy," *Baltimore Sun*, February 24, 1981.

On the other side, peasants know who their enemies are. *Campesinos* have reported armed men in civilian dress coming into their villages, indiscriminately or selectively killing people, all the while screaming that they are from the BPR or the FPL. But, the people say subsequently, "That's crazy, the Bloc (BPR) doesn't act like that." See T. S. Montgomery, "The Refugees from El Salvador," *Florida Times-Union*, February 23, 1981; and letter from the Christian community of Villa Dolores, Cabañas ("A la conciencia de todas las personas de buena voluntad" [To the conscience of all people of good will]), *CRIE* (Centro Regional de Información Ecuménica), No. 52 (June 9, 1980):10–11.

28. "Entrevista con Cienfuegos," p. 11.

29. First quotation from author's interview, February 20, 1982; the second from an interview conducted by the Agencia Periodística de Información Alternativa (Press Agency for Alternative Information–APIA), February 12, 1982.

30. Drehsler, "Revolution or Death."

31. "Plataforma Programatica del Gobierno Democrático Revolucionario" [Programmatic Platform of the Democratic Revolutionary Government], *Diario de Hoy*, February 28, 1980.

32. "Avanza la guerra popular revolucionario y se agrava la crisis de poder de la dictadura" [The popular revolutionary war advances and the crisis of power of the dictatorship is aggravated], Declaration of the FMLN General Command, *Boletin de Prensa* [Press bulletin] No. 38, August 12, 1981.

33. Drehsler, "Guerrillas Use Guns."

34. "Cartilla de alfabetización revolucionaria" [Workbook of revolutionary literacy] (El Salvador: Colectivo de Comunicación Humberto Mendoza [Communcation Collective–COLCOM-HM], n.d.). "Cuaderno de orientaciones para la alfabetización revolucionaria" [Teacher's guide for revolutionary literacy] (El Salvador: COLCOM-HM, n.d.). By late 1981, these two books were being used in literacy classes in the zones under FMLN control.

35. Drehsler, "Guerrillas Use Guns."

36. "En los Cerros de San Pedro."

37. Interview, February 1982.
38. Drehsler, "Guerrillas Use Guns."
39. Interview, February 11, 1982.
40. Interview with Norma Guevara and Marisol Galindo, Managua, Nicaragua, February 1, 1981.
41. Interview, February 11, 1982.
42. Interview, January 22, 1982.
43. Interview, February 11, 1982.
44. Interview, January 18, 1982. Although Zamora did not say so, Nicaragua offered an example of what he was talking about. The opposition daily *La Prensa* often reflected more closely the line of the U.S. State Department than the interests of the Nicaraguan people; a U.S. Embassy official described an opposition labor union as "our union" in an interview; there were close ties between the U.S. Embassy in Managua and the archbishop of Managua, Monseñor Miguel Obando y Bravo, who was an increasingly hostile opponent of the revolutionary government. These observations are based on more than seven months of residence in Nicaragua in 1981–1982 and numerous interviews.
45. Interview, February 11, 1982.
46. Interview, October 22, 1981.

CHAPTER 6. DESCENT INTO ANARCHY 1980–1982

1. The original letters, with signatures, were shown to me in mid-March by an officer who had been closely connected with the impeachment effort. He allowed me to hand-copy the letter.
2. Interview, Héctor Dada Hirezi, Cuernavaca, Mexico, March 22, 1980.
3. "Morales Erlich y Dada Hirezi candidatos a junta" [Morales Erlich and Dada Hirezi candidates for junta], *Prensa Gráfica*, January 7, 1980.
4. Shirley Christian, "Final Members Prove Snag for New Salvadorean Junta," *Miami Herald*, January 10, 1980.
5. García had the power had he been willing to use it. He also had the authority, as all directors and senior officers of all the security forces were army officers and therefore subject to the minister of defense.
   This account was given to me by an individual present at that meeting.
6. "LP-28 Tómanse PDC" [LP-28 occupies PDC], *El Mundo*, January 29, 1980.
7. An anonymous, detailed account by one of the LP-28 members who escaped appears in *Pensamiento Revolucionario*, No. 11 (1981):19–21. There are two interesting footnotes to this story. One is that the same officers who had announced their intention of attacking the National University on January 23 were the two officers in charge (officers of the day) the day the PDC headquarters was attacked. A then senior government official insisted in an interview that it could not have been a coincidence.† The second note is that the U.S. chargé d'affaires, James Cheek, was in the Ministry of Defense Com-

munications Center at the time of the attack.†

8. Interview, Héctor Dada Hirezi, Cuernavaca, Mexico, March 22, 1980; interview, Rubén Zamora, Mexico City, August 18, 1980.

9. The measure that Cheek was proposing would be unconstitutional in the United States, for it meant the suspension of habeas corpus.

10. Interview, James Cheek, Washington, D.C., April 29, 1980.

11. Interview, Rubén Zamora, Mexico City, August 18, 1980.

12. Héctor Dada confirmed the intent to carry out a coup in his letter of resignation to the junta, March 3, 1980.

13. D'Aubuisson was one of the seventy officers retired following the October coup. He was merely the point man in both coup attempts. D'Aubuisson became a familiar figure on Salvadorean television during the winter when he made several speeches in which he generally labeled anyone who supported any social or economic change a communist. Among those whom he attacked were Mario Zamora and Archbishop Romero, both of whom were assassinated soon after. D'Aubuisson also accused the political officer of the U.S. Embassy, Joseph Lee, of being the recipient of "all the information" from the BPR. Lee, for his part, had a policy of "talking to everyone," which automatically made him suspect in D'Aubuisson's eyes.

14. Guillermo Manuel Ungo, a member of the first junta, has related that in December 1979 an army colonel said that it would be better to go ahead and kill 100,000 people then; it would prevent having to kill 200,000 later.

The Salvadorean oligarchy was infatuated with what it regarded as Chile's "economic miracle," which was a product of the application of Milton Friedman's "Chicago School" economic theories. An ANEP official gave me a copy of a January 14, 1980, *Time* magazine article, "An Odd Free Market Success," and explained that ANEP would like to replicate the Chilean model in El Salvador. A translation of that article subsequently appeared as a *campo pagado* in San Salvador's major newspapers. See, for example, *Prensa Gráfica*, January 16, 1980.

15. "Dr. Mario Zamora Rivas fue asesinado" [Dr. Mario Zamora Rivas was assassinated], *El Mundo*, February 26, 1980; Aronette Diaz de Zamora, "Testimonio al pueblo" [Testimony to the people], *Prensa Gráfica*, February 26, 1980.

16. Dada was slandered by members of his own party following his resignation. He left immediately for Mexico because of threats against his life. José Napoleón Duarte announced that Dada had resigned for "personal reasons" ("Civilian on Ruling Junta in El Salvador Resigns," *New York Times*, March 6, 1980). The implication of the rumors was that the death of Mario Zamora had caused him to become emotionally unbalanced. The rumors were so vicious that Dada's wife, who had not yet left the country, prepared a statement for the newspapers. When none of them would accept it for publication, *Orientación* printed it, along with Dada's letter of resignation, in the March 16, 1980, issue. Archbishop Romero also read Dada's letter during his homily on March 9.

17. The reason given for this was that the Young Military knew of links

between Duarte and Minister of Defense García.†

18. "Carta de Renuncia al Partido Democrática Cristiana" [Letter of resignation to the Christian Democratic party], March 10, 1980 (mimeo). One of the signatories was Roberto Lara Velado, who had been the party's chief theoretician from its inception. They would be joined by at least two dozen other Christian Democrats in the following weeks. Subsequently, several other Christian Democratic ministers resigned their posts and left the country. All but two of them joined the MPSC. Meanwhile, many other Christian Democratic officials at the local and national levels remained in their positions and in the party but secretly joined the MPSC. In August 1981 José Napoleón Duarte ordered the preparation of a list of MPSC sympathizers still in the party, supposedly to exclude them from being candidates in the elections scheduled for March 1982.†

19. Between January 1 and March 3, 1980, 527 people were killed by security forces, ORDEN, or death squads. Between March 8 and May 25, 1,317 more people were killed by these groups. During the January 1–March 8 period, the OP-Ms killed 75, the overwhelming majority of whom were members of ORDEN or one of the paramilitary organizations (information from the Archdiocese of San Salvador and the Salvadorean Commission on Human Rights).

20. AIFLD is an agency of the AFL-CIO with known ties to the CIA. It was created to train peasant leaders under the program of the Alliance for Progress. AIFLD came to El Salvador in 1965 with an Agency for International Development (AID) contract. It held training seminars throughout the 1960s, set up cooperatives in the Salvadorean countryside, and founded the UCS in 1968. AIFLD was expelled from El Salvador in 1973 because the Salvadorean government opposed its leadership. It returned in June 1979 under stringent limitations. After the October coup AIFLD brought a large number of personnel into the country, installed them in two floors of San Salvador's Hotel Sheraton, and acquired a direct telephone line to the Salvadorean High Command. Roy Prosterman, director of the AIFLD program, is known for his role in the South Vietnamese agrarian pacification program called "the land to the tiller." See "Press Statement on the Role of AIFLD Agrarian Reform Process in El Salvador," EPICA, Washington, D.C., May 1980.

21. See, for example, Roy Prosterman and Mary Temple, "Land Reform in El Salvador," *AFL-CIO Free Trade Union News*, Vol. 35, No. 6 (June 1980):1–4; Statement by William G. Bowdler, assistant secretary of state for inter-American affairs, before the Subcommittee on Inter-American Affairs of the House Foreign Affairs Committee, 96th Congress, 2nd session, May 20, 1980; "U.S. Response to Crisis in El Salvador," A Dialogue between U.S. Ambassador to El Salvador Robert White and Tommie Sue Montgomery, October 8, 1980. Occasional Papers Series, Florida International University, Miami, Fla.

22. Norman Chapin, "A Few Comments on Land Tenure and the Course of Agrarian Reform in El Salvador," Agency for International Development, June 1980. See also Laurence R. Simon and James C. Stephens, Jr., "Salvador

Land 'Reform,'" *New York Times*, January 6, 1981.

23. Chapin, "A Few Comments on Land Tenure."

24. Ibid.; "Difficulties with the Implementation of Decree 207," Memorandum from Norman Chapin to Jack Vaughn, head, Latin American Bureau, AID, August 1980.

25. Memorandum from University of Wisconsin Land Tenure Center to Tom Mehen, Development Support/Rural and Administrative Development, July 18, 1980.

26. Two oligarchs were arrested for the crime three and a half months later, one in San Salvador and one in Miami ("Two Suspects Arrested in Salvadorean Killings," *Tampa Tribune*, April 16, 1981). Both were subsequently released.

27. An AID audit completed about the same time and official U.S. reaction to the UCS report were reported on in Karen DeYoung's article, "Salvadoran Land Reform Imperiled, Report Says," *Washington Post*, January 25, 1982. DeYoung wrote that "the land-reform program is divided into two operative parts." So, by early 1982, there was no longer even a pretense of intention to implement Phase II.

28. Frank Viviano, "El Salvador's 'Final Solution' for its Peasant War," Pacific News Service, June 26, 1981.

29. Inter-American Development Bank, *Economic and Social Progress in Latin America*, 1979 Report (Washington, D.C.: Inter-American Development Bank, 1980), p. 250.

30. Margot Hornblower, "The Exiles," *Washington Post*, March 22, 1981.

31. Inter-American Development Bank, *Economic and Social Progress*, pp. 250, 254. The 1980 CPI figure is from INFORPRESS, *Central American Economic Report* (Guatemala City, 1981), p. ES-10.

32. Inter-American Development Bank, *Economic and Social Progress*, p. 255; "Mas de 1000 millones de dólares se han fugado del país: Banco Central de Reserva" [More than $1 billion has left the country: Central Reserve Bank], *El Independiente*, January 15, 1980.

33. "2 millones diarios retiran de asociaciones de ahorro" [2 million (colones) withdrawn daily from savings associations], *Prensa Gráfica*, January 28, 1980.

34. In the 1960s a *zona franca* was created on the eastern side of San Salvador. Industries that located in this zone were exempt from Salvadorean taxes. In addition, the land was owned by members of the oligarchy, who made a sizable profit on the sale of land to companies like Texas Instruments.

35. "Millares sin empleo por cierre empresas" [Thousands without employment with business closings], *Prensa Gráfica*, January 12, 1980; "Que se evite colapso económico pide la ASI" [That economic collapse be avoided, asks ASI], *Prensa Gráfica*, January 21, 1980.

36. "ANEP retirase de instituciones oficiales" [ANEP to retire from official institutions], *El Mundo*, January 18, 1980. For several days ANEP ran, in all the San Salvador newspapers, reproductions of letters of resignation that various individuals had written to their respective agencies.

37. Productive Alliance of El Salvador, "Position Paper," no date (mimeo).

38. Press Release, Productive Alliance of El Salvador, June 26, 1980. Representatives Ken Hance (D.-Tex.) and Robert Lagomarsino (R.-Calif.) sponsored a meeting in the Rayburn House Office Building on June 26 so that the alliance could explain its position to the press and other interested persons.

39. Hornblower, "Exiles."

40. Oscar A. Romero and Arturo Rivera Damas, "La Iglesia y las Organizaciones Políticas Populares," Third pastoral letter of Oscar Romero and first of Arturo Rivera, El Salvador, August 1978, pp. 43–49.

41. See Michael Dodson and T. S. Montgomery, "The Church in the Nicaraguan Revolution," in Thomas W. Walker, ed., Nicaragua in Revolution (New York: Praeger Publishers, 1981).

42. Christopher Dickey, "Prelate Says Church Must Remain Neutral," Washington Post, March 9, 1981, p. A-1+.

43. "Reacciones Nacionales," Proceso, Vol. 2, No. 33 (August 31–September 6, 1981):5. Proceso was a small weekly news bulletin published by the UCA in San Salvador. Begun in 1980, it presented both information and analysis of the previous week's events, internal and international, in the political and economic spheres. It represented an effort to provide accurate, objective information that was simply not available through the Salvadorean mass media, all of which were owned by the oligarchy. According to UCA officials, a primary objective of Proceso was to reach the Young Military with alternative information.

44. Ibid.

45. "El Arzobispo de San Salvador afirma que debe haber diálogo entre las partes en conflicto antes de las elecciones" [The archbishop of San Salvador affirms that there must be dialogue between the parties in conflict before elections], Agencia Independiente de Prensa (AIP) telex news release, San José, Costa Rica, November 3, 1981.

46. "El Salvador: Elecciones no pueden esperar normalización del país" [El Salvador: Elections can't wait for normalization of the country], ACAN-EFE telex news release, San Salvador, November 20, 1981.

47. Letter of Apostolic Administrator of San Salvador Arturo Rivera Damas to Vice-President George Bush, April 6, 1981, mimeo.

48. "Statement from the Bishop, Apostolic Administrator, Priests, and Women Religious of the Archdiocese of San Salvador," December 5, 1980 (mimeo).

49. Interview with Father Walter Guerra, Mexico City, February 7, 1981.

50. "Former Salvadoran Official Captured," Washington Post, February 21, 1981; "El Salvador Confirms Liberal Colonel's Arrest," Washington Post, February 22, 1981; "Ex Junta Member Majano Said to be Bound for Exile," Miami Herald, March 22, 1981.

51. The course of U.S. policy from the October coup through August 1980 is discussed at length in T. S. Montgomery, "Política estadunidense y pro-

ceso revolucionario: El caso de El Salvador" [U.S. policy and revolutionary process: The case of El Salvador], *Estudios Centroamericanos (ECA)*, Vol. 35, No.
377-378 (March-April 1980):241–252; and "Política estadunidense y proceso
revolucionario: ¿Hacia la intervención?" [U.S. policy and revolutionary process: Toward intervention?] ibid., Vol. 35, No. 383 (September 1980):839–850.

52. The distinction between "lethal" and "nonlethal" weapons may be
clear on paper but blurs in the field. Part of the aid package included fifty PVS-
2B night-vision devices, electro-optic machines that are used for observation
and nighttime weapon targeting. In addition, there were private arms transac-
tions. In January 1980 the Commerce Department licensed export of $8,000
worth of "nonmilitary" shotguns and spare parts to El Salvador. During 1980
the State Department Office of Munitions Control expected to issue as much
as $250,000 worth of licenses, "mostly for carbines, handguns, and rifles." See
Thomas Conrad and Cynthia Arnson, "The Aid for El Salvador Is Called
Nonlethal," *New York Times*, June 15, 1980.

53. U.S. Department of State, Press Statement, January 17, 1981.

54. Karen DeYoung, "Envoy Reported Removed from Salvadorean Post,"
Washington Post, February 2, 1981.

55. "Communist Interference in El Salvador," Special Report No. 80, U.S.
Department of State, February 23, 1981.

56. For extended analyses of the White Paper, see John Dinges, "White
Paper or Blank Paper?" *Los Angeles Times*, March 17, 1981; James Petras,
"White Paper on the White Paper," *Nation*, March 28, 1981, p. 1; Jonathan
Kwitny, "Apparent Errors Cloud U.S. 'White Paper' on Reds in El Salvador,"
Wall Street Journal, June 8, 1981.

57. John M. Goshko, "Panel Rejects Reagan Cuts," *Washington Post*, April
30, 1981.

58. U.S. Department of State, Press Statement, March 2, 1981. For Fiscal
Year 1982 the administration proposed large increases in military aid to El
Salvador: $25 million in Foreign Military Sales credits; $1 million in Interna-
tional Military Education and Training grants; and $40 million in Economic
Support Funds. These funds were over and above the $25 million sent in
March 1981. If they were delivered it would mean an increase in U.S. aid to El
Salvador of 400 percent over the total aid given between 1950 and 1979.
Cynthia Arnson, "Background Information on El Salvador and U.S. Military
Assistance to Central America," Update No. 4, Institute For Policy Studies,
Washington, D.C., April 1981 (mimeo).

59. Reports of Radio Venceremos, August 11–20, 1981; "Mientras
'F.M.L.N.' respeta prisioneros Junta Duartista asesina a la población" [While
the FMLN respects prisoners, the Duarte junta kills the population), *El Nuevo
Diario* (Managua), August 19, 1981.

60. This information appeared in the Mexican and Nicaraguan
newspapers; it was also related to me by two officials of the FMLN.

61. "Ejercito destruye radio rebelde" [Army destroys rebel radio] (UPI
story), *Tiempo* (Tegucigalpa, Honduras), December 15, 1981.

62. Alma Guillermoprieto, "Salvadoran Peasants Describe Mass Killing,"

Washington Post, January 27, 1982, p. A-1; Raymond Bonner "Massacre of Hundreds is Reported in El Salvador," *New York Times,* January 28, 1982.

63. This attack on Usulután, although it achieved all the stated objectives of the FMLN, also revealed a chronic weakness: the shortage of big guns—60-, 90-, and 120-mm cannons and mortars. The army and security forces retreated inside the garrison, but the FMLN did not have the firepower to attack the garrison from a distance and thus force the army to choose between fighting in the streets or being killed inside the garrison. A senior FMLN official subsequently said that the FMLN were "in the process of acquiring" what it needed.

64. This battle took place at the Cutumay Camones, 17 kilometers north of Santa Ana. The FMLN column was caught poorly armed and with few munitions. This was, up to April 1982, not only the biggest military defeat the FMLN had suffered, it was the only major defeat. One reliable but unconfirmed report said that ninety-four combatants died at Cutumay Camones. The usual ratio of government *bajas* (dead and wounded) to those of the guerrillas ranged from 16 : 1 to 22 : 1 for any battle or offensive.

65. Press breakfast, Managua, Nicaragua, November 19, 1981.

66. PL 97113 (signed by President Reagan on December 29, 1981), International Security and Development Act of 1981.

67. "The Sting of El Salvador," *New York Times,* January 31, 1982.

68. These three parties were: (1) The Salvadorean Popular party (PPS), which was originally organized in 1975 by the coffee growers but lost much of its following to ARENA and the PCN; (2) the Renovating Action party (PAR), which was resurrected from the past (one report said that its principal activity consisted of delivering letters to various embassies in which its secretary general, Ernesto Oyarbide, laid responsibility for his future "accidental" death at the door of the extreme right; and (3) the Businessmen, *Campesinos,* and Workers (ECO), which registered as a party at the end of January 1982 and was concentrated in the department of San Vicente. The above information comes from Yan Verbeek, "Radiografía de unas elecciones con tiros y sin nacatamales" [X-ray of some elections with shots and without nacatamales (a Central American version of tamales)], *Barricada,* February 1, 1982.

69. "Reconocen representatividad political al FDR en El Salvador" [Recognize political representativeness of the FDR in El Salvador], Agence France Presse release, *La Prensa,* September 22, 1981.

70. Letter of the FMLN General Command to President Ronald Reagan, January 18, 1982. Reprinted in *Barricada,* February 1, 1982.

71. Verbeek, "Radiografía de unas elecciones."

72. Raymond Bonner, "Heavy Vote in Salvador Can Be Read in Many Ways," *New York Times,* April 4, 1982, "Week in Review," p. 1.

73. "Is El Salvador 'Another Vietnam'?" *Tampa Tribune,* March 26, 1981. The credit for mobilization of public opinion in the United States belonged largely to the Catholic and Protestant churches, the human rights organizations, and the Committee in Solidarity with the People of El Salvador

(CISPES), a nationwide coalition of more than 300 campus and community groups that supported the FDR and FMLN.

74. "A *Newsweek* Poll: 'Stay Out,'" *Newsweek,* March 8, 1982.

75. John Vanocur, "Salvadoran Opposition Rejects Talks with Right," *New York Times,* April 2, 1982, p. A10.

76. Portions of this section originally appeared in Tommie Sue Montgomery, "El Salvador: The Descent into Violence." Washington, D.C.: Center for International Policy, *International Policy Report,* March 1982, p. 11.

Glossary

Aparcero. A person who rents a plot of land for cash and/or for a portion of the harvest.

Arzobispado. The administrative offices of the archdiocese.

Audiencia. Court or governing body of a region; the region itself.

Cacique. An Indian chief.

Campo pagado. A paid political advertisement; includes manifestos, ads, commentaries, etc.

Colono. A person who works on an *hacienda* in exchange for shelter and (usually) a small plot of land on which to grow subsistence crops. The relationship of a *colono* to his *patrono* is very similar to that of serf to lord of the manor.

Communal lands. *"Tierras communales"* was an institution in America for centuries before the conquest. An area of land was held in common by a group related by blood or totemic bonds but was cultivated in the Mexica (Aztec) world individually. This institution existed in Central America, but in a less developed and less rigid form than in Mexico.

Compañero. Literally "companion, friend"; like the English "companion," the root is Latin, *"cum pani"* (with bread); someone with whom one shares one's bread. This etymological meaning is much closer to the Spanish connotation than "companion," a person who accompanies one. *"Compañero"* has become the traditional title used in revolutionary societies like Cuba and Nicaragua, replacing *"Señor"* and *"Señora."* It is often shortened to *"compa."*

Creole. A Spanish immigrant during the colonial period who usually intended to return to Spain after making his fortune.

Derechización. The process of moving to the right; applied to government policy, indicates repression by government forces and declining emphasis on social and economic reforms.

Encomendero. One who held an *encomienda* grant.

Encomienda. A grant of Indians, originally for labor and tribute, later primarily for tribute.

Finca. A cash-crop farm of less than 100 hectares; a coffee plantation of any size.

Golpe. Coup d'etat; the sudden overthrow of a government, usually by one faction within the army.

Golpista. A military officer who participates in the planning and execution of a coup d'etat.

Guerra Popular Prolongada. Literally, "prolonged popular war" – a concept of revolutionary struggle that emphasizes wearing down the existing regime through tactics such as hit-and-run attacks on military installations and sabotage of power and water sources, transportation, and strategic industries.

Grana. The cochineal insect, or the red dye it produces.

Hacienda. A large, self-sufficient plantation.

Hectare. 2.47 acres.

Ladino. A non-Indian, Spanish-speaking inhabitant of Central America. The term is far more common in Guatemala and Chiapas, Mexico, than elsewhere in Central America.

Machismo. The attitude that males are superior to females by virtue of their sex; also a "tough guy" image cultivated by males in an effort to impress other males or females.

Manzana. 1.73 acres, or 0.7 hectare.

Mestizo. A person of mixed Indian and White ancestry.

Milpa. A small plot of land, usually one hectare or less, which a peasant is given or rents from a *patrono* to grow subsistence crops like maize.

Oreja. Literally, "ear"; a government informer.

Patrono. The owner of a farm or *hacienda*; term is used in relation to the *colono* or *aparcero*; the boss.

Repartimiento. A system of draft labor on a rotating quota basis. Also forced purchases or sales of crops and other goods imposed on Indians or peasants.

Tribute. A forced contribution by Indians to the Spanish colonists. Tribute ranged from forced labor to a portion of one's crop.

Abbreviations

ADS	Salvadorean Democratic Association
AEAS	Association of Salvadorean Bus Owners
AGEUS	General Association of Salvadorean University Students
AID	Agency for International Development
AIFLD	American Institute for Free Labor Development
ANDES	National Association of Salvadorean Educators
ANEP	National Association for Private Enterprise
ANTEL	National Telecommunications Company
ARENA	Nationalist Republican Alliance
BPR	Popular Revolutionary Bloc
CACM	Central American Common Market
CCE	Central Elections Council
CEB	Christian Base Community
CEDES	Salvadorean Episcopal Conference
CEL	National Electric Company
CELAM	Conference of Latin American Bishops
CIA	Central Intelligence Agency
CISPES	Committee in Solidarity with the People of El Salvador
COCA	Central American Workers' Confederation
COES	Great Confederation of Workers of El Salvador
CONDECA	Central American Defense Command
CONIP	National Conference of the Popular Church
COPEFA	Permanent Council of the Armed Forces
CPD	Political-Diplomatic Commission
CPI	consumer price index
CRM	Revolutionary Coordination of the Masses
DRU	Unified Revolutionary Directorate
ECLA	UN Economic Commission for Africa
ECO	Businessmen, *Campesinos*, and Workers
EPR	Revolutionary Popular Army
ERP	Revolutionary Army of the People
FAL	Armed Forces of Liberation

FALANGE	Anticommunist Wars of Elimination Liberation Armed Forces
FAPU	United Popular Action Front
FARN	Armed Forces of National Resistance
FD	Democratic Front
FDR	Democratic Revolutionary Front
FECCAS	Christian Federation of Salvadorean Campesinos
FENAPES	National Federation of Small Businesses
FENESTRAS	National Union Federation of Salvadorean Workers
FESTIAVSCES	Union Federation of Workers in Food, Clothing, Textiles, and Similar and Related Industries
FINATA	National Financial Institution for Agricultural Lands
FMLN	Farabundo Martí Front for National Liberation
FPL	Popular Forces of Liberation
FRTS	Regional Federation of Salvadorean Workers
FSLN	Sandinista National Liberation Front
FSR	Revolutionary Union Federation
FUERSA	Salvador Allende University Front of Revolutionary Students
FUSS	Unitary Union Federation of El Salvador
GDR	Revolutionary Democratic Government
GPP	Guerra Popular Prolongada
INCAE	Central American Business Institute
ISTA	Salvadorean Institute of Agrarian Transformation
LP-28	28th of February Popular Leagues
MIPTES	Independent Movement of Professionals and Technicians of El Salvador
MLP	Popular Liberation Movement
MNR	Revolutionary National Movement
MPSC	Popular Social Christian Movement
OAS	Organization of American States
OP	Popular Organization
OP-M	Political-Military Organization
ORDEN	Nationalist Democratic Organization
PAD	Democratic Action Party
PAR	Renovating Action Party
PCN	Party of National Conciliation
PCS	Communist Party of El Salvador
PDC	Christian Democratic Party
POP	Popular Orientation Party
PPS	Salvadorean Popular Party
PRS	Party of the Salvadorean Revolution
PRTC	Revolutionary Party of Central American Workers
PRUD	Revolutionary Party of Democratic Unification
PUN	National Union Party

RN	National Resistance
STISSS	Workers' Union of the Salvadorean Institute of Social Security
STIUSA	Textile Union of United Industries
UCA	Central American University
UCS	Salvadorean Communal Union
UDN	Nationalist Democratic Union
UES	University of El Salvador
UNO	National Opposition Union

Bibliography

BOOKS

Anderson, Thomas. *Matanza* [Massacre]. Lincoln: University of Nebraska Press, 1971.

Baily, John, et al. *El Salvador de 1840 a 1935* [El Salvador from 1840 to 1935]. San Salvador: UCA Editores, 1978.

Baron Castro, Rodolfo. *La población de El Salvador* [The population of El Salvador]. San Salvador: UCA Editores, 1978.

Bermudez, Alejandro. *Salvador al Vuelo* [El Salvador: An Overview]. San Salvador: n.p., 1917.

Brannon, Max P. *El Salvador: Esquema estadística de la vida nacional* [El Salvador: Statistical outline of national life]. San Salvador: n.p., 1936.

Browning, David. *El Salvador: Landscape and Society*. Oxford: Clarendon Press, 1971.

Colindres, Eduardo. *Fundamentos económicos de la burguesia salvadoreña* [Economic fundamentals of the Salvadorean bourgeoisie]. San Salvador: UCA Editores, 1977.

Dada Hirezi, Héctor. *La economía de El Salvador y la integración centroamericana 1945–1960* [The economy of El Salvador and Central American integration 1945-1960]. San Salvador: UCA Editores, 1978.

Dalton, Roque. *El Salvador* (Monografia) [El Salvador (Monograph)]. San Salvador: Editorial Universitaria, 1979.

Durham, William H. *Scarcity and Survival in Central America*. Stanford, Calif.: Stanford University Press, 1979.

Guerra, Tomás. *El Salvador en la hora de la liberación* [El Salvador in the hour of liberation]. San José, Costa Rica: n.p., 1980.

Latorre Cabal, Hugo. *The Revolution of the Latin American Church*. Norman: University of Oklahoma Press, 1978.

Lernoux, Penny. *Cry of the People*. New York: Doubleday, 1980.

MacLeod, Murdo J. *Spanish Central America: A Socioeconomic History 1520–1720*. Berkeley: University of California Press, 1973.

Marins, José. *Comunidades Eclesiales de Base: Origen, contenido, perspectivas.*

[Christian Base Communities: Origin, Content, Perspective]. Bogotá: Ediciones Paulinas, 1977.

Mayorga Quiroz, Román. *La universidad para el cambio social* [The university for social change]. San Salvador: UCA Editores, 1978.

Menjivar, Rafael. *Crisis del desarrollismo: Caso El Salvador* [Crisis of development: The case of El Salvador]. San José, Costa Rica: EDUCA, 1977.

Montes, Segundo. *Estudio sobre estratificación social en El Salvador* [Study of social stratification in El Salvador]. San Salvador: UCA Editores, 1979.

Morán, Francisco. *Las jornadas cívicas de abril y mayo de 1944* [The civic marches of April and May 1944]. San Salvador: Editorial Universitaria, 1979.

Rutilio Grande: Martir de la evangelización rural en El Salvador [Rutilio Grande: Martyr of rural evangelization in El Salvador]. San Salvador: UCA Editores, 1978.

Ruhl, Arthur. *The Central Americans*. New York: n.p., 1927.

Theroux, Paul. *The Old Patagonian Express*. New York: Houghton Mifflin Co., 1979.

Urrutia Glamenco, Carlos. *La Ciudad de San Salvador* [The city of San Salvador]. San Salvador: n.p., 1924.

Villacorta, Emilio. *Por la patria y su gobierno* [For the homeland and its government]. San Salvador: n.p., 1919.

Webre, Stephen. *José Napoleón Duarte and the Christian Democratic Party in Salvadoran Politics 1960-1972*. Baton Rouge: Louisiana State University Press, 1979.

White, Alastair. *El Salvador*. London: Ernest Benn; Boulder, Colo.: Westview Press, 1973.

THESES

Chavarría Kleinhenm, Francisco. "Fundamentos políticos, económicos y sociales de la evolución y desarrollo del movimiento sindical en El Salvador" [Political, economic, and social fundamentals of the evolution and development of the union movement in El Salvador]. Thesis for the *Licenciatura* in sociology, University of Costa Rica, 1977.

Cruz, Octavio. "Conciencia y cambio social en la hacienda Tres Ceibas (El Salvador)" [Consciousness and Social Change in the Tres Ceibas *hacienda*]. Thesis for the *Licenciatura* in sociology, University of Costa Rica, 1978.

Elam, Robert Varney. "Appeal to Arms: Army and Politics in El Salvador 1931-1964." Ph.D. dissertation, University of New Mexico, 1968.

Sermeño Zelidon, Carmen. "Las nuevas formas de dominación política en El Salvador 1972-1977" [New forms of political domination in El Salvador 1972-1977]. Thesis for the *Licenciatura* in sociology, University of Costa Rica, 1979.

Wilson, Everett Alan. "The Crisis of National Integration in El Salvador 1919-1935." Ph.D. dissertation, Stanford University, 1968.

ARTICLES

Anderson, Jack. "Of Arabs, Weapons and Peanuts." *Washington Post*, July 10, 1980.

Arias Gómez, Jorge. "Augustín Farabundo Martí (Esbozo biográfico)" [Augustín Farabundo Martí (Biographical sketch)]. *La Universidad* (University of El Salvador, San Salvador), No. 4 (July-August 1971):181-240.

Armstrong, Robert. "El Salvador – Why Revolution." *NACLA Report on the Americas*, Vol. 14, No. 2 (March-April 1980):3-35.

"A sus ordenes, mi Capital." Editorial, *Estudios Centroamericanos* (ECA), Vol. 31, No. 337 (November 1976):637-643.

Bachmura, Frank T. "Toward Economic Reconciliation in Central America." *World Affairs*, Vol. 133, No. 4 (1971):283-292.

Burke, Melvin. "El sistema de plantación y la proletarización del trabajo agrícola en El Salvador" [The plantation system and the proletarianization of agricultural work in El Salvador]. *Estudios Centroamericanos* (ECA), Vol. 31, No. 335-336 (September-October 1976):473-486.

"Central America: Patterns of Regional Economic Integration." *Bank of London and South America Review*, June 1979.

"Central America: A Season of Martyrs." *Christianity and Crisis*, Vol. 40, No. 8 (May 12, 1980).

Colindres, Eduardo. "La tenencia de la tierra en El Salvador" [Land tenancy in El Salvador]. *Estudios Centroamericanos* (ECA), Vol. 31, No. 335-336 (September-October 1976):463-472.

Cuellar Zaavedra, Oscar. "Las tendencias de cambio en Centro América y el caso de El Salvador: El periodo 1960-1975" [Tendencies for change in Central America and the case of El Salvador: The period 1960-1975]. Central American University, 1977 (mimeo).

Drehsler, Alex. "Guerrillas Use Guns to Forge Marxist Society." *San Diego Union*, March 2, 1981.

————. "Revolution or Death!" *San Diego Union*, March 1, 1981.

Flores Macal, Mario. "Historia de la Universidad de El Salvador" [History of the University of El Salvador]. *Anuario de Estudios Centroamericanos*, Vol. 2 (1976):107-140.

Forché, Carolyn, and Wheaton, Philip. "History and Motivations of U.S. Involvement in the Control of the Peasant Movement in El Salvador: The Role of AIFLD in the Agrarian Reform Process 1970-1980." EPICA, Washington, D.C., 1980 (mimeo).

Grande, Rutilio. "Aguilares: Una experiencia de evangelización rural parroquial" [Aguilares: An experience of rural parish evangelization]. *Búsqueda*, Vol. 3, No. 8 (March 1975):21-45.

"H.O." "La iglesia y los acontecimientos de mayo en El Salvador" [The church and the events of May in El Salvador]. *Estudios Centroamericanos* (*ECA*), Vol. 34, No. 368 (June 1979):436–439.

Larín, Arístides Augusto. "Historia del movimiento sindical de El Salvador" [History of the union movement in El Salvador]. *La Universidad*, No. 4 (July-August 1971):135–179.

Masferrer, Alberto. "El Banco del Pueblo" [The People's Bank]. *Patria*, December 22, 1928.

_____ ."Como anda la justicia en esta San Salvador" [How justice operates in this San Salvador]. *Patria*, November 30, 1928.

_____ ."Sobre la carestía periódica del maiz en El Salvador" [About the periodic scarcity of maize in El Salvador]. *Patria*, April 4, 1929.

Mena, David. "Estado y grupos dominates en El Salvador" [State and dominant groups in El Salvador]. Paper presented at 3rd Central American Sociology Conference, Tegucigalpa, Honduras, April 24–29, 1978 (mimeo).

Paredes, Ivan D. "La situación de la Iglesia Católica en El Salvador y su influjo social" [The situation of the Catholic Church in El Salvador and its social influence]. *Estudios Centroamericanos* (*ECA*), Vol. 34, No. 369-370 (July-August 1979):601–614.

"Salvador Church Leader Suggests a New Coalition." *Miami Herald*, May 26, 1980, p. 15A.

Sorbrino, Jon. "La iglesia en el actual proceso del país" [The church in the current process of the country]. *Estudios Centroamericanos* (*ECA*) Vol. 34, No. 372–373 (October-November 1979):905–922.

Stein, Eduardo. "Los medios de communicación colectiva en El Salvador ante las exigencias de un diálogo nacional" [The means of collective communication in El Salvador before the demands of a national dialogue]. *Estudios Centroamericanos* (*ECA*), Vol. 34, No. 369-370 (July-August 1979):647–672.

Torres, Abelardo. "More from This Land: Agrarian Reform in El Salvador." *Américas*, Vol. 14, No. 8 (1962):6–12.

Wipfler, William L. "El Salvador: Reform as Cover for Repression." *Christianity and Crisis*, Vol. 40 (May 12, 1980):116–124.

Zamora, Rubén. "¿Seguro de vida o despojo? Análisis político de la transformación agraria" [Life insurance or plunder? Political analysis of the agrarian transformation]. *Estudios Centroamericanos* (*ECA*), Vol. 31, No. 335-336 (September-October 1976):511–534.

PERIODICALS

Búsqueda. Organ of the Pastoral Commission of [the Archdiocese of] San Salvador, El Salvador, 1975-1979.

La Crónica del Pueblo. San Salvador, 1979-1980.

Estudios Centroamericanos. (*ECA*). 1972-1980.

El Independiente. San Salvador, 1979–1980.
El Mundo. San Salvador, 1979–1980.
Prensa Gráfica. San Salvador, 1979–1980.
Orientación. Weekly newspaper of the archdiocese of San Salvador, 1979–1981.

DOCUMENTS

"Algunas características educacionales de la población salvadoreña" [Some educational characteristics of the Salvadorean population]. National Council of Planning and Economic Coordination, San Salvador, January 1976.

Arnson, Cynthia. "Background Information on El Salvador and US Military Assistance to Central America." Update No. 4. Institute for Policy Studies, Washington, D.C., April 1981 (mimeo).

Chávez y González, Luís. Fifty-first pastoral letter on the occasion of the first archdiocesan pastoral week. San Salvador, November 30, 1975.

The Church in the Present Day Transformation of Latin America. Washington, D.C.: U.S. Catholic Conference, 1970.

"Fé y Política" [Faith and politics]. Third Regional Meeting on Justice and Peace: Mexico, Central America, and the Antilles. Managua, Nicaragua, December 10–13, 1972.

Indicadores económicos y sociales Enero–Junio, 1979 [Economic and social indicators January–June 1979]. Ministry of Planning, San Salvador, 1979.

"Justicia y opción por el pobre" [Justice and option for the poor]. Seventh Regional Meeting on Justice and Peace: Mexico, Central America, and the Antilles. Alajuela, Costa Rica, October 16–21, 1977.

"Movimientos apostólicos en América Central y su incidencia en lo socio-político" [Apostolic movements in Central America and their occurrence in sociopolitical life]. Fifth Regional Meeting on Justice and Peace: Mexico, Central America, and the Antilles. Belize, August 18–22, 1975.

"El pensamiento social de la iglesia" [The social thought of the church]. National Commission on Justice and Peace, San Salvador, n.d.

"Persecución de la iglesia en El Salvador" [Persecution of the church in El Salvador]. Interdiocesan Social Secretariat, June 1977.

Plan de desarrollo económico y social, 1968–1972 [Social and economic development plan, 1968–1972]. National Council of Planning and Economic Coordination, San Salvador, 1967.

Plan Nacional: Bienestar Para Todos: 1978–1982 [National plan: Welfare for all: 1978–1982]. San Salvador: Ministry of Planning and Coordination of Social and Economic Development, 1978.

Rivera Damas, Arturo. "Reflexión pastoral sobre la iglesia particular de Santiago de María" [Pastoral reflection about the particular church of Santiago de María]. Second pastoral letter of the Bishop of Santiago de María. December 2, 1979.

Romero, Oscar A. "Misión de la iglesia en medio de las crisis del país" [Mission of the church in the center of the country's crisis]. Fourth pastoral letter. San Salvador, August 1979.

Romero, Oscar A., and Rivera Damas, Arturo. "La iglesia y las Organizaciones Politicas populares" [The church and the popular Political Organizations]. Annexes to the pastoral letter. El Salvador, October 1978.

Romero y Galdámez, Oscar A., and Rivera Damas, Arturo. "La iglesia y las Organizaciones Politicas populares" [The church and the popular Political Organizations]. Third pastoral letter of Monseñor Romero and the first of Monseñor Rivera Damas. El Salvador, October 1978.

U.S., Congress, House. "Human Rights in Nicaragua, Guatemala, and El Salvador: Implications for U.S. Policy." Hearings before the Subcommittee on International Organizations of the Committee on International Relations, 94th Congress, 2nd session, June 8 and 9, 1976.

"Violación de los derechos humanos" [Violation of human rights]. Inter-American Commission on Human Rights, Organization of American States. San José, Costa Rica, 1979.

Index

ADOC shoe factory, 202–203(n7)
ADS. *See* Salvadorean Democratic Association
Agency for International Development (AID), 169–170, 218, 219(n27)
AGEUS. *See* General Association of Salvadorean University Students
Agrarian reform, 83, 117, 178
  criticisms of, 170, 219(n27)
  Molina proposal, 4, 90
  1980 promulgation, 132, 168–169
  supported by Central American University, 109
  under Arturo Arajo, 49–50
  See also National Agrarian Reform Congress
Agriculture
  diversification, 40, 67
  as "key to wealth," 34
  See also Coffee; Cotton; Economic cycles; Sugar cane
Aguilares, San Salvador, 104–106, 109, 115, 123, 181, 210(n18).
  See also Christian Base Communities; Grande, Rutilio
Aguirre y Salinas, Osmín, 61, 63
Ahuachapán (department), 123, 170, 203–204(n21)
AID. *See* Agency for International Development
AIFLD. *See* American Institute for Free Labor Development
Alas, Higinio, 117, 212(n35)
Alas, José Inocencio
  exiles, 212(n35)
  and formation of FAPU, 115–117, 121, 213(n7)
  kidnapped, 97–98, 110
Alvarado, Gonzalo de, 33
Alvarado, Pedro de, 33
Alvarengo, Ramón Alfredo, 195(n8)
Alvarez, José Eduardo, 209(n7)
Alvarez Córdova, Enrique
  assassination of, 140, 214(n26)
  as minister of agriculture, 82
  president, FDR, 133
American Institute for Free Labor Development (AIFLD), 123, 124, 218(n20)
  and 1980 agrarian reform, 168–170
Anderson, Thomas, 1, 201(n42)
ANDES. *See* National Association of Salvadorean Educators
Andino, Mario, 15, 23
ANEP. *See* National Association of Private Enterprise
Añil. *See* Indigo
ANTEL. *See* National Telecommunications Company
Anticommunist Wars of Elimination Liberation Armed Forces. *See* FALANGE

237

Also of Interest from Westview Press

El Salvador, Alastair White

† *Nicaragua: The Land of Sandino*, Thomas W. Walker

† *The End and the Beginning: The Nicaraguan Revolution*, John A. Booth

† *The Dominican Republic: A Caribbean Crucible*, Howard J. Wiarda and Michael J. Kryzanek

The Dominican Republic, Ian Bell

Arms and Politics in the Dominican Republic, G. Pope Atkins

† *Brazil: A Political Analysis*, Peter Flynn

Brazil in the International System: The Rise of a Middle Power, edited by Wayne A. Selcher

† *Post-Revolutionary Peru: The Politics of Transformation*, edited by Stephen M. Gorman

Colossus Challenged: The Struggle for Caribbean Influence, edited by H. Michael Erisman and John D. Martz

† *Latin American Foreign Policies: Global and Regional Dimensions*, edited by Elizabeth G. Ferris and Jennie K. Lincoln

Development Strategies in Latin America, edited by Claes Brundenius

Technological Progress in Latin America: The Prospects for Overcoming Dependency, edited by James H. Street and Dilmus D. James

† *The Continuing Struggle for Democracy in Latin America*, edited by Howard J. Wiarda

Corporatism and National Development in Latin America, Howard J. Wiarda

Latin America, the United States, and the Inter-American System, edited by John D. Martz and Lars Schoultz

† *From Dependency to Development: Strategies to Overcome Development and Inequality*, edited by Heraldo Muñoz

Insurgency in the Modern World, edited by Bard E. O'Neill, William R. Heaton, and Donald J. Alberts

† Available in hardcover and paperback.

About the Book and Author

Revolution in El Salvador: Origins and Evolution
Tommie Sue Montgomery
Introduction by Román Mayorga Quiroz

El Salvador is experiencing the most radical social change of its history. The resilient Farabundo Martí Front for National Liberation (FMLN) and its political arm, the Democratic Revolutionary Front (FDR), are battling the Salvadorean government head on. The United States, playing no small role, is apparently attempting to keep the popular organizations from coming to power, as they well might in a full-scale civil war, while trying also to head off an extreme right-wing government. This small Central American nation, where a few individuals have controlled the agricultural, financial, and industrial resources to an extent unparalleled even in Latin America, is now in the midst of a potentially long-term crisis.

Dr. Montgomery examines the historic and economic roots of the crisis, giving particular attention to sociopolitical developments since 1970. Her opening chapter tells for the first time the full story of the October 1979 coup d'etat, an event that encapsulates the interactions and contradictions of the various actors on the Salvadorean political stage. Chapters 2 and 3 trace the history of El Salvador from 1524 to 1979, focusing on the two actors—the oligarchy and the armed forces—that created the Salvadorean economic and political system and then devoted themselves to maintaining the status quo. Separate chapters highlight two other actors that have challenged that status quo since 1968: the Catholic church and the revolutionary organizations. The last chapter begins with the resignation of the government in January 1980 and follows events into the spring of 1982. Dr. Montgomery ends with a prognosis: No lasting, viable political solution is possible without the participation of the FDR/FMLN.

Based on eleven months of field research and more than one hundred interviews with Salvadoreans from the far right to the far left, this book presents new information on the October coup and the revolutionary organizations. It also reveals the church's role as a seedbed of the popular organizations—a part it has not previously played in Latin America—and explores the possibilities presented by the emergence of a progressive group of young army officers, who could form a new coalition between the military and the popular organizations.

Dr. Montgomery has been an assistant professor at Brooklyn College, City University of New York, and a visiting scholar at Union Theological Seminary. She is currently associated with CINASE (Centro de Investigación y Asesoría Socio-Económica) in Managua, Nicaragua.